(IT'S GREAT TO)

SUCK

AT

SOMETHING

(IT'S GREAT TO)
SUCK
AT
SOMETHING

The Unexpected Joy of Wiping Out
and What It Can Teach Us About Patience,
Resilience, and the Stuff That Really Matters

KAREN RINALDI

ATRIA BOOKS

New York   London   Toronto   Sydney   New Delhi

ATRIA
BOOKS

An Imprint of Simon & Schuster, Inc.
1230 Avenue of the Americas
New York, NY 10020

First Atria Books hardcover edition May 2019

ATRIA BOOKS and colophon are trademarks of Simon & Schuster, Inc.

For information about special discounts for bulk purchases, please
contact Simon & Schuster Special Sales at 1-866-506-1949
or business@simonandschuster.com.

The Simon & Schuster Speakers Bureau can bring authors to your live event. For
more information or to book an event, contact the Simon & Schuster Speakers
Bureau at 1-866-248-3049 or visit our website at www.simonspeakers.com.

Interior design by Laura Levatino

Illustrations by Niege Borges

Poem "Kindness" by Naomi Shihab Nye, originally published in *Words Under the
Words* (Far Corner Books, 1995), included with permission from the author.

Excerpt from "Burnt Norton" from FOUR QUARTETS by T. S. Eliot.
Copyright © 1936 by Houghton Mifflin Harcourt Publishing Company,
renewed 1964 by T. S. Eliot. Reprinted by permission of Houghton
Mifflin Harcourt Publishing Company. All rights reserved.

10 9 8 7 6 5 4 3 2 1

Library of Congress Cataloging-in-Publication Data is available.

ISBN 978-1-5011-9577-8

<u>DISCLAIMER</u>: I COULDN'T POSSIBLY LIST ALL OF THE THINGS YOU MIGHT SUCK AT THAT WOULD CAUSE YOU OR SOMEONE ELSE HARM. INSTEAD, I ADVISE THAT YOU PROCEED WITH CAUTION IF YOUR WAY TO SUCKITUDE INVOLVES ANYTHING DANGEROUS: SURFING, FOR EXAMPLE, OR WINGSUIT FLYING. USE COMMON-SENSE AND MAKE SURE YOU ASK FOR AN ASSIST. DON'T GO IT ALONE UNLESS IT'S MACRAMÉ, CROSSWORD PUZZLES, OR ANYTHING ELSE YOU CAN SUCK AT FROM THE SAFETY OF YOUR COUCH.

For Rocco and Gio

THE SUCKING MATRIX

Sucking and knowing that you do—this is where you want to be

SUCKING AT SOMETHING

You're a little dangerous

Suck at something sweet spot

CLUELESS

AWAKE

Humility taken a step too far

SME (Subject Matter Expert)

GOOD AT SOMETHING

"You grow up the day you have
your first real laugh at yourself."
– ETHEL BARRYMORE

"Success is stumbling from failure to failure
with no loss of enthusiasm."
– WINSTON CHURCHILL

"Ever tried. Ever failed. No matter.
Try again. Fail again. Fail better."
– SAMUEL BECKETT

"All it takes is just one wave. Not even that, one turn . . .
just a moment, it keeps pulling you back to have
another moment, and it never ends."
– GERRY LOPEZ (*STEP INTO LIQUID*)

Contents

Introduction

Let's say that you don't already suck at something.

First of all: that's delusional.

But even if it is somehow true, I'm going to show you how you're missing out on something wonderful.

In this book, I'm going to encourage you to find and embrace something you suck at. I want to share with you just how great it can be to suck at something: to really, really struggle to do something unremarkable, uncelebrated, and without much to show for it. And to do that unremarkable thing with love and with hope in your heart. To do it with joy.

I know this joy firsthand because I surf, and I'm bad at it. Surfing isn't a new kick, and it's not a phase. I'm not in that honeymoon period of surfing when I'm trying it out, seeing if I'll get the hang of it, romancing it. By any objective measure, it's a big part of my life, and has been for a while. I've been surfing eight months out of twelve for seventeen years (and yes, to those devoted surfers out there reading this, you have every right to scoff). I've arranged my middle-aged life around getting in the water as much as I can. I chose a career path that would allow me to pursue it, risked hard-earned money to support it, and coerced my family into a lifestyle only some of us appreciate. And—I still suck at surfing.

But I love it. I think, in its way, it loves me back.

I have put so much of myself into the waves over the years, but no matter how much I give, I always get more back. It's an unfair exchange—in my favor—and it has nothing to do with my aptitude.

You, too, have this potential to suck at something. It doesn't take any-

1

thing more than just being yourself, having a bit of courage, a sense of humor, and a willingness to start something new, or to return to something old, to start growing again, even if the end result won't get you in any record books. This book won't make you a master of anything.

On the other hand, it won't hurt your chances. A recent study whose results were published in the *Journal of Psychology of Science and Technology* found that Nobel laureates "were significantly more likely to engage in arts and crafts avocations" than mere members of the National Academy of Sciences—who themselves were also far likelier to have hobbies than the public at large. There's some politesse in that phrase "arts and crafts avocations," so let me translate: these Nobel Prize winners like to do things like play the cello and do macramé when they're not staring down microscopes. And no one is paying to listen to that music, or for their knotted wall hangings.

The very-super-seriously-successful suck too. They just do it intuitively. The rest of us have to figure it out for ourselves.

So what's stopping us? Nothing more than the fact that sucking has a bad rap. It's a reputation thing. There's nothing inherently unpleasant about being substandard at something (think about it: how would our species ever have learned anything if that had been the case?). It's just that our culture maligns and mocks ineptitude. So much of our public life is oriented around hiding our weaknesses or denying they even exist. Because we are so geared toward success and reward above all, we fail to set aside space in our lives to cultivate new talents and interests. That kind of cultivation will inevitably include fits and false starts. We'll almost certainly look foolish. We'll fail. And, so, too many of us skip doing it altogether.

When we approach something new, it seems like our first response is to try to dominate it. If we can't, we ignore it. By ignoring it we solve one problem: we don't have to be inadequate at something; but we create another: we diminish our own lives. We add another blank spot. Adulthood becomes a kind of accumulation of blank spots. A strategic anti-growth, surrounded by space we're too scared to enter. All because we can't stand knowing about something we won't command. But if we avoid the vulnerability of living in the space of the new and challenging, then we'll get old and stagnant real quick.

I believe there's an even better argument for living in that sucky space more often. I believe happiness itself is found in accepting, even dwelling in, what we fail to excel at.

This isn't easy. We've all felt the particular pain and unhappiness that can make us uncomfortable in that zone between discovery of something that enthralls us and disappointment in ourselves as we fail to master it. Discomfort is the least of it. In this book, I make a case for discomfort. While it may sound counterintuitive right now, it's where a lot of good stuff is hiding. Quitting before we even start is the tragedy. The other side of frustration and discouragement is tenacity and hope. Let's live in the doing. The process itself is where we should find satisfaction. Success is a reward we should not come to expect. Once success is attained, if ever, we should be humbled by it.

In our workaholic, goal-driven, relentlessly meritocratic life we have gained so much but lost many things as well. Patience, humility, and self-awareness all get sacrificed in a uniformly goal-setting and -seeking life.

What would happen if we put the need for stroking and reward behind us, just for a bit, and faced the truth that we all suck at some things? If we're honest with ourselves, we never have a good day if it depends on whether our egos get stroked or not. This doesn't mean we have to deny the pleasure of knowing and appreciating our talents.

But we can bring this into better balance—I'm pretty sure we spend more than enough time hawking our strengths. Social media is all about it, and it's a race to the bottom when it comes to our well-being. It turns out that when everyone just shares their very best aspects, it's a lot harder to be satisfied with our own.

What would happen if instead we celebrated our failed efforts? Or got past celebration entirely, and just let ourselves live with ourselves: our complete, imperfect, untalented selves?

The fact is: there are few tasks at which any of us truly excel. By avoiding what we suck at, we're unnecessarily avoiding so much of the stuff of life. There's so much more than just talent. Talent is certainly useful, and for many of us, it helps earn our livelihood. But there's more to life than usefulness. What can talent teach us about determination? Or patience? Or willpower? Or peace?

Aptitude is easy.

The truly strong spirit pursues something that holds no promise of reward except for the fact of doing it.

Perhaps that strength is similar to what Josef Pieper, a German philosopher writing shortly after WWII, had in mind when he wrote his classic *Leisure: The Basis of Culture*, in which he said that "The idea of leisure is diametrically opposed to the totalitarian concept of the 'worker,'" and proceeded to celebrate human activity detached from so-called "social usefulness."

Nothing is less socially useful to me than surfing. I don't know if my board is the only thing that stands in between me and, say, fascism, but I think I understand what he means. My surfboard may be your guitar, or pottery clay, your putter, or bag of latex twisting balloons. The instrument or action is simply the means by which we practice transcending our usefulness. Whatever the tool or method, by allowing ourselves to suck at something, we will have more patience with ourselves for getting better at the things that really matter. Like being decent human beings.

That's one mission of this book. We'll rethink what we thought we knew about some of the basic building blocks of our lives: our free time, our work time, and the disproportionate science and vocabulary we've developed to speak about and understand those things. We'll bust some of the myths that keep us from trying new things in the first place—the drive of perfectionism, the delusion of nostalgia, the lie of first-times, and all of those trivialized touchstones to which we grant meaning: "Do what you love, and you'll never work again"; and "Winning isn't everything; it's the only thing."

But, there's more to it than that. I didn't set out to write this book because surfing appealed to the contrarian in me.

In 2013, when I got back onto my surfboard three months after being diagnosed with breast cancer, I wasn't thinking about productivity and how I might get back to work with more energy if I caught a few waves.

I wasn't thinking about anything but being out there. Likewise, the second mission of this book is this: celebrating the life-making art of doing something seemingly irrelevant, especially when the rest of your life is being pulled toward one resounding, overwhelming, all-encompassing, and weighty relevance. Sucking at something can help us to reframe the most difficult moments of our lives.

Sure, I've gotten better at surfing since then, but even still—I can't be clearer about this and once more for the cheap seats—I suck at surfing. And the joy I get from doing it is not contingent on rare moments of accidental accomplishments. The joy I get is the joy of trying. Success, when it happens, is a welcome reward, but it's the wrong end of the funnel.

I don't think my experience is so unique.

A little while ago the *New York Times* published a piece I wrote called, naturally, "(It's Great to) Suck at Something." At the same time, I posted a video of myself surfing—a video I have kept close for many years, because it's embarrassing. See, plenty of people in my personal and professional lives already knew about my preferred pastime. And, well, I had to let them assume that I was okay at it, or even pretty good (a natural assumption to make based on how much time I've poured into it). So, the video was a bit of an admission.

Have you ever had a friend show up in your neighborhood, and you realize suddenly that you perhaps let that friend believe you were a little more put-together than you really are? And you're kicking yourself that you didn't bother to clean the gutters yet this summer, or take out the recycling, or do one of a million things you would have if you had known you were going to be on the spot?

This was like that, except I basically invited the world over, and the front door was rusted off its hinges.

And it's one of the best things I've done in ages. I've heard from so many people, from readers all over the world, who were delighted to read my story. Not because they care about surfing (and, wow, some people have strong feelings about surfing!), but because it was a story about someone sucking without shame. Many of them were secretly sucking, too, and it was great to hear there's a burgeoning tribe out there. But I also heard from plenty of people who were not trying because they didn't feel like they could. Now I want to invite the world through that rusty-hinged door and to the joys that sucking can bring, an invitation to try new things without the pressure of having to be any good at it. Who knows? You might stumble onto something for which you have innate talent that you never knew you had. But that's not the end goal because there is no end goal, not even for the potential experts.

My story is not so unique that I should have gotten as much feedback as I did—and with this book I'd like to make it less unique. That's really the biggest mission: I want to start a whole new bookshelf. A new genre of dinner table conversation. A new community.

We do not tell stories about sucking. I think that's why so many people thrilled to mine. All of the stories we tell each other, from Hollywood to the hair salon, are stories about triumphs and upswings. When we do share horror stories, we tell them for laughs: Well, I won't be going there again . . . I won't be seeing him for a second date . . . I won't pick that song for karaoke next time.

The implication is: How funny it was that, for a moment, my life was something less than perfect.

Our lives are far from perfect, except for fleeting moments when the perfect wave comes through, and your body and mind are both ready for it, and for a moment you hitch a ride on what feels like a ripple on the silk of life itself.

The rest is tumbling beneath the wave.

But there's so much to celebrate in the rest of the stuff, in those billions and trillions of potential moves—we just need to start being willing to suck.

That's three missions:

1. Suck passionately: To learn about the real tonic power of the pursuit of our passions, to see how our brains aren't built for monomania, but for a full-spectrum life.

2. Suck unproductively: To investigate the special quality that studied irrelevance can have in our own lives, especially during times when the world would seem to be suggesting that we should only be focusing on what's making us miserable.
3. Suck communally: To hear stories about sucking at something, and to start sharing your own.

My conditioning for sucking started before I learned to surf and comes as the benefit of a lifelong love and professional devotion of being a dilettante. As an editor, I rely on the expertise of others to deliver deep dives into subjects that I midwife into books. As a publisher, I launch those books into the world. The privilege of getting intimate with some of the greatest minds never grows old. Along the way, I've learned a little about a lot of different subjects. I get to be a skipping stone on the surface of life's mysteries. It wouldn't be too farfetched to say that sucking at things is my profession.

Curiosity and greed for learning keep me vigilant for the new insight, adventure, aha moment, and because of what I do for a living, I get to have them every day. This book is the happy mishmash of what (I hope) I do best, and what I do worst. In these pages, I look to the wonders of science, philosophy, literature, history, and culture, and talk to experts in those fields to help me unpack it all. Surfing and sucking at it is the foundation that keeps me grounded when my mind gets untidy. (Any avocation of your choosing can serve as a similar grounding.) In the end, I hope to shed some light on our experiences and offer some new ways of looking at things. Maybe we'll even have a jolly good laugh at ourselves.

But before we head out into the waves, I want to explain what got me obsessed with this idea in the first place.

It started with an innocent enough question. My son Rocco was eight years old. At pickup outside of his school, I was chatting with John, another PS 41 parent. "So, how's Rocco doing at school this year?" he asked.

It was a subject that was never far from my mind. Early in the new school year, we'd already begun the annual investigation into Rocco's dif-

ficulty with fine motor skills and with what we would come to learn as his
struggle with sensory perceptions. The problem manifested in all sorts of
ways, one being that he couldn't write with a pen or pencil—at least not
in a way that he, let alone anyone else, could decipher. He was supposedly
old enough to have mastered readable handwriting and yet the skill eluded
him. Typing on a keyboard wasn't a problem, but writing on paper took
such effort that it made schoolwork literally painful for him, and teachers
had difficulty evaluating Rocco's work. It caused enormous frustration for
Rocco at homework time. One evening, as we sat at the dining room table
trying to slog through his homework, he told me it actually hurt him to
write, which in turn interfered with his thinking. We knew Rocco understood what was being asked of him, but putting thoughts through pen to
paper stopped him cold. There were often tears.

"Oh, he's having some trouble with his handwriting," I told John.
Rocco was standing next to me. He wasn't embarrassed. He knew it as
well as anyone. He nodded in agreement. "He's trying," I continued, "but
writing causes him some stress so homework is difficult for him."

John didn't miss a beat. He smiled at my son, pushed his hands deep
into his coat pockets, and looked up toward the heavens. "Oh, yeah,
Rocco," he sighed. "It's so great to suck at something."

Rocco's worried expression melted away. He smiled. His face lit up
with what I knew was a feeling of recognition and relief, the kind you feel
when something old and beloved, something you thought you'd lost, suddenly falls out from deep in your closet and into your hands.

While Rocco didn't have a choice but to suck at fine motor skills, it
was the acceptance of his handicap—and the momentary celebration of
it—that gave him the freedom to go forward as he is, not as he thought he
should be.

A reflex benefit of this book will be to learn how to stop beating yourself up for sucking at some things you can't help but suck at. But that's not
the main point. I want to inspire you to find something you love to do—
even though you might suck at it—and to do it anyway as a way to joy. To
celebrate not excelling as a path to freedom.

Over the last decade, I have found that people will bare their souls when given the opportunity to talk about failing at something important to them. It's always a beautiful conversation. I hope this book encourages more of us to have these kinds of conversations with one another, to open a door of acceptance that we are all dying to walk through. Ultimately, it is about connection with one another, which can only happen if we first connect with ourselves.

Back to that fateful afternoon when I was picking up my son—it turned out John was right. But way more important than that, Rocco heard him. He still can't handwrite worth a damn, but ten years later he became valedictorian of his high school graduating class without that skill.

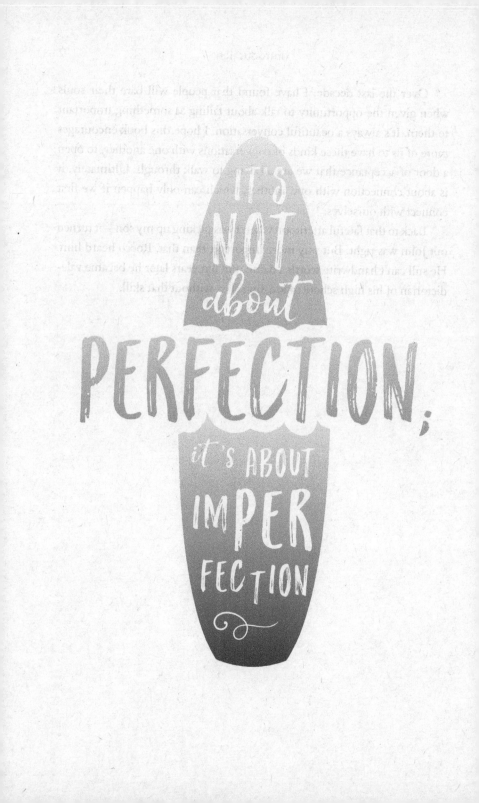

IT'S
NOT
about
PERFECTION,
it's ABOUT
IM PER
FECTION

WAVE 1

My First Wave: An Invitation to Suck

Rule #1:

You have to care about what you suck at, or else it doesn't count.

Lesson #1:

First times are overrated.

Benefit #1:

You appreciate how hard so many things really are, especially those things the truly talented make look so easy.

Let's get things straight from the outset. I didn't start surfing so I could suck at it; I wasn't a guru of sucking from the get-go.

Like all delightfully deluded kooks (the surfing term for newbies and shitty surfers), I'd thought, sure, it might be hard at the beginning, but I can do this. I mean, how hard can it be, really? A Darwin Award–winning question if there ever was one.

I'm not ashamed of my early bravado. Frankly, a little bit of delusion is probably a good thing. It's often the ignition that propels us toward trying something new. But the fuel of delusion burns quickly once we start to realize that the activity in question won't yield quite so easily to our will. It's always harder than we thought. How many times have you said that very thing, "Wow—that was harder than I thought." This alone should be enough to convince us that sucking at something is as inevitable as sunrise on an eastern shore and we would all do well by accepting it as fact. That's all to say that delusion can only take us so far. It took me to the water's edge.

Something else had to actually get me wet.

The current trend of "hacking" our brains, our health, our lives, in order to perform better, reach our goals, and be better than our peers, has us all maniacally focused on the win. But we don't seem to be getting anywhere. We are living in an era of aspirational psychosis, believing in those picture-perfect lives we see on social media and in commercials. How does your life stack up in comparison? Not so great, right? We are bombarded every day with imperatives to strive to have more, be more, be better. It's the capitalist way. Without something to strive for, what would we spend our money on? But we're being had. All of this pressure leads to paralysis and makes it harder to start something new. The voice in our head warns us that we might fail, so best not to try.

What might seem like a counterintuitive call to action to suck at something is really the start of a more fulfilling life. I want to push you into your first wave and get you to your feet. But first you have to find the thing you are going to suck at—which brings me to the first rule of sucking: It has to mean something to you. If you don't love bread, sucking at baking doesn't count. If making music doesn't move your soul, then your screechy violin will be for naught. You have to give a shit in order to let go of your desire to excel at it.

If you don't want it, you're going to quit. It's that simple. There's every single reason to quit: you're wasting time, you look foolish, you're not getting measurably better. Wanting to do something you suck at is precisely and perfectly unreasonable. It must be so.

After my first surf lesson, it took me five years to catch a wave. Five years is an absurdly unreasonable amount of time given the task at hand. Five years of practice until I could paddle into, catch, pop-up, turn, and glide along the face of a wave. That is, five years to actually surf.

Surfing, it turns out, was harder than I thought.

Those five years weren't empty. They were full of failure, full of realization, full of learning. After a while, after I kept trying to do something that I was supposed to give up, I started to shed some other shibboleths of success. I learned to quash some of those pesky myths we carry around that weigh us down as surely as the 168-pound Olo surfboard made of wiliwili wood that Hawaiian kings would ride in the early days of surfing. Let's put those ancient boards down and pick up some lighter sticks. The idea is to get upright on a wave, not to be a king of Hawaii.

FIRST TIMES ARE OVERRATED

When you try something new, there is going to be the unavoidable first time. People tend to be nostalgic about first times and log away a lot of soft-focus memories. Since politeness dictates that we let people participate in their own mythmaking, we're generally happy to allow one another fabricated reminiscences. No one calls one another on their bullshit when it comes to origins. First loves, first cars, first jobs. But if we're honest with ourselves and think lucidly about the first time (for anything), chances are it sucked. Prodigies not included. For the rest of us: That first love broke your heart, that first car was a lemon you had to hot-wire to get started, and that first job was sorting the mail and getting coffee for a boss you hated.

A victimless crime, perhaps. Except that when we're dishonest with ourselves about our first times, we're making it harder to see how far we've come since then. We're unnecessarily shorting our own accomplishments. Honesty, in this case, actually magnifies and expands the truth about what we've done.

It doesn't matter how bad a first time was. A key component to sucking at something is acceptance that first times are overrated. This is true even for what comes naturally. Try it. You can do it in private, in your head right now as you read. I'll go first: If I catalog my epic firsts, they are none too pretty. My first kiss was full of so much saliva that it made me want to vomit. The first time I had sex, I wound up with crabs. My first marriage literally could've killed me. The first time I gave birth, I nearly bled out. Still, if I hadn't kept trying in spite of the fact that I sucked at all of those things, I would never have experienced the most awesome sex of my life and a long marriage (okay, it took until the third time, but you already know I'm a slow learner). My sons are the happy-making result of both of those experiences.

Sucking can be epic and important when it comes to sex, love, marriage, work, birth, death. That means that learning to accept sucking when the stakes are low will ultimately help us when we suck at the big stuff. Practice will give us some muscle memory to deal with it. The stakes are never as low as the first time.

Here are some of my other epic failed firsts: The first time I cooked for a dinner party; the first time I tried going on a trail ride on a horse without a guide; the first time I ordered a meal in French—it was my first day in Paris. I'd moved there after college with little but a misguided fantasy that it would become my home for the rest of my life. I'd been a committed Francophile since middle school, fortified by my language and literature studies in high school and college. I thought I was fluent until I wound up with a plate of grilled kidneys I mistakenly ordered from the menu and ate while gagging because I didn't want to admit to my incorrect translation.

Have you had the opportunity to try any of those things—and haven't taken it? Were you afraid of looking dumb? Or of getting the proverbial plate of grilled kidneys?

It's endless, this list of things that are harder than they seem. And the first time you try, it'll suck. Be ready for it and forget about laying down tracks to some knee-jerk nostalgia about how mind-blowing that first time was. There'll be no contribution to that great scrapbook of life. I hope that comes as a relief.

There are some things that you'll have a harder time avoiding. Have you ever applied for a mortgage to buy a house? If not, then get ready because it is one of the greatest of all-time sucky things to do.

The opposite of delusion isn't just honesty. It's self-belief. And self-belief is a far more dependable, and longer-lasting, fuel.

Luckily for me, when I decided to start surfing, I already had some of that self-belief banked.

In the universe of physical endeavors, I was in my comfort zone. I had been physically active my entire life, but when it came to the life of the mind, well, that was where my insecurities resided. They were always there, like sparkly dust motes in a ray of light shining through a living room window, but I had at least learned by adulthood to wave them away when I needed to rise to the occasion.

But sports were second nature. Okay, I couldn't throw a ball, or run long distances. And yes, it had taken me two years of jumping in front of the bay window of my childhood home—an ersatz mirror in which I could watch my progression—to figure out how to do a spread-eagle, touch-toe jump so I could make the cheerleading squad. But all that jumping made my legs really strong, which helped me to throw a shot put for the track team and beat out girls twice my size. Cheerleading captain–star shot putter: I covered the spectrum by any measure. So, you get the idea: I was strong and determined and confident-ish about it. Surfing would just be another physical endeavor I would practice and get pretty damn good at.

Delusion, pure and simple.

Over the years, I had dabbled in many sports, among them boxing, cycling, weight lifting, running, skiing, horseback riding. I could have pursued any of those with a lifelong passion and I would probably have been better at all of them than I am at surfing. But even as I write, I am aware of the tug of nostalgia about these earlier pursuits. I probably sucked at them too.

THAT BITCH, NOSTALGIA

It's only relatively recently that we've begun to wear rose-colored glasses when looking into the past. Nostalgia was considered a "neurological disease of essentially demonic cause" in the seventeenth century. Coined by Swiss doctor Johannes Hofer in 1688, the word derives from the Greek *nostos*, which means to return home, and *algos*, which means sickness. The term was often applied to soldiers who longed for home (who can blame them?), but it was treated as a pathology. Apparently, Swiss soldiers fell prey to it when they heard a certain Swiss milking song. The heartrending nostalgia they felt when they sang the song interfered with their effectiveness as soldiers so much that singing it became punishable by death.

The idea of nostalgia as something positive is a new concept. Studies now show that nostalgia can give us a sense of well-being. It helps us to make meaning of our past—arguably a force for good. It drove Odysseus back to Ithaca, makes Londoners remember the Blitz with fondness, and keeps high school reunion venues flush with paying celebrants. But I think our forebears were onto something. There's room for a reconsideration of the grass-is-always-greener coloring of nostalgia. Was it really always better then? And if so, where does that leave us now? Current science also cautions against this kind of nostalgia as magical thinking that works against coping mechanisms. And so much of being able to suck at something depends on staying firmly in the present.

Still, you might have to dig into your past to find out what it is you are going to love sucking at.

I started to surf because it terrified me.

I'd grown up with recurring nightmares and dreams about the ocean. They began before I have memory of my age, and continue, in a different form, today.

In the dream version, a giant wave is coming toward me, and instead of wanting to escape it, I surrender to it and become one with its power. Oftentimes, I lie down on the sand and let the wave overtake me. I understand, in my dream-state, that I will be able to breathe underwater if I am held there. I don't fret about turbulence or what will happen when the wave actually crashes. As it approaches, I am calm, and when it arrives, I accept its power as my own. It is a beautiful dream.

In the nightmare version, a giant wave is coming toward me, the same as in the dream, but there is a wall, cliff, or some kind of structure behind me. I have nowhere to run, even though I have a clear understanding in this sleep vision that I need to get the fuck out of there. But, no luck. I am doomed. In this scenario, I will get hammered and I understand that I can't breathe underwater. With this awareness comes the certainty that I will die. The surrender and peace of my dream is replaced with panic and terror in my nightmare.

I grew up with these conflicting images dancing in my head. They were there when my family vacationed at the Jersey Shore throughout my child-hood. They were there when I swam with my friends as a teenager and panicked when my feet no longer could gain purchase on the sandy ocean bottom. They were there when I found myself walking along the shoreline in Laguna Beach and realized that even though the tide was low, there was a cliff behind me and I didn't know how fast the tide would come in and what depth it would take on: my nightmare vision in real waking time. They are there still when a wave jacks higher than I expect it to, and I lose my breath with anticipation about what will happen when I dive under to avoid it. They are there when I get caught in a riptide and feel myself being pulled out to sea. They are there when an outside set wave looms on the horizon and I can't make it up and over the top to the other side. While these oceanic fears may be instinctual and relevant to my life as a surfer, our underlying fears of being overwhelmed apply to anything unknown or unpredictable. For many of us, public speaking is just as terrifying as a jacking wave.

It took me thirty years to overcome this inhibitory fear of the ocean, her waves, and what swims beneath her surface. But the fear is counterbalanced by a compulsion to be near, in, and on her. I am pulled toward the big blue, even though its power and what lives in its depths freak me the fuck out. I'd spent half a lifetime watching surfers with envy. Not by their ability to surf the wave—I've already admitted my imbecilic thought that, if I tried, I'd have that covered pretty quickly. I was wowed by their seeming fearlessness to just be out there, even though it's what I wanted so badly to do.

This isn't something particular to me. Nor is it particular to me that I first felt the overwhelming need to get to the ocean in my middle age. There's even some biological basis for seeing the urge as literally rejuve-nating: at birth, water makes up around 75 percent of our bodies. That can decrease to between 50 and 60 percent in old age. Surely this march toward desiccation calls our bodies back to the elements.

My particular romance with sucking began with something elemental—in my case, the pull of the ocean, and all of the fear and struggle and chal-lenge to survival it represented. But the form it took was less important than the fact of my compulsion to act on it. All animals experience fear; acting in defiance of it is so much of what makes us human. Nonetheless, the first time we take that action will not be a triumph. It'll be a tremble.

Hannah Arendt calls action "the one miracle-working faculty of man." She writes in *The Human Condition*, "The life span of man running toward death would inevitably carry everything human to ruin and destruction if it were not for the faculty of interrupting it and *beginning something new* [italics mine], a faculty which is inherent in action like an ever-present reminder that men, though they must die, are not born in order to die, but in order to begin."

Arendt's concerns with political and social theory apply to the call to do something new because, as she also writes, "the faculty of action . . . interrupts the inexorable automatic course of daily life." With that automation comes a complacency that gets us nowhere. It is better to act than to wish that we had.

It is better to suck than not to suck at all.

My first son, Rocco, arrived late in my life. I'd already been married and divorced twice and set out to have a child on my own. As life has taught me over and over again, what I thought would happen and what winds up happening are often two very different sides to the same delusional certainty that we are somehow in control. So, at thirty-seven, I gave birth to my first son and along with new life and the placenta that sustained him, I expelled old fears. Out with the silly neuroses I'd held my entire life . . . and in with more profound ones, such as: how do I protect this child, whom I love more than seems possible, from all of what may cause him harm and heartache? It was a kind of hell on earth, but also divine. A nightmare-dream.

The convolution in my somewhat overwhelmed brain was the condition from which arose my desire to surf. For years I had looked longingly at people riding waves but wouldn't dare try it myself. Now my old fears receded like the water's edge before a tidal wave and in rushed the fears that pervade motherhood—along with the nagging one that I would grow old without ever paddling out and going for a wave at least once. I was no longer afraid to give it a go. Frankly, I had bigger things to be afraid of. Suddenly, I was imbued with a certain "fuck yeah" attitude. Ocean nightmares be damned.

I was so serious about a shift toward ocean living (and perhaps so high on my own hormones) that I moved my family from New York City to the Jersey Shore. Never mind that I did no research about what it would cost in life-hours to get from Seaside Park, New Jersey, to Manhattan every day for my job. Clearly, I suck at reality checks as well. I hadn't even tried surfing yet, but in my commitment to try it, I went all in. And, because life likes to mess with us—especially when we exhibit the kind of cluelessness I subjected myself and my family to—the week I signed up for my first surf lesson, I found out I was pregnant with my second child. The dream would have to wait.

Over three thousand commuting hours later, I was out of shape and overweight and completely out of my mind with exhaustion. But I still wanted to surf, dammit. My kids were now four and two. It was getting late in life for this folly. Still, and finally, on a midsummer morning of my forty-first year, I sheepishly phoned a local surf instructor, and asked for a lesson. When the weather and swell cooperated—wind light and offshore, waves super-small (read: barely there), calm and clean current—he called and said, "Conditions are good. Can you meet me in twenty minutes at Thirteenth Avenue beach?"

My husband, Joel, asked if he could come along, and I begged him to stay home. I couldn't bear a witness to my self-inflicted humiliation.

When I arrive at the beach, the instructor asks, "Okay, Karen, so . . . do you snowboard?"

"No."

"Do you skateboard?"

"I've tried."

"Do you water-ski or windsurf?"

"Nope."

"Okay, then," he offers gamely, "we're gonna get you up anyway."

We wade out into the water with a yellow 10' soft-top beginner's board, resembling more a small flat boat than a surfboard. I lay on top of it, sloppily and awkwardly. There is so much board beneath me that it remains steady even though I am feeling anything but.

At this point on that fateful morning, I am confronted by the irrefutable and humbling reality of what I am to this patient young man: a middle-aged, out-of-shape kook whose only value is that I can afford the hourly fee for a private lesson. I have to fight back the impulse to just call it quits even before I start, but instead I resign myself to try this once and then to forever put this dream aside.

My instructor was a man of his word: before my hour is up, I stand up on my first wave. It was knee-high and slow, a pulse more than a wave. He pushes me into it and yells, "Up! Now!" I practically crawl to my feet, ride the wave straight to shore, and fall off when I don't know what else to do. The force of the water from falling into the crashing wave dislocated the tenuous hold my breasts had on the bikini top I wore. I bubbled to the surface with it dangling around my neck. Any embarrassment I felt was immediately overcome by *stoke*. There's that word, forever connected to surfing at its most pernicious—the purview of the insouciant and inarticulate. "I'm just so stoked, man . . ."

But it rocks, that word. It sounds exactly how it feels. I was so stoked.

I apologize to my instructor for the flash of my breasts—no fun for him, I assure you—and happily pay his fee. I ask him to meet me the same time the next day and I run the half-mile home. (All of a sudden, my old athlete body recovered some muscle memory.)

Those two surf lessons changed the course of my life.

What if I'd never succumbed to a delusion? Things surely would have continued apace—for better and worse, I imagine. I will be forever grateful that I tried something I would never get good at—but I didn't know that yet.

The fact is, that wasn't my first wave. Not really. I try not to dress up a past memory with shimmery false qualities or by falling prey to that bitch, nostalgia. In the painfully beautiful novel *The Sense of an Ending*, Julian Barnes writes, "what you end up remembering isn't always the same as what you have witnessed."

That first day was followed by countless others of me trying, and failing, to catch a wave. Joel bought me a 9' orange soft-top for my forty-first birthday later that summer and I spent the next two years lugging that monster to the beach where I floundered in the slop with it. Our local surf shop owner, Mike Colombo, wouldn't even sell us a real board. He told me, "As a beginner who is also the mother of two young sons, it would be irresponsible to sell you a fiberglass board. Learn how to handle this foamy in the water and then I'll sell you a real board."

Two years later, I bought a 7'4" "fun-shaped" board that was too narrow and had too much rocker for me (the degree to which the nose of the board curves up). I never scored a wave on that one either. Mike clearly thought I was progressing more quickly than I was. I admit to having had thoughts of giving up, but by this time, I understood a few things, one of which was: I was gonna need a bigger board. And even though Mike was being helpful in directing me to one board or another, it was up to me to find one most appropriate for my skill level.

In most endeavors, the more talented usually can't wait to tell you what you're doing wrong or to offer advice—wanted or not. Weirdly, in surfing, few people chime in to give you pointers. They mostly let you go about fucking it up on your own. This has to do with the irrefutable fact that surfers want waves for themselves (this is not a character flaw so much as an innate preservation of something they love too much and get to do so little) so encouraging you to continue is not in their self-interest. A successful surf brand from the '80s, Gotcha, became popular with a logo that said: If You Don't Surf, Don't Start. That about sums up the unspoken surf culture.

So, with no one to tell me what I should be riding, and with nary a wave in my up-until-then sad history of surfing, I bought a plain white 8' Blair epoxy board for added float and stability, which would become a kind of mysto board in my quiver. (Translation: a board in my collection that I return to again and again because its mysterious special qualities help me catch some of my best waves.)

My real first wave happened five years after the summer I took that first surf lesson. It took five years of getting rolled and roughed up, of paddling out alone; years of riding on the inside, where the force of the white water from a breaking wave pushes you jerkily to shore. This is the kind of surfing you see in surf camps for first-timers. Fun enough at first, it gets to be a drag after a while. It's exhausting to keep fighting the white water while hanging onto your board on the inside as opposed to sitting on your board in the calmer waters of the lineup, enjoying the ocean as you wait for a wave to roll through. Besides, it isn't surfing. It's something else not worth naming. There were years where my family watched me, shaking their heads. My father—who at eighty-eight still comes to dinner every Saturday—would stand on the beach and witness my struggle. He'd ask, "Why do you keep trying?"

NEW THINGS

What was it that kept me at it for five long years?

I didn't have a great answer for my dad at the time.

Part of what kept me going was that I felt I had accomplished something by the sheer fact that I'd overcome my fear of the ocean, at least enough to get into it, often alone, and for hours at a time. To get into it with a board and to try to surf seemed heroic. But that is attaching a sense of accomplishment that I didn't actually feel.

I felt something else. It always felt new. Each time I paddled out, I felt a frisson of being somewhere I'd never been before and doing something I shouldn't be doing. That had something to do with the activity itself, where the conditions are never the same as they were even half an hour earlier or would be fifteen minutes later. The wind switched or kicked up, the swell grew or died out, the tide was coming in or going out. There are countless factors contributing to the shifting conditions. The novelty reestablishes itself, over and over. The waves never form the same way twice. This sense of newness is something surfing has in spades.

Novelty is so powerful, and it's not as subjective as you might assume. It's not just in the eye of the beholder.

Mammalian brains are wired to search for new environments—it's what keeps foraging species from starving to death. Think about taking your dog for a walk. Is it different—is he different—when you take him on that typical morning walk around the block, and when you take him on that extralong weekend hike? Is he especially keyed up and crazy on that hike? Does he get so excited that he exhausts himself? He's driven to seek out the new. The only thing holding him back is his leash and that nap that he so desperately needs.

We've known for a long time now that learning something new activates a variety of neural responses, many of which are beneficial beyond the behavior memory pigeonhole. Novelty can improve the mind as a whole.

This curiosity, or drive for novelty, also has a positive effect on longevity in humans; it helps maintain a healthy central nervous system. Studies show that more curious senior citizens actually outlive their less curious peers. New tricks are exactly what an old dog needs.

Even the anticipation of novelty can increase dopamine, the powerful neurotransmitter that makes us swoon as we fall in love, cements our addictions, and, according to behavioral neuroscientist Bethany Brookshire, is what puts the sex, drugs, and rock 'n' roll into sex, drugs, and rock 'n' roll. Even more fundamentally, dopamine is instrumental in our motor functions, which is why a decrease in dopamine is one of the main characteristics of Parkinson's disease. The complexity of dopamine makes it impossible to qualify it as a necessarily good thing or a bad thing—it's also what we feel when we gamble or do meth—but one thing is for sure, when we get a hit of it, it feels good and we want more of it.

If a longer life and a dopamine high aren't enough of a reason to start something new, there is the more ornery benefit that when you suck at something, no one asks any favors of you when you're doing it. People will give you space. I promise. Sucking doesn't attract a crowd.

In those heady years of raising my children and forging ahead in my career, surfing was the one thing I did regularly that I didn't have to succeed at. It was the one space in my life where the expectations were low enough I could take full and solo ownership of them. No one bothered to ask me to get better at surfing. They knew they'd get nothing from it. Instead, I got to control my own pace. Surfing—sucking—was my domain.

MY REAL FIRST WAVE was really my upteen-hundred and fifty-somethingth wave and I wasn't even supposed to be in the water. I'd sprained my wrist and the inflammation was acute enough that I couldn't pick up anything with my right hand. My doctor told me to stay out of the water so I could rest it. I asked for an alternate solution, but he just shook his head. (Ignoring doctors' warnings will become a refrain in these chapters.)

Since staying out of the water really wasn't on the table—it was a beautiful day, the waves were clean and well formed, my son-in-law, Christopher, whom I adore and don't get to surf with nearly enough, was heading out for a session—a resourceful friend gave me a work-around. At his suggestion, I wrapped my wrist and hand in an ace bandage and then covered the ace with gaffer's tape, creating a waterproof seal. My right hand and wrist became a shiny gray-taped club. I carried my board on my left side to the beach and I paddled out with a splish-clump, splish-clump, splish-clump, clawing my way to the lineup.

Even though I was game to get out there, once I sat outside, I started to think about how it was going to hurt like hell when I tried to pop up. I say "tried" because, even though I'd been riding teeny waves and white water for years, I still hadn't managed to drop into, turn, and ride the face of a significant wave. I would try, as ever, dammit, and remain ever hopeful.

BREAK IT DOWN

It might be helpful to understand the various aspects of surfing that make it so damn hard. Any sport or effort can be broken down into its component parts to illustrate what needs to be learned to reach competency, a useful exercise to appreciate why sucking at something isn't something to be ashamed of.

I invite you to break down your own pastime too. This guidepost is meant for two exercises. First, break down something you do really well into detailed action points. This will make you feel like you kick ass. Eventually, you'll do it for the thing you suck at, something you struggle with, or simply something you'd like to try. My hope is that the exercise acts not as a deterrent, but as an appreciation about how fucking hard things are so you can get on with it. Step by step.

I'll go first. Here's what a beginner needs to learn before she slides on water:

1. You have to manage your board in wildly moving water. Even before you jump on the board to paddle out, you have to make sure you are in control of your equipment as you enter the ocean, lest it be wrenched away from you and fly back into you, or worse, into a fellow surfer or swimmer. Many injuries happen in the shore break the moment a surfer stops paying attention to her board.

2. Once you are in a good place to start paddling, you need to lie prone on your board in the exact right position so the board doesn't tilt sideways, and in the most efficient front to back position to get the most out of your paddling. You'd think this would be instinctive, but I assure you, it is not.

3. As you paddle out to the lineup, you have to confront the waves that are breaking in front of you. If the waves are small, you get over the top of the white water by paddling through or by lifting your body off the board to let the white water rush between you and the board. Once waves reach a certain size, the power of the white water will push you back toward the beach in a cycle of Sisyphean efforts to keep moving forward that results in moving nowhere at all. To avoid that pointlessness, you must duck dive under the wave, if you are riding a shortboard; or if you are riding a longboard, you turtle roll to let the wave roll over the underside of your board with you safely underneath it. Don't let cutesy duck and turtle designations betray how hard these basic actions are to learn, especially when the surf gets big. You duck dive with a shortboard by pointing

the nose of your board down and under the oncoming wave, then you press down on the back of the board with your knee or foot at the properly timed moment to gain momentum to dip under the rolling breakwater and come up on the other side of it, where the water is calm. For a turtle roll—which is performed on bigger, higher volume boards with which it is impossible to duck dive—you grab the rails and roll sideways so that you are under the water and the board is on top of you. You hang on with your hands and legs to the board as the onslaught of white water rushes over you. Once it passes, you flip over again and continue paddling. The key here is to not let the force of the water pull the board away from you.

4. Once you are out in the lineup, you catch your breath as you sit on the board facing the horizon. Sitting on the board is also a skill that you have to learn. The water is moving around you, so you are always responding to the environment. If the water is choppy or there is swell coming from different directions, you can bob around like a cork. Learning to balance by sitting is not hard, but it is something that takes some practice. Some people sit way forward and let the tail stick out of the water. Others sit back and let the nose lift out. The cool cat long-boarders kneel as they paddle and wait—I still can't do this after all this time. (Though I keep trying.)

5. Now that you have reached the lineup without killing your-self or anyone around you, you have to learn how to choose a wave to paddle for, which is the hardest part of surfing for me. Reading the incoming swell lines is key to surfing and the skill level varies in knowing which waves to go for and which ones to let pass, even among the pros. Me: yeah, I suck at it. I surf best when someone more adept at reading the lines is calling me into the waves. My son-in-law says he just feels it. My son

is legally blind out there (he sucks at wearing contact lenses) and yet he can call a proper wave coming toward him or me. I still don't understand how he does this if he can't see it.

6. Once you choose which wave you are going to go for, you have to make sure that you have priority. This means that there isn't another surfer closer to the peak of the wave, who has the right of way to go for it before you do. Dropping in on someone is one of the great no-no's in surfing. You should never go for a wave already claimed by someone else. If there is nothing else you learn from this little surf lesson, this should be the one. The tenth commandment applies in surfing, absolutely. Covetousness can get you kicked out of the lineup, or worse.

7. Okay, so now that you have chosen a wave, established that you have priority (keep in mind this is all happening in like, fifteen seconds or less), you have to paddle like crazy to catch it. The factors involved in catching a wave depend on swell speed and direction, wind speed and direction, bathymetry (the ocean bottom), wave height and steepness, among other factors. The trick is to time your paddling so that you catch up to the speed of the oncoming wave and lock into its energy as you and it move forward together. Catching a wave is one of the greatest feelings in the world. It's like a direct plug-in to the universe. I can't make too much of it—it's one of the reasons this damn impossible sport has commandeered my life and the lives of millions of others, in spite of how hard it is to do.

8. Once you catch the wave, you have to pop to your feet while deciding which direction to point the board, either right or left, depending on which way the wave is breaking. Popping up also takes *a lot* of practice. One of the reasons why the barrier to entry for surfing is so high is because so many factors

have to line up perfectly before you even have the opportunity to try to do the thing you set out to do in the first place, which is riding a wave while standing. The time you spend actually surfing is a minuscule fraction of the time you spend setting it all up. Studies show that pro surfers spend only 8 percent of their time in the water actually surfing. Most of the time is spent paddling, around 54 percent. For me, that number is more like 0.004 percent surfing (during a successful session), with 80 percent paddling. There isn't a sport in the world where the metrics are working harder against mastery and in favor of just giving up.

9. Once you're up and headed in the right direction, you steer the board along the wave's face and around the people who might be in your path. This is something you see surfers do in videos all the time with a precision that belies how hard it is not to slice right over them. Too often, you have to bail because other wave-riders (surfers, boogie-boarders, bodysurfers) are in the way, or because the wave closes out (crashes with no shoulder to ride). For less-skilled surfers, these pullouts outnumber the times you achieve the satisfaction of completion. You can guess how often I have to bail.

10. Absent of bailing, wiping out, closeouts, etc., you try to keep the ride going for as long as possible by responding to what the wave is doing at that very moment. Shifting your weight and turning your body is key here—but you are doing this on a board that is moving on water that is also moving and changing at every instant. Making sections (different parts of the wave, as it shifts along the way) is what you're going for here. There will never be a wave or a situation that repeats itself, so each time you get to this point, a different response is called for. It also greatly varies depending on the board you are riding.

11. After you complete the wave, there is the kick out. One of my favorite things to watch is the way pro surfers kick out of a wave. Some do it with grace, others with humor, others with aggression. You can coolly float out the back while still standing or dive off your board and over the lip or breakwater. You can roll through the face of the wave and back out the other side. You can cannonball into the soup or kick your board forward as you fall strategically backward away from the chaos of the breaking wave. The idea is to get out of the wave before you are all the way to shore again, unless the ride takes you there, because the closer you are to shore, the longer the paddle is back out to the lineup. For a kook like me, a kick out is never really a kick out, but an attempt to fall without hitting the board or another surfer.

12. Whatever the outcome of 1–11, you swing your board around, head for the horizon, and do it all over again.

THERE. That's the basics.

Mastering these basic skills will not make you a perfect surfer. It will not even make you a good one. It's just the starting point. A starting point that, for me, never ends.

Hence the reason for the number one principle of sucking at something: you've got to want it. You've got to want something even more than you want perfection.

Right now: write down the basics of something that you've got dialed. Maybe it's as seemingly simple as perfect scrambled eggs on toast for breakfast or doing your makeup or shaving before work. Maybe it's swimming laps at the Y for your morning workout, completing a series of Turkish getups with a kettlebell at the gym, or a yoga sequence you practice before bed. Maybe it's something necessary like navigating rush hour or the public transit system. Break it down like you would for a total beginner. Do it in as many steps as possible: be comprehensive, be deliberate, and be clear.

Did you have any idea how crazily complex that thing really is?

Appreciating how hard things can be is the first step toward the liberation of lower expectations. The freedom to suck at something.

FIND YOUR THING

Now that you've proven you're already an expert in some areas, you can feel less self-conscious about finding something new that you can suck at. It might take some misses to land on the thing that will keep you working hard in spite of failure, but I promise: when you alight on it, your life will change for the better. It took years to find surfing as mine; and surely part of what makes it so compelling to me is my personal history with waves as my white whale. Concomitant fear and obsession was a siren call I finally could not ignore. On your journey to find your white whale, you may have to swim with smaller fish.

Before surfing, there were other activities I loved, but from which I ultimately moved away. There was a time when horseback riding became a favorite activity. Needless to say, I sucked at it. I just didn't know it until it was almost too late.

In 1992, I moved to Los Angeles. During my brief tenure in the City of Angels, I would drive weekly to a ranch in the hills above Malibu to escape city traffic and to ride a devilish stallion named Tempest. I rode under the instruction of a gun-toting, leathery, blond cowgirl. One day, she hiked me up on the moody stud bareback, just to watch him buck me off. By clinging fiercely to his mane, I managed to stay upright. Cowgirl thought it was a riot.

"Oh, yeah," I thought, stupidly, "I got this!"

After eight months with Tempest, I figured I knew something about horses. When I moved back to New York, I missed riding. One crisp fall morning, I ventured to the old Claremont Stables on the Upper West Side, assuring the staff that I was expert enough to take a horse out on my own for a spin on the Bridle Path in Central Park.

We'd been out of the barn for all of one minute when it started to go wrong. Somehow, I got us going the wrong way down Amsterdam Avenue. Daisy, excited by the sense that we had already veered off the expected direction toward Central Park, and no doubt confused by an erroneous signal I'd given her, began cantering down the city street. We were soon confronted by a hairless blue and white monster coming straight toward us. It was the M11 bus, driving north up Amsterdam on its dutiful route uptown. With the bus bearing down on us, I dropped the reins and swung my hands above my head and shouted, warning the bus to stop before horse and human flesh were scattered across Eighty-Seventh Street and Amsterdam. With my hands free, my body swung dangerously to the right and I nearly toppled out of the saddle. Had that happened, I would have been unmercifully dragged across the pavement to certain death. It was sheer luck that I managed to stay upright on that poor horse.

Daisy quickly got the drift that I had no business being on her back and had the decency—through no direction from me—to hightail it back to the stable.

The Claremont staff asked me, "What happened?"

"Oh, I'm not feeling very well," I lied to explain the lack of color in my face. "I decided against the ride . . . What's that? A refund? Oh, no, no thanks, I'm good."

I couldn't get me and my humiliation out of there fast enough. That was the end of my very short riding career.

My past is full of trial and error and failure. I have been down for the count while boxing. I flushed a tampon out of my body while waterskiing when my legs, instead of holding parallel, spread-eagled through the water, causing the cotton plug to lodge inside my one-piece bathing suit. I've barreled down snowy mountains without knowing how to stop and have had close calls while rollerblading and cycling and skateboarding. In spite of the bruises and awkward moments, I regret none of these efforts. And, while none compelled me to continue while sucking, I think some conditioning took hold for when I stumbled onto the real thing.

Most important, I didn't *need* to commit to each and every thing that I ventured into. You don't either. Pressuring yourself for commitment is just another obligation that moves you further from the freedom that sucking can bring. The point is to start something new with an open heart. Commitment will come or it won't. The beauty of it is that when you let curiosity lead you to an undiscovered passion, you'll find relief from having to excel and a welcoming community you didn't know existed.

Here are some prompts to get you started:

1. What did you want to do when you were a child but were too afraid to try or didn't try because someone told you—"oh, you'd never be good at *that* . . ."?

2. What is it you see some people doing and think, "If only I could do that!"?

3. What terrifies you? Does conquering that fear compel you?

4. Answer this question: If I could leave my job right now, where would I go and what would I do? (I'm not prompting you to irresponsibility; rather, suspending obligation for a moment might free your mind to wander into unchartered territory.)

5. When you are scanning the magazine rack at the airport or bus depot, which do you secretly want to buy and read, but don't feel that you should because you don't really do that stuff?

A few words of caution: Keep it from becoming transactional. If you are going to start throwing pottery or knotting macramé, don't get caught up in the investing in that cute little storefront to sell it. If you want to write poetry, forget—at least for now—getting published. If you want to sing, don't start auditioning just yet. If you love Scrabble, the national championship is not where you set your sights, but rather concentrate on making pointy words when playing against your not-so-clever aunt or know-it-all nephew.

One thing is abso-fucking-lutely true: you will never be *the best* at any of these things, so best to get over it now. Let me help.

As a checkpoint—or just for fun—follow the decision tree on the next page to guide you along the way.

BAD VIRTUES

We're closing in on eight billion people in the world. How many "bests" can there be? And where does that leave the rest of us?

I admit to having a strong aversion to the idea of perfectionism. My opposition to it has an emotional valence because I know I can succumb to its siren song. Perfectionism is so, so comfortable. It's a common excuse I encounter when I speak to people about how great it is to suck at something. Striving for perfection is a glossy way to say: afraid. Afraid to look foolish. Afraid to have to start somewhere. Afraid to suck.

Part of the problem, I learned very quickly, is how perfectionism can be regarded as a virtue, when in fact it's just another self-defense against being vulnerable. And an inspiration for ad copy. A certain luxury European car company recently put out this commercial: A hot new model is humming along a curving road at high speed, the music is pumping, and the voice-over says: My dad always told me, "it doesn't matter what you do in life . . . Just be the best at it." Oh, sure, and that means buying this $60,000 car, I guess.

Since you and I are on the quest to suck, together, we're going to have to bust down the door on the myth of perfectionism. We're going to have to call it what it really is: fear. And we're going to also have to make a nuanced distinction between striving for excellence and holding out for perfection. One of these pulls us along; the other holds us back.

This won't be so easy. Our sophisticated complex of ideas around perfection is pretty ingrained.

To understand the origins of our drive to perfection, we can look to the father of individual psychology and psychotherapy, early twentieth-century Viennese doctor Alfred Adler, whose work centered on the idea that human striving from inferiority to superiority drove all of our actions. He called this striving, "The urge from below to above that never ceases."

THE SUCK AT SOMETHING (SAS) DECISION TREE
Find out if you are living the Suck at Something life

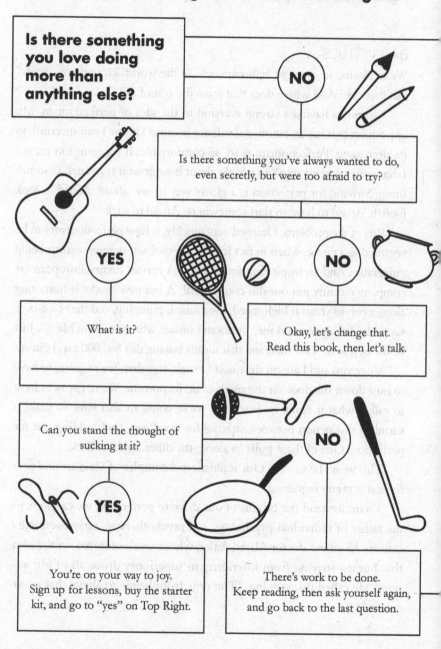

Is there something you love doing more than anything else?

NO

Is there something you've always wanted to do, even secretly, but were too afraid to try?

YES

NO

What is it?

_____

Okay, let's change that. Read this book, then let's talk.

Can you stand the thought of sucking at it?

NO

YES

You're on your way to joy. Sign up for lessons, buy the starter kit, and go to "yes" on Top Right.

There's work to be done. Keep reading, then ask yourself again, and go back to the last question.

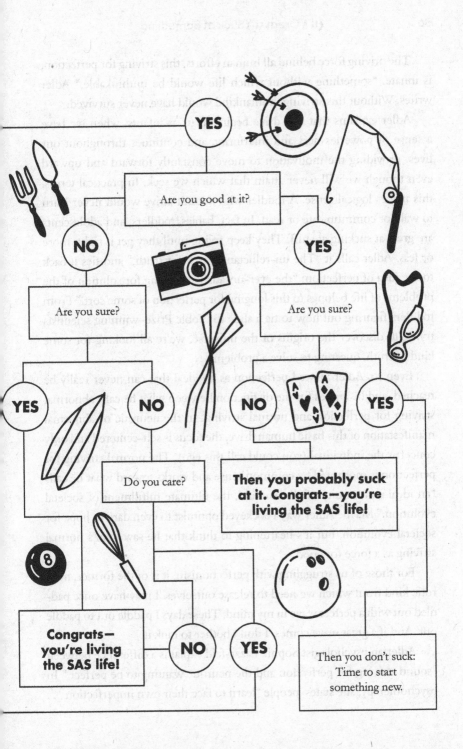

The driving force behind all human efforts, this striving for perfection, is innate, "something without which life would be unthinkable," Adler writes. Without this striving, humankind would have never survived.

Adler explains that this drive begins in us as infants, when we have a sense of powerlessness and inferiority, and continues throughout our lives, providing the motivation to move constantly forward and upward even though we will never attain that which we seek. In practical terms, this makes logical sense. A toddler who doesn't strive would never learn to walk or communicate or read. In fact, babies, toddlers, and adolescents are great at sucking at stuff. They keep trying until they get it right, more or less. Adler calls it "The un-reluctant search for truth," and ties it back to the idea of perfection: "the ever-unsatisfied seeking for solution of the problems of life belongs to this longing for perfection of some sort." From toddlers figuring out how to tie a shoe to Noble Prize–winning scientists trying to discover the origins of the universe, we're all looking for some kind of truth, questing to solve a problem.

Even so, Adler viewed perfection as an ideal that can never really be reached, and he argues for the distinction between what he calls abnormal striving for perfection and normal striving. In the neurotic or abnormal manifestation of this basic human drive, the focus is self-centered and only concerns the individual (you could call this ego). The normal striving for perfection is motivated by common sense and works toward what he calls "an ideal community of all mankind, the ultimate fulfillment of societal evolution." Maybe Adler was a cockeyed optimist to even dare to hope for societal evolution, but it's heartening to think that he saw man's normal striving as a force for good.

For those of us struggling with perfectionism, it is of the former, neurotic kind from which we need to release ourselves. I may have once paddled out with a perfect wave in my mind. These days I paddle out to paddle out. And if a great wave comes, I don't bother to rank it.

Adlerian psychologist Sophie Lazarsfeld explains a difference between "sound striving for perfection and the neurotic wanting to be perfect." In psychotherapy, she states, people "learn to face their own imperfection . . .

They acquire the courage to be imperfect." Recent studies support the idea that depression and low self-esteem can result from not accepting imperfection. It's a trap. And the feelings of deficiency that "not being perfect" engender in us have nothing to do with sucking at something. Deficiency requires believing in a measuring stick so high in the air it's not even worth grasping at.

Perfectionists will always be disappointed. They have a built-in defense mode that prevents them from enjoying activities, whether connected to work or play. How can anything be satisfying or any fun if doing something perfectly is the end goal? They are bound to fail. There is no way around it. One of the greatest actors of all time can't watch herself in the movies she performs in because all she can see are her mistakes. It's painful, this refusal to accept ourselves for our efforts in the face of the impossibility of perfection.

If we understand perfectionism in the way Adler first postulated, we can begin to understand that this striving is innate—a natural impulse to improve. As long as we accept that we will never get to perfection, or become the "best," maybe we can be more satisfied as we bust our asses along the way. At the very least, we can learn not to use it as an excuse for never trying something in the first place. In reality, too, it's actually hard not to improve at something a little bit.

There's a strong connection between holding ourselves to an impossible standard (but really thereby letting ourselves off the hook of trying) and unfairly judging other people. Rudolf Dreikurs, another Austrian-born psychiatrist working in the US, who developed a system for working with troubled children, cautioned in a 1957 address to the University of Oregon that we were becoming:

> [A] mistake-centered [society where] this mistaken idea of the importance of mistakes leads us to a mistaken concept of ourselves. We become overly impressed by everything that's wrong in us and around us. Because, if I am critical of myself, I naturally am going to be critical of the people around me. If I am sure I am no good, I have at least to find

that you are worse . . . Anyone who is critical of himself is always critical of others. And as long as we are so preoccupied with the fallacious
assumption of the importance of mistakes, we can't take mistakes in
our stride.

Dreikurs was pointing to our pathological focus on what we do wrong,
instead of focusing on what part we get right. And that was decades before
the internet would make a national pastime out of trolling.

The nuance I referred to earlier in this chapter is contained in this
difficulty: it's only great to suck at something if we accept it, embrace it,
and see it as a piece of the equation rather than some error. You can't want
to feel (too much) frustration after sucking. In the same way that beginner
runners will feel muscle pain for a few miles, you should seek feeling that
good stress, the kind that comes with going a few extra blocks farther than
last time. Otherwise we'll quit or lash out (or both) at others for our own
perceived deficiencies.

Dreikurs was not discouraged, though, believing that "if we learn to
function, to do our best regardless of what it is, out of enjoyment of the
functioning, we can grow just as well, even better than if we would drive
ourselves to be perfect." In other words, be happy in the doing, and not
necessarily in the succeeding. We need to let sucking at something be a way
to work toward healing the rift in our perfectionist soul, by, as Lazarsfeld
said, helping us to find "the courage to be imperfect."

In the rare instances when we aren't lashing out at those who suck
worse than we do, there are those to whom we assign roles of perfection,
putting them on a pedestal they didn't ask for. Doing so appeals to our
sense of aspiration as it also contributes to our self-doubt. We believe that
the enormously talented have degrees of perfection they get to enjoy while
we can only dream of being lauded in the same way.

Many years ago, I had the privilege to work with one of my heroes of
seeming perfection: Mikhail Baryshnikov, arguably the greatest male ballet
dancer the world has ever seen. I grew up mesmerized by his power and
grace, his beauty and talent. Our first meeting took place in a diner across

from Lincoln Center. I was eight months pregnant and could barely fit into the booth. Our time together was short because he had a daily appointment he couldn't miss, which was a good thing, because as I exited the taxi for our scheduled appointment, I got hit with a killer contraction. As if to confirm my estimation of Baryshnikov as a master of the universe, he guessed the moment he set eyes on me that I had just gone into labor. I'd thought I was hiding it pretty well. (I also sucked at carrying my sons to term—both were born four weeks early.)

I lied and told him, "No, no, I'm fine. Just some Braxton Hicks. It's cool."

Baryshnikov wasn't buying it. "I've witnessed this when each of my four children were born; I know what it looks like and I think you are in labor." (His agent told me later, "Misha has that effect on people.")

Turned out Baryshnikov was right.

"I tell you what," I said to him, "let's have this meeting and I will head straight to the hospital right after. Deal?"

"Deal."

Since we were now on intimate terms considering he was witness to one of the most primal moments in my life, I braved a question to the master. "Now that you know what I'm doing after our meeting, tell me what you will be doing."

To my great surprise, he answered, "Dance lessons."

I think I said something totally uncool, like, "What?!"

The greatest dancer in the world was taking dance lessons. It wasn't about striving for perfection (though he gets pretty damn near close); instead, he told me, he never stopped learning. This gave me plenty to think about over the next two weeks of bed rest before I gave birth to my second son.

ONE FINAL BENEFIT OF GIVING UP perfection is that it means you don't have to think as much. Since perfection is inherently a measurement (how close is this to what it should be?), you'll always be judging what's here and now with what it might be. That's too many things to think about.

On that day of my actual first wave, I splish-clumped my way into a clean left-hander. I paddled and felt the push of the wave lift me and, with my focus on trying not to further injure my wrist, I awkwardly pressed down on the board using my left hand and clubbed right and somehow managed to pop up. Before I knew what was happening, I was gliding effortlessly down the face of the three-foot wave and instinctively turned left (most goofy-foots' preference—meaning my right foot was forward) to catch the section and navigate around other surfers. I completed the ride nearly to shore. I didn't even know I knew how to do that. And then, suddenly I did. I surfed! Those five years of trying became useful only when I stopped thinking.

When we were walking back to the house after our session, I asked my son-in-law, "Did you see that wave I caught?"

This business of having a witness is some serious shit. In surfing, this is especially true. Surfers like people to watch, which is what turned the GoPro camera into a billion-dollar company.

"I saw you made it," he said coolly, unimpressed.

"You know it's taken me five years to catch that wave?"

"Yep. I know. How'd it feel?" he asked.

"It felt good," I told him. "It felt really good."

That was it. It was one of the best conversations of my life.

Eighth-century Zen master Tennō Dōgo told a novice monk, "If you want to see, see right at once. When you begin to think, you miss the point."

Thinking, I'd begun to understand, can be seriously overrated.

ROAD RULES TO SUCKING AT SOMETHING

(a cheat sheet)

1

The thing you suck at has to mean something to you.

2

Don't compare yourself to others.

3

Do what you love without expectation of gain or reward.

4

The pleasure you find is in your own sucking at something, not in the sucking of others.

5

Silence your inner critic by eliminating the question: "Why don't they just____?" (There is no *just*. Things are always harder than they seem.)

6

You shouldn't suck at team sports (unless you are invited) or at tattooing, unless you're doing it for free.

7

Do no harm to others in what you suck at.

WAVE 2

My Pura Vida Wave: Chasing a Dream and the Demons Away

Rule #2:
Do what you love without expectation of gain or reward, or, You are not your work.

Lesson #2:
If you fight the wave, the wave always wins.

Benefit #2:
Playing is good for you.

I bought a piece of property I'd never seen, from a man I didn't know, in a country I'd only visited once. It was the single biggest leap of faith I'd ever taken. Not one of my three marriages had been as risky. No job leap, even backward, put me in more dire financial straits.

I was aware of all of that. And yet, on May 24, 2010, when I wired every last dollar in my savings account to a bank in Costa Rica, I didn't think twice. In fact, in a fit of rationality, I used the fact that I had just cleaned myself out as a negotiating tactic: "That's all there is," I told the seller. "Nothing more where that came from. It's yours if you want it."

Three weeks later, via email and phone calls, it was all done. I had closed on a one-third-acre property on the Pacific coast of the Nicoya Peninsula in the small surfing community of Guiones. Almost immediately, I received a letter from the Internal Revenue Service.

"Send a bunch of money to Central America," my accountant told me, "and you get audited by the IRS." Luckily, my purchase hadn't been illegal, just wildly irrational. The audit brought that home to me. It felt faintly ludicrous. I wonder if the IRS agents felt sorry for me.

The IRS wasn't the only voice of reason. My husband had concerns as well. Understandably.

Joel and I had been together for fifteen years. We'd bought and renovated two homes together. One transaction nearly ended our marriage. We'd been involved in lawsuits and disputes with developers and architects. Joel's first novel was about being a squatter in an East Village apartment, a saga later turned into a feature film. That real estate story does not end well in any iteration.

Why we would enter another venture during a most precarious time of our lives, with four children to care for, was a mystery to anyone who knew us.

One secret factor is that my facility with numbers far outweighs my facility with catching waves. (It is good to suck at something; it is also very good to not suck at other things.) In short, I was able to figure out, with reliable accuracy, how far we could push it before everything fell apart and when, if it came to it, we'd be wise just to walk away. We'd relied on my sense of risk in the past, and each time we'd managed to squeak by without losing everything.

Besides, I trusted the real estate agent, Erik. He and I had spent a total of three hours talking by phone. I knew about how exhausted and exalted he was by his two young children, about his back problems, about how—because he'd imagined an office job in his home state of Florida might kill him—he'd come to live his dream life surfing and working in Costa Rica. We were new old friends.

Joel was more skeptical, and he had a right to be. Like any seasoned adult, we'd seen our share of people who lied and cheated and stole because they could. Sure, we'd encountered assholes, though we didn't feel particularly bruised by any of it. We took our hits, learned our lessons (sort of) and moved on. Risk wouldn't be risk if things didn't go south sometimes.

RISK IS UNDERRATED

A natural annex to the principle of sucking at something is this: when the world reveals itself, inevitably, as the dangerous place it can be, go further. Go deeper. Get in over your head. Protect yourself, but don't allow the world to scare you away from its abundance just because there are pitfalls.

Like anyone else, there have been times when I trusted the wrong person and got into some seriously sketchy situations. When I married a man who betrayed me in a way that threatened my life, I married again after just one date. When a boss put me in a professionally compromised position, I called him out on it, which led to my firing. I had no contract and no net to protect me. The stakes had deepened now that my family and their livelihood could be at risk too. My perhaps injudicious response to each trauma has been the same: Instead of retreating into more cautious behavior, I have remedied a dangerous world by putting myself into an even riskier one. It was my way of testing the universe. A cosmic dare.

I'm not talking about recklessness here. In times of great distress, I most feared embitterment, manifesting as a bedrock of mistrust that would calcify my soul into a never-ending cycle of reliving whatever terrible thing had happened. The only way I could fight retreating into fear and suspicion was to believe in the basic goodness in the world. I made it a practice to trust again, no matter what kind of crap I'd encountered. Some might call this naive, but I look at it as a kind of survival mechanism.

Buddhist nun and meditation teacher Pema Chödrön teaches in her invaluable book *When Things Fall Apart*, "Reaching our limit is like finding a doorway to sanity and the unconditional goodness of humanity, rather than meeting an obstacle or a punishment."

Chödrön recounts the story of how, when the Buddha was about to reach enlightenment, he was confronted with the malevolent forces of Mara, or obstacles to spiritual enlightenment. These Maras shot swords and arrows at the Buddha, but instead of doing harm, their weapons turned into flowers. Chödrön explains, "Whether we experience what happens to us as obstacle and enemy or as teacher and friend depends entirely on our perception of reality. It depends on our relationship with ourselves."

I'm all in for turning swords into flowers.

My husband had more prosaic concerns.

"You mean to tell me you're going to wire all of our cash to Central America without even checking references on this guy?" he asked, referring to the absurd transaction I was about to blindly make.

"He seems like a really nice guy," I told Joel. "I trust him."

"You don't even know him," he rationally objected.

"Yeah, I know. But, I can't imagine why he'd lie to me."

"That's not the point."

"So . . . you think I shouldn't do this?"

Silence. Joel made his point.

"Okay, okay. I'll get references on him."

Sulking was a childish response to the pinprick burst of my naive fantasy bubble that there was some real estate angel just waiting to make my day by offering me a jungle lot in a fire sale. When I told Erik I wanted some names to use for references, he said, "It's a small community down here. I couldn't hide if I wanted to."

I would later learn that the community was built on ex-pats running from the law—but that was in the '70s when the only way into or out of town was via horseback. Forty years ago, surfing and drug-running were symbiotic, alternative lifestyles of choice. A far cry from the organic-living, yoga-practicing, early-to-bed and early-to-rise surf-stoked community that now dominates the place.

Sometimes sucking at something means bending reality sideways to get a different perspective. It all started the year before, when the whole family had traveled to a little surfing enclave in Costa Rica called Playa Guiones. By the end of the vacation, we'd already started joking about buying a place down there, but it was just vacation-instilled silliness. Life interferes with dreams, of course it does.

Three weeks after I'd inquired about a turnkey house, I got an unexpected call from Erik.

"Hey, Karen, I don't know if you are planning on coming down anytime soon, but something has just come up that I thought I should tell you about . . ." He went on to explain how we'd have to close in a month. Cash only. Would I be interested? If I wanted it, I'd have to make an offer that weekend.

Joel didn't like it one bit. I was completely intrigued.

"I'll get right back to you," I told Erik.

When I got off the phone, I was flush with excitement. I'd always wanted to build a house from the ground up. Joel knew I had the itch; here was my moment to scratch it. But I was going to need a very long arm.

"You're crazy," Joel told me.

But Joel's words couldn't offend me at this point. I was in la-la land, doing the thing I do when I get that buzz. I call it "doing the numbers." There is a meditative quality to scratching out financial scenarios: financing, cash flow, investment risk, as if I will discover some magic math that will compensate for never having enough capital, time, or leverage. We were still living paycheck to paycheck with no cushion except for what I was about to risk on this escapade. That cushion was only a year old and I was about to blow it on a hunch.

"I think we can do this," I breathed out loud to no one.

Joel was listening. He is always listening when I think he isn't listening and rarely listening when I address him directly. If that is not the definition of marriage, I don't know what is.

"Do what?"

"Buy this property, build a house. It'll be fun. I'm going to ask Erik to video the property for us to look at. Isn't that a good idea?"

Genius.

The next day, Erik emails a shaky handheld video recording as he slowly walks among the forty-foot guanacaste and pochote trees toward the back of the property line and scans east to the dense forest below the small hilltop. When the camera pans to the front of the property, its view registers and pauses on a For Sale sign nailed to a tree. I already want it taken down.

Here is the first thing I asked myself as I watched the video: how is Erik walking through this uncleared forest wearing only flip-flops? Aren't there deadly spiders and snakes and scorpions lurking under every leaf and fallen tree branch? I mean, I know there are, because we saw them every day walking to the beach and back when we visited a year earlier.

The prospect of venomous insects and snakes had been the reason I decided against a trip to Costa Rica fifteen years earlier. The country boasts the densest biodiversity in the world, with many endemic species thanks to its various terrains and the fact that it borders two oceans—the Pacific on the West Coast and the Caribbean (part of the Atlantic) to the east. My fearful brain translated that as: that's a lot of animals—some you never want to meet. That was before I had children and surfed, when creepy crawly things in nature freaked me out. But, things change. Oh, how they change.

Erik's video was selling, to say the least, because I called to tell him, "We're in." And before you could say "army ants!" we were working with a San Jose attorney to close on a piece of land I'd not walked on but virtually via YouTube.

We did attempt to close on the property in person. But I was blessed with the only eleven-year-old surfer who would choose school over surfing because it was the right thing to do. We argued about it one morning on the way to school. A conversation that says more about how I sometimes suck at parenting than I should be willing to admit.

"Hey Rocco, we have to go down to Nosara to finish buying the property, but it has to happen in the next couple of weeks." I knew I was on shaky ground, but I thought I'd give it a go.

"What about school?" he asks, completely aware of where I am going with this, and not happy about it.

"What about it?" I try to fake it. Impossible. Rocco knows what I am thinking before I know what I am thinking.

"Won't I be missing some days? I do not want to miss school."

"You'll only miss three or four days . . . we'll figure out a way to make it up. Besides, you'd be missing school to go surfing. Who wouldn't rather do that?" I say this with a false bravado. It is cruel and selfish, because as much as he loves Costa Rica and surfing, his unwavering, instinctive sense of right and wrong is being challenged by—who worse?—his mother. He takes school seriously. On most occasions, I am pleased by that fact. Now, in a pathetic role reversal, I whine and try to coax him into a trip.

He looks at me with stubborn refusal. "I will not go. Why can't we wait until school is over?"

"We can't wait. But if you won't go, Grandma and Grandpa can stay with you and your brother while Papa and I go down." This is a low blow and I know it. Rocco's eyes well with tears. He loves his grandparents and he doesn't want to miss this momentous trip. But those are not the issues. It's my fucked-up priorities and his sudden awareness of them that is the issue. At this point I totally suck at being a mother, but something inside me is screaming: don't you know how important this is to me?

But how could it be? How could this crazy transaction—this securing of a place I hardly know anything about, so I can conceivably surf more often, if badly—be more important to me than the priorities of my beloved son?

Rocco brought me to my knees in submission the moment he was born. I had never truly known surrender and love—even though I had loved plenty, it was not like this. Not like the love I felt for my little boy. People speak of shifting priorities when they have children, but they don't mention the shifting of every molecule of your being. That is how I felt when Rocco and then Gio were born. I thought my heart would burst from my love for them. Whatever came before was unrecognizable. Through my boys, I have known the greatest love, and everything else is everything else.

Rocco's fierce determination to not miss school and to defy his pleasure-seeking, childish mother set me straight. Priorities realigned, I decided we would all make the trip together after school let out for summer break. At that point, it would be too late to turn back. My savings would have already changed hands, a deed would be in my possession, and a piece of the Costa Rican rain forest would be ours. So, while Rocco and Gio continued third and fifth grades without interruption, I closed the deal.

On June 15, 2010, I received an email from my attorney in San Jose with the notice that we had closed on the property and the relevant documents were on the way to America. When they arrived, I opened a package to find a handwritten deed in blue ballpoint pen ink. I also suck at speaking Spanish, but I imagine it stated that we were now the proud owners of lot number K-17 in Guiones. The deed sat in my filing cabinet where I put it the day it arrived. I trusted the deed was sound.

A STAR FALL, A PHONE CALL, SYNCHRONICITY

What may seem like a random act of impulsivity to build a house in Nosara makes a bit more sense when seen through the sunset rose–colored glasses of the life-changing family surf vacation we'd taken just eighteen months earlier. I hadn't taken a non-work-related trip in over a decade, before the boys were born.

I still sucked at surfing, but once you've sucked at something long enough you start to get a yen to do it in under more propitious conditions. Once I was convinced that I might actually be able to surf, I began to dream of surfing someplace besides New Jersey. I am not hardy enough, or skilled enough, to make it into North Atlantic water before May or after December. Cold, dark, heavy Atlantic winter ocean is great for the young and the talented, but for me, it was just ornery water. If I was really going to do this, I needed warmer waters. That meant getting a lot closer to the equator than Ocean County, New Jersey.

While risk-assessment still dominates my professional life, I've learned to abandon myself more and more to chance—or, to put it somewhat more poetically, to serendipity, which is what brought me to Nosara.

I've come to realize that serendipity is really the only possible lodestone for when you give yourself over to sucking at something. In other circumstances, you'll be directed by the milestones of mastering that new activity. Your vector is obvious: First you get on a tricycle, then you get on a real bike, then you get rid of the training wheels. The question "What comes next?" is implicitly answered by the purpose. When you don't suck at something, your path is clear.

And more boring.

Part of sucking at something is learning to welcome serendipity into your life. Call it a knock-on effect of having the universe reiterate how unexceptional you can be. Submission is a hell of a drug.

I have tried to untangle the web of small actions that led to the unlikely circumstances that I would build a house in a place I had once refused to visit because of the size of its insects. If I hadn't called Erik during a rare free moment on a Saturday afternoon—and spoken to him about his family, which made me trust him—would I have been hell-bent on this particular place? The inexplicable coincidences that occurred from the outset of our adventure and continue to this day make it seem, if not fated, somehow connected to something larger than mere coincidence.

It's a senseless exercise, the if-this-then-that kind of thinking, but it's hard not to go there. We try to make sense of things to better understand them. But it's not in the causal relationships where we find meaning.

Our acceptance of a synchronistic beauty lends meaning to our lives in ways too mystical to comprehend with the logical mind. We look for signs to guide us, though they may be as fleeting as the shooting stars you see just outside of your peripheral gaze when you look up at the night sky. We are skeptical—*was that a meteor whizzing by, or did I imagine it?*—so we toss them aside in favor of more rational determinism, thinking that it protects us and puts us in control.

The ability to suck at something entails letting go of this lie of control. My favorite surf mantra is Surrender-Control-Surrender, beautifully depicted in the mesmerizing photo of the legendary Midget Farrelly, the first world champion surfer. In the LeRoy Grannis photo, taken in 1968, Farrelly is poised on the nose of his board, feet parallel, knees slightly bent, arms relaxed and held straight in front of him with his hands pressed together and his head bowed, as if in prayer. The moment captured the extreme control Farrelly must have to assume a supplicant's position on the moving wave. A snapshot image of simultaneous surrender and control.

I keep copies of Grannis's photo at home, in my office, and on my phone; I keep the image of it in my head and return to it every day.

It's not just a surfing thing. This nexus of surrender, serendipity, and meaning (and sucking) has been deeply investigated under one name or another over the years. I'm here to promote its potential to improve your life, but others have mapped out its theoretical underpinnings.

Carl Jung was very much taken with the idea of "synchronicity" and tied it to the notion of *unus mundus*—literally "one world"—meant to signify the concept of unity. His close work with physicist Wolfgang Pauli, who won the Nobel Prize for his work in quantum theory, veers into the mystical but looks for science-based proof that meaningful coincidence happens because of a time-space connection between psychic and physical events. Inspired by his early conversations with Albert Einstein, Jung became interested in the psychic conditionality of time and space. Because seemingly random events can coincide outside of someone's immediate perception but simultaneous with their psychological and emotional experience, Jung believed that these synchronistic events proved that "the psyche cannot be localized in space, or that space is relative to the psyche." In other words, there are things that happen that carry meaning but for which there is an acausal connection. Jung spent years working with Pauli to find scientific grounding that tied these phenomena to our conscious and unconscious mind, admitting that synchronicity remained mysterious. However, Jung believed that these linked occurrences that go beyond mere coincidence or causal circumstances "are so improbable that we must assume them to be based on some kind of principle, or some property of the empirical world."

Jung and Pauli didn't finally land on an equation for synchronistic events. Still, the lifelong efforts of these masters of science to understand meaning, Einstein included, proves their conviction that science undergirds meaning; they spent a good portion of their lives working to prove and measure it. It's no wonder that science and philosophy developed together since the ancients. Empiricism is necessary to advance hard science, but it's where science and meaning meet that humankind truly advances.

Those who followed in Jung's footsteps and discipline, such as the author Remo Roth, have gone even further in investigating a way of thinking that doesn't depend on seeing causes and effects behind everything, our current go-to duality mind-set. Roth suggests that when we can put aside this need to be in touch with a chain of causality, we become receptive to opportunities that wouldn't otherwise be available to us. By being receptive, we begin to notice things we wouldn't have noticed before and who knows what a more open perception might bring? Sucking at something helps to keep us noticing.

I think the missing piece of the equation is control. The need to see cause must implicitly be the need to see the way we might control the thing in front of us. After all, a cause is something we can wrap our heads around. So, we live under the pretense that we can control everything and fit it to our vision of the way we think things should be. Life doesn't roll that way. Instead, if we let go of our erroneous sense of control—the idea that where there's a will there's a way, and accept instead that shit happens so we might as well go with it—therein lies our path to happiness. Sucking at something puts you on that path. Sucking helps you turn swords and arrows into flowers.

THE RIDE ALONE on that first trip to Costa Rica from the airport in Liberia to the destination of our coastal enclave was adventure enough. We had rudimentary instructions and little clue about how long the drive would take. Eight of us crammed into the largest SUV we could rent, but which was still too small to hold us comfortably with our luggage. It was hot: about 99°F of equatorial sun. We were thirsty and tired. My youngest, Gio—a vocal eight-year-old who habitually represented the voice of discomfort for all—complained the entire way and for good reason. As the smallest of our tribe, he was wedged in the far back seat between his siblings and cousin.

There were no real directions, few road markers, and we were unprepared for the hour and a half of off-road driving to get to Nosara. Parched, we stopped at a roadside stand selling small, perfect watermelons. We picked three small ones and handed them over to the *chica* running the stand who unceremoniously whacked open the small *sandia* with her short machete. Standing along the dusty road, we gulped down the sweet red-pink watermelon fruit, leaning forward to avoid dripping juice all over our clothing.

The roads to and from Liberia are all single lane. There was a road crew paving the narrow road up the mountain on the other side of Nicoya, the only sizable town between the airport and Nosara. We were stopped by a workman who handed Joel a red flag on a pole, which he understood he should hold until we reached another crew about a mile farther down the road, where he handed them back the flag. The road crew then released waiting traffic headed back in the other direction until—we imagined—the same red flag was given to the last car and the process would repeat.

Having been chosen as the bearer of the red flag to the other side was seen by the whole family as a great welcome. Everyone in the car cheered as Joel proudly held the flag out the window of our car to the other side of the work site, where he handed it to another of the road crew who then gave us what seemed a benediction: *"Pura vida!"*

Clumsily translated as "pure life," it is the expression we would come to learn and use ourselves, signifying the spirit of this welcoming, beautiful country. Pura vida is said as a hello and a goodbye, a welcome, an all-is-well, a have-a-good-day, and everything lovely in between. This, our first exchange in what would become our adopted home, seemed a kind of tacit belonging, a red flag of welcome that would last throughout the entire trip.

I had booked a rental unit online and was half expecting it to turn into a disaster. Once we arrived in Playa Guiones, hand-painted signs tacked to trees gave general directions and we easily found the Harbor Reef Hotel—the outfit that managed many of the rentals in the vicinity. The Tico behind the desk at the main office gave us keys to Villa Belitza and pointed us down a dusty road. A few circles around the pothole-littered dirt roads got us there in fifteen minutes. We would figure out later that it was only a hundred yards from the main office. The saffron-painted stucco house with a clay-tiled roof stood back from the street through an iron gate. The house was bigger than I expected. The interior was clean, spacious, and welcoming. The terra-cotta floors, heavy teak furniture, and solid construction were in the typical style of the area. We could not see the crashing waves through the jungle flora, but we could hear their pounding white noise above the birdcalls.

Night descended quickly and with it the shrill call of cicadas. From dusk to twilight, the air reverberated with an ear-piercing, pulsing screech, the sound of a single giant organism that permeated the jungle. Once dark, the insects went silent.

"Dark" does not quite describe it. By 7:00 p.m., we were starving, and completely exhausted from the day of travel, which had begun at 4:00 a.m. Adrenaline subsided into basic desires: Food. Sleep. We walked to the Harbor Reef restaurant since it was the only place apparent to us. We were, literally, the blind leading the blind. We couldn't see our hands held out in front of us, let alone the road back toward the main building. The sky was clear, but the moon hid behind the jungle canopy. We stumbled along, too stupid to be afraid of what we might step on. One of the first rules of traveling to a place off the grid: bring flashlights.

Christopher was up first the next morning and in the lineup by 6:00 a.m. The waves were sizable those first few days: a few feet overhead on set waves. But the water was warm, the waves empty, and the sun was just rising over the mountains. He came back from his first session as happy as I had ever seen him, admitting, "It was a bit spooky being out there alone."

I didn't really understand what he meant at the time, but I would have that same feeling years later during a dawn patrol session—just me and Rocco out in the waves. It is both everything you hope for in that there is no competition for waves, but then there is also no competition as prey. You're it in both cases. You're well aware of the order of the universe out there.

We quickly fell into a blissful pattern of rising before dawn, surfing all morning, and eating lunch, followed by games of Scrabble and cards, a siesta, sunset sessions, ravenous dinners, and sleep before 9:00 p.m. We were awakened every morning by the calls and noises of birds, insects, and

howler monkeys, who deafeningly claim their territory at least twice a day:
at dawn and at dusk. One afternoon, Joel got into a shouting match—really
a grunting and roaring match—with the alpha of our local troop.

Chris and I were returning to the house from a golden sunset session when we heard, or rather we felt in our chests, the unfathomably
loud grunts and growls of a howler. These diminutive primates have the
longest-ranging calls of any land animal, capable of being heard three miles
away. Up close, it's a terrifying racket when you hear it for the first time, as
if the jungle itself were raising an alarm. We found our family in the back
of the house, watching another primate family move across the trees. Joel
was provoking the alpha male—they are the ones who produce the gut-
tural and forest-shattering noise—as if to engage in a territorial fight. The
howler's neck was thick, his black eyes focused on Joel and the decidedly
nonhowler, strange noises he was making. The monkey answered back
more fiercely than his size would betray. His large *cojones* swung in the
breeze. The argument continued until the adolescents and the mothers,
with their babies clinging to their backs, had moved safely away from the
big white hairless monkeys on the ground.

When the wild animals weren't entertaining us, there were plenty of
domestic ones to keep things interesting. One afternoon as we were driving down the main road, we were stopped by a herd of cows. A particularly aggressive long-horned bull played a game of chicken with our car—I
thought for sure he was going to ram our front end—but he made a quick
hard right turn at the last second to avoid hitting us. Horses trailed along
the side of the road with no apparent destination or leader. Where were
they going? The beach and shore break were lousy with dogs, happy-to-
be-running-on-the-beach-chasing-fish-and-coconuts dogs.

One of them adopted our family as his own. A wiry, brown, short-
haired mutt with a long muzzle and pointy ears followed us home one day
and decided to stay. We named him Hector. He was ours for the week and
we loved him.

Even all of the warnings we'd received about crime in Central America
seemed unfounded. We lost our new Flip Cam on the beach. A palm-

sized video camera that became popular for a minute before iPhones and GoPros forced their obsolescence, we'd videoed our entire week with the camera and hadn't yet loaded it onto a computer. Joel thought the cam had fallen behind the log we camped out by on the beach, but he didn't find it when he searched for it there later that day after he realized it was missing. I just assumed it was stolen. Optimistically, Joel posted a sign on a fence post at the entrance to the main beach:

LOST ON BEACH: FLIP VIDEO CAMERA.
LEAVE WORD FOR JOEL AT JUNGLE JAVE CAFÉ.

The next day, Christopher was returning from dawn patrol and saw, on the opposite side of the same fence post:

FOUND CAMERA ON BEACH.
STEVE @ NOSARA PARADISE RENTAL. CASA CAPITAN.

When we knocked on the door of Casa Capitan, a lovely couple handed us our prized camera. They wouldn't take a single *colón* for it.

About six days into our trip, a truck backed into our gated property and beeped its horn. When the kids and I opened the front door, we found a delivery truck with its back panel open to reveal a cache of German breads, cakes, and pastries. No one asked what German pastries were doing in a jungle enclave. We were famished, and the truck was welcome, if a bit unexpected.

The best part of the trip was how I settled into the energy and attitude of the average age of our brood. With kids ranging in age from eight to twenty-eight, I became the mean age of all of them, which put me at about nineteen. Except for Christopher, we were all in various stages of sucking at surfing. Every day we carted seven boards to the beach and, together, we flopped around in the surf for hours on end. My time surfing in New Jersey was often interrupted by obligations of one kind or another. In Costa Rica, my only obligation was to a good time.

PLAY LIKE YOU MEAN IT

I hadn't had a week of all play and no work since . . . forever. I didn't check in to work once all week, a liberating exercise and one I have yet to repeat. The playfulness of all the kids was contagious and I caught the bug pretty much from the moment we got off the plane.

About halfway through the week, I spotted and visited the local tattoo artist and afterward I tried to convince us all to get matching tattoos before we left. Even my eight-year-old, Gio. (Rules seemed pretty fluid in the jungle.) Maybe I was getting carried away. Joel added some leavening to my sunbaked teenaged behavior. But this sense of play felt new. I was happier in the moment than I had been in years. So what if I had lost some basic adult reasoning? I was reminded of that old trope best known from *The Shining*: "All work and no play makes Jack a dull boy." Gotta have some fun or shit turns bad.

When you really start sucking at something, much of the rest of the world will insist—out of habit and out of politeness—on calling it leisure. That's fine. They're close enough. And while too often in our society "leisure" puts some of our most meaningful activities into a tiny box, there is something in the concept of play that we can use for our purposes.

Stephen King wasn't the first to make resonant the old proverb, which entered the modern lexicon in the seventeenth century as Welsh historian James Howell's most popular proverb. But the distinction between work and leisure dates way back to the ancient Greek philosophers who divided the two for the purposes of praising the virtues of leisure. Clearly surfing wasn't a consideration then or Homer would have had Odysseus diverted to some thumping breaks on his journey home.

The pursuit of play didn't die out with the Greeks. The eighteenth century saw the great Friedrich Schiller, poet and philosopher, warn against being driven purely by work in his *On the Aesthetic Education of Man*. He writes, "Man only plays when he is in the fullest sense of the word a human being, and he is only fully a human being when he plays." I was all human that week in the jungle and I liked it.

It's hard to suck at something if you don't have a sense of play, and if you don't know how to play, you'll never suck at something. But what, exactly, do we mean by "play"? Like porn, it seems to be one of those "I-know-it-when-I-see-it" kind of things. One person's play is another person's torture (see: Frisbee golf or surfing, for that matter).

Anthropologically, animals and humans play in preparation for some skill that will be necessary or useful later in life. Certainly, the swordplay of fourteenth-century young noblemen profoundly influenced life span. Learn to fight well or die. Much of animal play is geared toward learning basic survival skills. Lion cubs hunt their mothers' switching tails and stalk their siblings so they can land that zebra to feed themselves when they set out on their own. Play is considered an instinct but if it is instinct, doesn't it have to serve an evolutionary purpose? How we determine what is play and what is pleasurable practice toward a goal has been the subject of study for ages.

At the close of the nineteenth century, the subject of play went pro. The philosopher Karl Groos wrote what has become an essential guide to play as a field of study. He'd first written about animals and play and by extension, he applied his work to the upper echelon of the animal kingdom. In his *The Play of Man*, Groos lends scientific grounding to Schiller's maxims. After writing his first study, *The Play of Animals*, he concluded "that among higher animals, certain instincts are present which, especially in youth, but also in maturity, produce activity that is without serious intent, and so give rise to the various phenomena which we include in the word 'play' . . . [T]hus, when an act is performed solely because of the pleasure it affords, there is play." Seems obvious enough. But beneath that German stolidity is a wonderful idea: play exists for you and me for no reason at all, and it's available to us until the day we die.

About this instinct or impulse to play, Groos and his contemporary theologian Max Reischle, believed that play contributed to the ethical development of individuals and that "Human society reaches its fullness only among well-rounded individualities, since they alone are properly fitted for service to the whole." To the issue of an evolutionary imperative to play, we, as a society, do better if we stretch our experiences. Monocultures are depleted—both in the natural environment and in the environment at the core of our being, which in turn affects society as a whole.

In one of my favorite surfing movies of all time, *Step Into Liquid*, professional surfer and writer Sam George answers, when asked what purpose surfing serves, "If I come out of the water in a much different, better mood than when I get into the water, that somehow translates into my life and I end up being a happier, nicer person as a result, then I guess you could argue that surfing is good for society." Mood-enhancement is the least of it.

Konrad Lange, another contemporary of Groos, writes, "in the various occupations of mankind, as a rule, but a limited number of the mental powers are employed, and these not fully so. Innumerable springs of feeling are hidden in the human breast untested and untried." He goes on to explain how this has a disastrous effect on the human race. But why must we stay untested and untried? Let's get out there and do something. Something decidedly not connected to work. Something we might suck at.

Going by Groos's expansive definition of play, we can also see that it doesn't just mean running around on a playground, and it doesn't necessarily entail stopping by a sporting goods store. Yes, this is a book where surfing figures wildly, and yes, etymologically, play connotes activity (from Old English *plega* meaning "brisk motion"), but if it includes anything we do just for the "pleasure it affords," then surely that can include more reflective or stationary activities. Better yet, find something that can do both. Even the more contemplative or passive parts of surfing provide as much pleasure as the activity itself. When I float on my board, pointing toward the horizon, I watch for signs of a coming wave, I listen and feel the wind and the movement of water around me. I exist as one with the ocean and enter a kind of meditation.

WHAT DOES THIS have to do with serendipity? With submitting yourself to something bigger, more mysterious?

So much. Because as oxymoronic as this'll sound: playing is hard. For all of us. So few of us really ever do it. So few of us really want to play. If it were so easy, we wouldn't have perennial debates about work-life balance. If we all were great players, we'd all have park-side apartments or houses—because there'd be ten times as many parks.

The commitment to play is hard not just because we all have so many responsibilities. Playing is hard because playing, like sucking, means giving up on being the master. When you play, you submit yourself to spontaneity. That requires humility. Watch some kids playing some obscure, temporary game on a playground sometime. If they all had our hang-ups, they couldn't possibly permit themselves to dissolve into the chaotic giggling crowd that all those games end up in. Play is hard because play means you have to give yourself up. You can't take yourself seriously at play.

It hasn't helped that our culture has entirely mixed-up ideas about work and play and the mythical intersection of the two.

The study of play versus work has concerned thought leaders for years, yet we seem to be no further, or further away still, from a balanced life. Somewhere along the line, as one recent billboard proclaimed, we embraced the idea that "We are what we do." This is meant to proudly identify us by what we accomplish professionally, and to indicate that work for work's sake is enough. A dangerous trap.

WORK IS OVERRATED

Signs condoning a life given over to work are everywhere we turn. That billboard echoes the moronic but pervasive saying: "Do what you love, and you'll never work a day in your life." I've said as much myself. I love what I do, and my work life is intimately integrated into my personal life. I will be forever grateful that I found meaningful work that also supports my family. But let's be clear. When I am working, I work. It is not the same as play. Part of the appeal of surfing for me is that it has little to do with my working life. (I say little because there will always be those welcome overlaps, bringing together the world of water and waves to the world of words and wisdom. But those rare Venn diagrammatic intersections are not what keeps me centered.) Getting away from work is essential, not only for the individual, but for the culture at large. Wouldn't it be great if cocktail party conversation changed from the default, "Hi, so what do you do?" to "Hi, so what do you suck at?"

I often think about a *Surfer* magazine cover feature about Andy Irons, one of the greatest surfers of all time. The headline read: "I Want to Fall Back in Love with the Sport that Gave Me Everything." Andy Irons was a world-champion surfer whose stoke was not guaranteed even though he spent his life surfing the greatest waves in the world and was celebrated as unquestionably one of the sport's all-time best. I remember thinking when I saw that headline that even surfing is work for some. That doesn't take away how awesome that is, but it reinforces that where there are expectations of performance, the dynamics change. No activity is inherently play or inherently labor.

If that sounds a little existential, that's not a mistake. I think that play and work are mind-sets that you bring to an activity, making it your own, instead of some essence of activities that you uncover. I couldn't resist bringing up this idea to my friend Andy Martin, a Cambridge don of French literature, and, of course, a surfer. He has surfed the world over while being able to speak of Sartre on intimate terms—no small feat. When I asked him what Sartre would make of sucking at something as a way to combat existential angst, he refers me to *Being and Nothingness*, where Sartre talks mainly of skiing, then veers off into a consideration of sliding on water.

"What Sartre is saying is that everyone—when surfing or skiing or whatever—is trying to be a Socratic philosopher, which is to say die, transcend, and become godlike. To overcome our human fallibility. So, when I am skiing, I want to be nothing less than the Skier—in some semi-allegorical way. Perfect. Impeccable. Sartre's technical way of talking about this is 'the for-itself-in-itself.' Everyone wants to be a god. But here we come to the sense of failure built into consciousness itself. There is an inevitable asymmetry between the dream and the experience."

This myth or desire of gaining perfection is built in, Sartre is saying. And, of course, we will never fully attain perfection. It's why sucking can be so damn hard. It'll always feel incomplete.

Sartre tries to reckon with the challenge. As Martin explains, "The melting snow provides Sartre with a metaphor of the whole phenomenon. In effect, philosophically speaking, he is saying, I am flawed, but with absurd built-in aspirations to the sublime. The manic-depressive curve is right there. The sense of disappointment. Cognitive dissonance. Every now and then the two coincide, briefly, and in that moment, there is a taste of immortality."

While you might think this means that we have to reach a kind of perfection for a taste of immortality, I believe that since we aren't going to get there, we can find and enjoy lesser moments by finding moments of the sublime through acceptance of our flawed status. And we do this by giving ourselves the freedom to play and suck at it.

But we can't get there if our sole purpose is, well, purposeful. If we have a purpose in the first place. Obsessing over results is for utilitarians. But you, as an honorary kook while reading this book, are a good existentialist. Me too. As Sartre says, play is freedom. A person whose sole focus and purpose is "seriousness," in the Sartrean definition of it, lacks the space and time for intellectual or spiritual contemplation and growth. The idea is particularly relevant today in light of the ways in which we glorify workaholism as a badge of honor. The workaholic uses his working life as a way to push away other fulfilling aspects of his life—whether from fear, misdirected competitiveness, lack of imagination, or total "seriousness." We all know the workaholic who uses work as an excuse for not fully living or enjoying his life: why he is not a more present father or partner; why she can't get to the gym more often. Why the laundry isn't done, or why we can't visit our aging parents more. Why we can't take the time to learn something new even if we are going to suck at it.

What's more perplexing is our tendency to boast about how hard and how long we work. It's like boasting about not sleeping. I don't know about everyone else, but I love to work less and get enough sleep. It makes me think I'm doing something right. But I'd be boasting in turn (and lying) to say that I don't fall into the same work-as-badge trap.

One of the most eye-opening things Gio has ever asked me was, "Mama, why do they make you work so much?"

I paused before answering, because in that innocent enough question was the shameful answer.

"They? There is no 'they,'" I told him, instantly aware of my dysfunctional time management skills.

"Then why do you work so much and then complain about it?"

Another bull's-eye shot to the heart by my then nine-year-old.

This pull toward work is a kind of false paean to a sense of purpose and part of what makes it hard being comfortable with sucking at something. But there is a profound difference between dedication to one's work and the complete immersion that blinds the worker to all other experience. Ultimately, this single-mindedness to work can close off our minds to what makes us human. This remains true for anyone along the socioeconomic spectrum—energy allowing, of course—as what we choose to suck at has nothing to do with a cost of admission, and more about a mind-set.

It isn't so much what we actually do in our play or leisure that matters. Josef Pieper reminds us that it's bigger than that. He writes, "Leisure, it must be clearly understood, is a mental and spiritual attitude—it is not simply the result of external factors, it is not the inevitable result of spare time, a holiday, a weekend or a vacation. It is, in the first place, an attitude of mind, a condition of the soul . . ."

The prospect of leisure concerns philosophers and scientists from diverse disciplines. It follows that its consideration would fall under the purview of economists since time taken for leisure directly affects work time, and therefore, productivity.

Influential British economist John Maynard Keynes, in his 1931 essay, "Economic Possibilities for Our Grandchildren," predicted that by 2028, the global economy would be so large and efficient, that the workweek would shrink to fifteen hours. The problem, as he saw it, was how people would fill all of their leisure time once they had it. "Must we not expect . . .

a general nervous breakdown?" he asks in his essay. Keynes betrays his lack of confidence in the strength of our mental and spiritual attitude that Pieper refers to when he writes, "we have been trained too long to strive and to not enjoy."

Keynes nailed it on the growth of the global economy and while he totally missed the mark on the shortening of the workweek, he was right to be concerned about man's ability to enjoy leisure. Not only do people work nearly as much as they did in the early part of the twentieth century, the distribution of hours worked has reversed: people who gain affluence via their working life are working more than laborers and everyone seems to have less leisure time, not more. The growing gap in wealth distribution means the labor force isn't enjoying leisure time either. So where does this leave us?

In 2008, with the century mark coming up on Keynes's prediction, a group of world-renowned economists considered why we work so damn much. With contributions from sixteen leading thinkers, the analyses presented in the book *Revisiting Keynes* varied from the social benefits of work, to an increase in consumerism. We have to work more to be able to keep up with the Joneses. What makes it worse is that, compounded with an increase in wages, comes an increase in the cost of leisure.

Income inequality is to blame as well. Studies show that the greater the income inequality in a work environment, the more hours worked by everybody in the environment. This effect is encouraged by the tournament-style economic system and performance-related compensation systems, which Harvard economist Richard B. Freeman explains, "gives the person who puts in an extra hour of work a potentially high return." Whoever works most wins!

Americans, it won't come as a surprise, are the worst offenders. Freeman writes, "The United States is the most striking counterexample to Keynes's prediction that increased wealth would produce greater leisure." He goes on to explain that "Americans are so committed to work that they don't take four vacation days from the two weeks that they typically receive, whereas Europeans take almost all of their four- to five-week vacations."

The rote argument goes that Americans work more and therefore, the correlation between hours worked and high output justifies the workaholic culture the United States foments. But does it make us more productive? And more important, does it make us happier?

Where productivity is concerned, studies show again and again that at a certain point, there is a fall-off benefit when hours worked exceed a certain limit. Longer hours benefit no one. Not the employee. Not the employer.

In January 2017, France implemented a law stating that employers must give the right to employees to stay off work-related emails during nonworking hours. What people do with their time is up to them, of course, but the law acknowledges that professional duties are infringing on personal lives. Institutionalizing boundaries can go a long way to creating a culture where time off is valued. There seems to be something so un-American about that French policy, but statistics show that the French work 15 percent less than Americans and are just as productive.

Who's winning here?

And as for happiness, I guess it depends on where you get your jollies. According to Freeman, "Many people go to work for reasons beyond money . . . Workplaces are social settings where people meet and interact. On the order of 40 to 60 percent of American workers have dated someone from their office." But that's because people are always at work—where else can they meet someone to love? But why not at the yoga studio, or the next potter's wheel over, or in the lineup? Besides, work-related romance is about to get pretty sticky in the post–Harvey Weinstein age. Maybe we would all do better looking for love elsewhere.

Another contributor to *Revisiting Keynes*, Columbia University economist Edmund S. Phelps, argues that work positively provides a place for people to exercise their minds and develop new talents. In a time of steady technical progress, he postulates, "an increasing number of jobs will offer the change and challenge that only predominantly capitalist economies, thanks to their dynamism, can generate."

Clearly, work can be enjoyable. I'm not going to argue that point. Those of us lucky enough to work in dynamic environments can find social and intellectual benefits from how we earn our daily bread. But no matter how you look at it, work is meant to be about accomplishment in some material way, and a move away from that imperative helps us to grow in important, unquantifiable ways.

Recent science bolsters an argument in favor of my proximally induced devolution into childhood (tats for the entire family!), Schiller's two-and-a-half-centuries-old philosophy, Pieper's anti-totalitarian argument, Sartre's existentialism, what kept Keynes up at night—all of it is supported by heeding the relatively recent studies of Berkeley professor of psychology Alison Gopnik, a leader in child development and learning.

As we'll see time and again, children seem to have a special and innate grasp on the wisdom of sucking. In Gopnik's popular TED Talk, *What Do Babies Think?*, she compares the thinking processes of babies to that of adults. She explains how adults "spotlight" on what we pay attention to in order to properly reap the benefits from the executive functioning part of the brain, where calculated decisions are made (If I work more, I get more!). Arguably, executive function is necessary to keep us safe, employed, productive, and socially adept. Babies, by contrast, have more of a "lantern of consciousness." They aren't good at focusing, because the inhibitory parts of the brain haven't started working yet to drown out other stimuli. Everything around them is interesting and they take it all in. That is also how creative, imaginative, and innovative learning happens. While we would be fucked if we didn't learn to focus on specific tasks to get stuff done and keep ourselves functioning and alive, we could benefit from thinking more like babies and children from time to time in order to be open to learning.

You could tie this all the way back to Plato and Aristotle, who made clear that leisure and play are the way we open our minds to intellectual and spiritual growth. Elemental to our lives as civilized beings is this ability to responsibly push aside our goal—and reward-driven impulses—to make way for something we can suck at and enjoy without having to be productive.

Somewhere along the progression of going from childhood silliness to adult play-to-win, we lose something. Our minds get overridden by goal setting and reward getting. Our culture has become so success-oriented that even kids don't get to play for fun anymore. When they do play, everyone gets a gold star or a trophy just for showing up. Four-year-olds are tested to get into the right nursery schools. High school students are driven to breakdowns as they strive for acceptance into the most prestigious universities. Those universities are pressure cookers of competition and performance.

All of this success-as-symbol-of-worth isn't working for our children. Kids are more medicated than ever. The CDC reports a fivefold increase in psych meds for minors between 1994 and 2010. The goal-focused world we live in now is the anti-formula for creating resilient, confident kids and young adults. As parents, we can remedy this unfortunate trend by setting better examples.

In this case, "being a better example" might not look like trying to be superhuman in front of the kids. It might mean, rather, looking more like them. Letting things happen. Submitting before serendipity.

SURRENDER TO PARADISE, SUBMIT TO HELL

Our second trip to Costa Rica was as landowners. We were buzzing from excitement, which must have somehow numbed us to the task at hand. Finding the 1,242 square meters of jungle we now owned should have been difficult. But once we reached the Playa Guiones community that we would eventually call home, we bounced along for a mile and a half, taking rights and lefts like we knew where the hell we were going.

"How do you know where to turn?" Joel asked.

"I don't, but I am following Erik's video in my mind. I think we are close."

A few of those turns led us to dead ends, but we finally climbed a steep, muddy, truck-gouged hill as if being pulled along by an invisible cable. My brain kept switching from "Where the fuck are we?" to "This is our new home!" And there, as we approached the end of the road, I recognized the For Sale sign on a particular tree. "Hey," I thought, "why is that still there?"

Out loud, "That's it! That's our property!"

Joel said, "Are you sure?"

The anticipation and excitement I'd been feeling suddenly abated and I was overcome with an uncharacteristic calm. "Oh, yeah, that's it."

The lot was to our left, the next to last property on the road. To our right was a tangle of thick forest, through which we could glimpse the big blue Pacific in the distance, her swell lines pulsing toward shore. We heard her waves as white noise climbing up the hill to our perch and we were intoxicated by the smell of ocean, carbon-rich earth, and the sweet scent of flowering trees.

I jumped from the car, headed straight for the tree bearing the offensive For Sale sign, and tore it off. I stepped into the flora-filled lot wearing only flip-flops, understanding immediately that fear mostly happens in the abstract.

What we knew as the K-section of Guiones was still only theoretical. Sure, we had that video from Erik that bounced along the dirt road leading to our plot of land. But during our first trip to Nosara, we never ventured farther than a half-mile radius from the house we'd rented. It was like falling in love. The rest of the world falls away and you only have eyes for what is right in front of you. It was no small thing that our first experience in Costa Rica was magical for all of us. Had that trip been disappointing, we'd be safely cash-secure with money in the bank, and a significantly smaller lien on our apartment. Instead, we were cash poor, and had all of that potential in front of us for a happy life in the jungle.

Now, to build.

And where to start but with our new (and only) friend in Nosara. Erik turned out to be a six-foot-three blue-eyed surfing Viking, not the rather stocky, dark-haired, and deeply bronzed man I'd pictured from our conversations. I should have seen it as a sign—not portentous, but a humility-building corrective that we had no fucking idea about anything in this madcap venture. Later, we would hear horror stories about people trying to build in Costa Rica. Those naively optimistic Americans, Canadians, and Europeans who entered this friendly country, only to spend years struggling to see their home to completion or never getting there. People lost their life savings, got into legal morasses. For me, I had a feeling that everything was gonna be all right.

A better story might be that all went to hell the moment we blindly entered the process of building our house in paradise, four thousand miles from our New York home. But that's not what happened. Erik turned out to not only be a stand-up guy, but he also remains a great friend to this day. We met local architects who understood exactly what we wanted. Even with a language barrier, they listened to our ideas and came up with a Japanese-inspired modern design that matched the vision I'd had for the house. It turns out that our house spurred an architectural language for the community and its influence can now be seen in the vernacular architecture everywhere you turn.

When we hired our builder, we did so without meeting him except by email. I had seen some of his work when we met with Erik, who showed us houses by different crews. We liked the work of this one contractor in particular because he clearly understood modern finishes. We accepted his bid and before we even signed the contract, he broke ground and started working.

I emailed Marion Peri, the owner of the company we agreed to hire, as we were hashing out the details of the contract. When he told me that the gray work was already started, I asked him, "Don't you want to be paid before you start?"

"It's okay," he answered. "I'm not worried about it. You're good for the money."

How could he know that?

Over the course of the next year and a half, we planned around the boys' vacations to travel to Nosara at every chance to oversee the project. The builder we hired turned out not to be the middle-aged Tico I expected him to be, but a gorgeous and ebullient young Israeli man who'd married a local woman and was raising a family with her in Nosara. The first thing he said to Joel when we introduced ourselves from across our property during our first visit to the building site was, "You're Jewish, right? Come to seder tonight at our home! My parents are visiting from Tel Aviv."

We ate roast pork (yes, *pork*) in their house on the Rio Nosara, which we learned would flood during the rainy season every year, surrounding the house with muddy water and bringing with it the caiman known to attack the family dogs. Marion and his family have become our extended family in Nosara.

Despite the warnings—mostly from friends who thought us mad— building our dream house in Central America resembled nothing of the chaotic nightmare of construction projects the world over. If I was looking for signs about the reliability of my fellow humans, they were everywhere I turned, like the hand-painted signboards tacked up all over Nosara point- ing visitors to the unexpected wonders of this marvelous place. Following those signs deepened my faith again that the world can be a beneficent place and that those moments proving the opposite are the exception. At least, for the moment, it was where the better part of my delusion resided, and I was happy to live there.

IT WAS THE WAVE in Guiones that had brought me to Nosara in the first place. That wave would teach me more about surrender and how to surf than any other. A thumping beach break on a big day, it could also be the perfect waist-to-head-high gentle wave I needed to get up and ride. That wave instilled in me the visceral knowledge of letting go of attempted con- trol as a way toward the thing I really wanted—which is riding a wave. Until I surfed Guiones, I'd muscled my way into the lineup and into a wave. Paddling with too much force, pushing up with all my might, surf- ing for me was Herculean. I never felt strong enough, nimble enough, youthful enough to earn an ease of entry onto the face of the wave. I spent precious energy working against the ocean and I don't need a lot of words to explain where that got me. Nowhere.

There were myriad reasons for why I sucked at my beloved obsession, but a fundamental misunderstanding about how to work with the wave, as opposed to against it, had thus far eluded me. The lesson that changed all that came, as most do, via failure.

Exhausted and defeated after a bout of illness during one of our trips, I couldn't muster the might to pop up when I caught a wave. My arms collapsed against the board. My body felt extra heavy against the force of gravity, which was not my friend that day. To compensate for the power I didn't have, I succumbed to my weakness and instead allowed the wave to do the work of putting the board under me so I could pull my feet under to stand. Instead of muscling the pop-up, I submitted to the physics of the situation. While it felt like magic to be able to pop up without excess effort, it was a surfing lesson based on relatively simple science that didn't occur to me until that moment. Like a Newtonian fluid that becomes more resistant the harder you hit it, so the act of pushing against a wave makes it harder to ride and leaves you . . . nowhere.

If you fight the water, the water wins.

By releasing my failing strategies and just feeling the wave, I finally understood that so much of the difficulty I'd had surfing came not from the challenges of the sport itself (which are significant enough), but from the excess effort I wasted as I worked against the environment around me instead of responding to its invitation.

As above the water, so below, which is where surfers wind up when they miss or fall off a wave.

The better I got at surfing (in the relative sense—I will always suck at this), the bigger the waves I wanted. I'm not talking about going from four- or six-foot waves to eight- to ten-footers. I mean going from one- to two-foot waves to head high ones. I make the distinction here because every beginner surfer exaggerates wave size and every expert surfer minimizes it. It's the opposite of the classic fishing story where the fish gets larger with each telling. In surfing culture, you could be looking at bombs (big waves) and surfers will shrug and say, "yeah, that's three to four feet max." In Hawaii, that rule more than doubles in the opposite direction. So, an eight- to ten-foot California wave is a four- to six-foot Hawaiian. This has to do with how the wave is measured—either from the back of the wave (Hawaiian method of measurement) or from the crest to the trough (everyone else's). It also has to do with machismo.

What's the opposite of macho? That's me. Unless it's waist high, it's ginormous. And waves *always* look smaller from shore. Always.

The bigger the wave, the bigger the wipeout. I hadn't purposefully gone for bigger waves until I surfed Guiones and that meant more wipeouts. Those first ones scared the shit out of me. They scared me so much that one bad tumble would put me back on the inside or even back to the shore. That is, until I applied the same thinking to wipeouts as to catching waves. If I let the wave do what waves do—which in these circumstances means giving me a good thrashing (called getting worked or rag-dolled)—and I just let it happen without trying to control the situation, eventually the wave would let me go and I could surface. Fighting the force of the water was useless. By relaxing as the wave had its way with me, I felt calmer, used up less precious oxygen, and received fewer injuries. Fight the wave and the wave always wins. This has become a mantra for me. Relax, and instead of opposition, there is oneness. Don't fight the wave. Become it.

A lesson I try to carry with me into virtually any situation.

Andy Martin and I speculated that Sartre also understood something about surfing, even if he didn't know such a thing existed. Sartre wrote at length about skiing, and he believed that the ideal act of sliding (which happens to be a term regularly used for surfing) "is sliding that does not leave any trace," i.e., sliding on water. Sartre was referring to the recently invented sport of waterskiing—it was 1943 and while there were surfers in the world, they numbered under a thousand, so it is unlikely Sartre came across any of them. The existentialist wasn't a beach guy anyway. That was his frenemy Camus's turf. As Martin puts it, "Sartre heaped scorn on all that beachside bewitchment." Still, Sartre submits that, with regard to water, "sliding appears as identical with a continuous creation." Continuous, that is, until the wipeout. And then we're back to being all too human.

This act of creation includes an act of conquest as well since man must climb the mountain in order to slide down it—or, he must paddle out and catch a wave in order to ride it. The mountain and the ocean, both being indomitable, lead man to the very nature of his quest for being. For Sartre and his fellow existentialists, it is a constant struggle, wanting to be the thing he also wants to dominate. In the end, his frustration with harmony is what keeps man embattled with existential angst. If I could, I would tell him: Don't fight the wave. Become it.

OUR COSTA RICAN ADVENTURE turned into a new way of life for our family. We made friends and experienced uncanny—and yes, meaningful—coincidences each time we visited. It became the only place where I would stop being productive and simply be. My surfing improved. After a session, I got into the habit of sitting on the back patio of the house and staring at the trees and the monkeys and lizards that occupy them. I watch the hummingbirds and butterflies flutter around the bird of paradise plants for hours on end. It is where I do the least and feel most alive.

But here's the thing about paradise, it is also hell.

When life gave me lemons, I made lemonade, but then I spilled the sugar and it brought ants. Lots of them, as in: biomass!

We'd built a house with no doors, in a jungle that doesn't sleep. Where the animals move in, many unwelcome (with the exception of our neighbor's pooch, whom we nicknamed Jungle Pug). We were awakened by earthquakes; one cracked our foundation. We'd go days without water, and the electricity would turn off several times a day. We were attacked by aggressive bees and swarming tiny ants; things went awry every day that we were there.

We like to believe that there is a place where lost cameras find their way back to the rightful owners and friendly dogs move in as temporary pets you don't have to take full responsibility for. Where bakery trucks show up just because you're hungry. But that is just one side of paradise.

The other side is messy and can suck big-time. That doesn't mean you turn away from it. Head straight into an adventure with no expectations for what it may bring, and you find not what you were looking for, but something way more important.

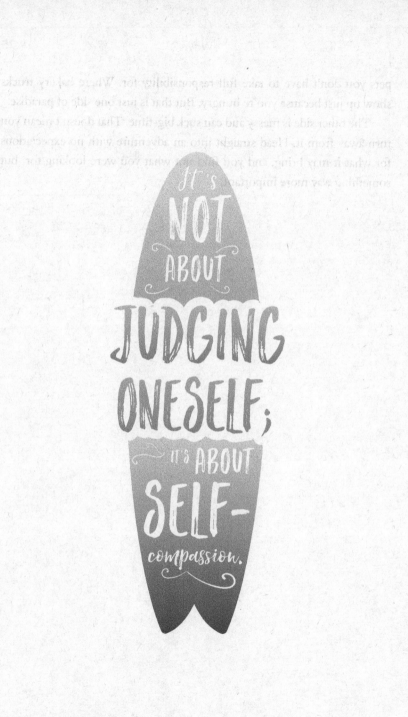

It's
NOT
ABOUT
JUDGING
ONESELF;
it's ABOUT
SELF-
compassion.

WAVE 3

My Worst Wave: Tearing Myself Another One

Rule #3:

Don't compare yourself to others.

Lesson #3:

It's going to get ugly.

Benefit #3:

You come to know yourself—possibly the hardest task in life.

Getting finned is part of surfing. Anyone who surfs will eventually take a trip to the emergency room—if you are lucky enough to have access to one—to get stitched up, have a bone reset, or, in the most extreme cases, be brought back to life. Waves are stronger than we are, and surfboards can become weapons of individual destruction. Surfboard fins are made from a variety of hard materials, most of them either molded composites or layered fiberglass, finely honed to cut through the water. They work much the way dolphin or shark fins work, by providing drag and balance in order to slice through the water for greater speed, efficiency, and control, depending on the type of fin and how many there are on the surfboard. Since humans are biologically impaired by not being equipped with their own fins, we have to rely on man-made versions attached to our surf craft.

Over the years, I've heard horror stories of severed ears, a lost testicle, and a person who literally tore himself another asshole. A boy was scalped, an Achilles' heel torn. One of the most brutal survival stories is the well-told tale

77

from Susan Casey's book *The Wave*, of Brett Lickle's near-death experience on a hundred-foot wave when the razor-sharp fin of his tow-in board flayed open the back of his calf. Had he been surfing with anyone other than his superhuman water partner, Laird Hamilton, who stripped off his wet suit to use as a tourniquet until he could get Lickle to safety, he surely would have bled out in the stormy Hawaiian sea. The story goes that Laird swam to shore and ran bare-skinned for help: a naked Neptune saving his friend's life.

Whenever you hear stories of surf accidents, there is often a sense of noble courage attached to them. In Brett Lickle's case, he and Laird were attempting to ride the biggest wave ever. Two of the greatest surfers the sport of kings has ever seen attempt to reverse-scale a mountain of water, man versus nature. When nature wins, we bow to the seemingly fearless souls who attempt the stuff of our nightmares or dreams, depending on our fears or aspirations.

Even though the laws of probability dictate that absolutely everyone who surfs with any regularity will get hurt—it happens to everyone, from the novice to the pro—each time I am injured, I am filled with self-doubt and self-criticism. I've torn the meniscus in my left knee, sheared my calf muscle, broken my finger, been concussed several times by taking a rail to the head, and had my entire right side go numb from being bent in half backward after one notorious wipeout at Ocean Beach, San Diego. I knew I was bent in half when my feet slapped the back of my head—bringing with it a wave of nausea at the realization of the unnatural contortion my body had just made. Once I resurfaced and made it back to shore, the friend I was surfing with took that story—and the stupid move I'd made that put me in danger—and dined out on it for days.

And lest I be accused of being Pollyannaish about sucking—getting hurt will be a part of the deal. You're going to get tossed around and whacked on the head. But you can say the same about your work, or when you do whatever you're good at. The difference is this: when you make a mistake at work, it matters. Oh, you may have a humane boss and a positive HR department, but every time you fuck up, you have one less opportunity to fuck up again. The laws of scarcity apply here.

When you fuck up while doing the thing you suck at—it doesn't matter. It'll hurt, but that's it. There's no greater meaning, and it's limitless. You're not on any clock.

It'll make you stronger, in fact. Because every time you kook out on a wave, it's a rehearsal for when you fall behind at work or make a mistake that takes weeks to set right. Sucking is failing and falling within limits. You'll get to go through the process and experience how fucking up really isn't the end of the world. That'll make you better equipped to handle more of it in the future.

DESIRE ISN'T YOUR FRIEND

The offshore wind groomed small clean waves on a late summer day. The lineup was crowded for our local and fickle break on the Jersey Shore. There were about twenty of us out, friends, family, groms, near-pros, and a few middle-aged longboarders (myself included). It was a glorious day in the water. The sun was shining, the water a perfect 72°F and unusually clear. The ocean, so full of life, inspired one of our friends to exclaim, "It's like an aquarium out here!" Schools of baitfish and something bigger were popping out of the water, running from whatever was chasing them. Every once in a while, the water surrounding my surfboard would swell and explode as thousands of small silvery fish broke the surface and schooled over the deck. One large pod after another of bottlenose dolphins appeared just beyond the lineup, arching gracefully and momentarily above the waterline to breathe before silently diving below again. Some would stop their trajectory south to swim in circles and slap the surface of the water with their flukes to stun bait balls of fish, making it easier to feed.

Every surfer out there knows that where there is abundant sea life, there are bigger fish we don't like to name. It's something we talk about on land, but rarely, if ever, in the water. It's not so much superstition as it is respect for the order of the universe, especially once we leave terra firma and abandon our predatory status and become prey.

The day was a beauty, though as surf goes, it was hardly the perfect wave; but we work with what our ocean sends us. Hollow and breaking over a sandbar into shallow water, I was taking care about which waves I paddled for and which I let pass. I pulled out a few times to avoid colliding with another surfer or with the sandy bottom. Two hours into the session, I hadn't caught and ridden a single wave. And even though the day was perfect—just being in the lineup with friends was happy-making—I wanted a wave. I am rarely greedy about what I get, but I was watching others get their short but successful rides and I was missing every one. My blissful state was souring into desire unfulfilled. That's how it all started to go wrong.

AFTER ALL THESE YEARS of sucking at surfing, I've had to adopt some coping mechanisms that allow me to continue (surfing and sucking) without going mad or, worse, giving up. In one such practice, I put myself in a state of mind where I am not wanting. By quelling desire, I convince myself that being in the water is enough, that paddling out is enough, and that sitting on my board is enough. If a wave comes to me, I tell myself, I will think of it as a gift from the sea. If I paddle for and make the wave, then it is a blessing. The action and result of riding that wave successfully is but a momentary reward—one I (should) neither expect nor desire.

But if I'm honest with myself, I don't always succeed in thinking in those terms. It's one thing to diminish the necessity of catching a wave when you're sitting in front of a computer. But when you're actually out there and you see other people, some hardly more talented than you, getting some? Well, that's when you need to tap into some wisdom from the experts.

Jaimal Yogis, for instance. He's the author and filmmaker of *Saltwater Buddha* and a follow-up book, *All Our Waves Are Water*, two entries in his lifelong quest to tie the two disciplines of spirituality and surfing together to make some sense of the world around him. I spoke with Jaimal about sucking and I hardly needed to explain myself. He got it immediately, echoing one of the basic tenets of how great it is to suck at something at the outset of our conversation. "We really suck at allowing ourselves to do things that suck. It's not that surfing sucks, but learning it is hard, and mastering it to perfection impossible." Jaimal compares it to the Zen practice of solving the riddle of a koan. "Someone is given an impossible question to answer and they will eventually give up because they cannot answer it. Finally," he explains, "they will have to surrender to the fact that there are things you cannot know." Or do—no matter how badly you want to.

The secret is to keep doing them without need for answers, success, or resolution.

In order to rid ourselves of the need for a particular outcome, it helps to understand where it all starts. Our original desire, according to Vietnamese Buddhist monk Thich Nhat Hanh, is for our survival once we leave our mother's womb. The Chinese and Vietnamese refer to the womb as the palace of the child. In that palace, we are safe. Our mothers feed us, breathe for us, and expunge our waste while we float in the safe cushion of amniotic fluid. Once we are forced from the womb, we are exposed and vulnerable. We have to learn how to do all of this on our own. That first breath is difficult as we have to push out lung liquid to make way for air.

That original desire for survival after being born is carried into our childhood and adulthood. While we learn to breathe and eat and function on our own, we still experience that deep original desire, felt as a kind of inchoate craving. I'd experienced this craving my entire life but without understanding what it was that I craved. When I started to learn to surf, I was able to watch it take form in my desire to surf. I felt this before I even knew what it actually felt like to ride a wave.

Of course, it has little to do with a wave. My wave could be someone else's swing to the putting green, or another's shot at a goal, the mastery of an ancient language, someone's flying lotus, or another's trying to play a particular phrase on a violin. It isn't about the specific desire, just the fact of anticipating a desired outcome. In the case of surfing, I am often returned to a very close approximation of that original desire to fill my lungs with air whenever I am held down by a wave and come close to running out of oxygen before surfacing to take a breath. This is especially true when there is extreme pain involved. Maybe it's taking the point further than is necessary, but I do feel reborn whenever I surf.

But then, as Thich Nhat Hanh explains, "to say that craving is the cause of all our suffering is too simplistic." He tells us that we need to understand the cause of our suffering in order to find a way to heal ourselves. When that suffering is the result of a desired outcome, the practice of aimlessness or *apranihita* can help.

The Buddhist practice of aimlessness is especially useful in the realm of sucking. In the famous Heart Sutra, we learn that there is nothing to attain, and if we can stop chasing after some ephemeral moment and live in the present, if we accept and practice aimlessness, we will find that we already have what we crave. Hanh writes of the Heart Sutra, "If we cannot stop running, we will miss the miracles of life available inside and around us . . . Practicing aimlessness, you don't need to run after anything anymore."

The trick is to be present without being driven by wanting something. Master Hanh sums it up beautifully. "When we are in touch with things by means of the mind of love, we do not run away or seek, and that is the basis of freedom. Aimlessness takes the place of grasping."

I don't need that wave. I don't need to surf well or beautifully in the first place. We care about those successful outcomes because we attach meaning to them. And the more we attach meaning to a specific result, the more important it becomes. Letting go of this need for meaning is what can bring freedom and "freedom is the only condition for happiness." So, the freedom to suck can make us happy. But this business of letting go isn't as easy as it sounds. It demands practice.

It's practice that I definitely need.

On one waveless (for me) morning, I admonished myself when I got caught inside: "You stupid fucking jerk!" That was not freedom or touching things in the mind of love. That was me yelling at myself.

A moment later, when I realized the spin I was getting myself in, I burst out laughing. *What a jerk for calling myself a jerk*, is what went through my mind. But the second jerkiness was funny to me. Laughing at myself switched the experience from an unsatisfactory one to—while not quite satisfactory—something else. Something not terrible. I turned back and headed back to the lineup. Practice takes practice.

The idea that sucking at something—and falling on your face—will help you when you fail at something more significant doesn't just exist in koans. Acceptance as a practice has support in what we've known about neuroscience since the early days of that profession.

Practicing in the right mind can change our perceptions because the human brain is plastic. The term is "neuroplasticity" and it means exactly what it sounds like. It's what gives us the ability to continue learning and changing throughout our lives. Even better news for those who suck at something, when we keep our brains challenged, they stay healthier longer. Imagine a future of aging kooks running around having a blast doing things that don't really matter. They'll be a whole lot healthier and sharper than if they'd stayed at home.

Neuroplasticity is based on the law that "neurons that fire together, wire together." Donald Hebb, known as the father of neuropsychology, came up with the concept in 1949 to explain how learning happens and habits form. Simply put, the neurons in our brains release neurotransmitters that communicate with other neurons. This neural transmission creates resilient pathways that get stronger and stronger the more often those transmissions are made. It follows that positive experiences reinforce more positive experience.

But it's a value-blind phenomenon. Our brains don't distinguish neural pathways as "good" or "bad," they just are what they are. So, neuroplasticity works equally well for the more negative aspects of our thinking too. If we keep telling ourselves we won't be happy unless such and such a thing happens—and then it doesn't happen—we reinforce our frustration and unhappiness.

If we create a habit of wanting only a certain outcome, we can get stuck on focusing on the result. It's a totally different mind-set from learning. There are rewards associated with improvement, but learning is a process of gathering, not of sowing. Learning opens us up to the world.

That's a way that sucking at something is akin to learning. When we accept sucking at something, we throw out our milestone-oriented mindset. By setting ourselves up for an expected reward, our efforts become transactional and things can go wrong. Especially if it never actually comes. Our brains can get caught in a negative feedback loop of wanting something that might never happen quite the way we want it to. If we perceive that we are continuing to fail and fail and fail, we can become enormously frustrated and deny ourselves the pleasure of trying in the first place.

STORIES MATTER

Alas, you are coming to this book with a lifetime of neural pathways already crisscrossing your mind. Many of them negative. Perhaps most. Me too.

Then the question is: what is there in sucking at something that can help us reroute and reset those pathways? Sure, we can go out and create new ones—but how to deal with old, distracting negativities?

In his bestselling book *Capture*, Dr. David Kessler tells us that the best way to get rid of a negative feedback loop is to replace it with a positive one. He calls the phenomenon "capture" to describe how what takes hold of our attention is then reinforced by continued focus. The stimulus can be as simple as an annoying voice at the table next to yours in a restaurant: once your brain locks onto it, you can no longer listen attentively to your dining partner or enjoy your meal. This is a benign example of capture, but it shows how quickly something can commandeer our attention and we get stuck in a loop. On the other side of experience, it can be as complex as a sudden spiritual awakening. That new focus does a lot. It diminishes the influence of the old neural rut.

Kessler asserts that "We can gradually reshape our minds, even transform our way of experiencing the world, though overcoming one form of capture often depends on discovering another."

But still, that doesn't go all the way. We'll need to find new positive paths to put down. Kessler writes, "Over the course of a lifetime, each of us creates a coherent account out of the jumbled, often fragmentary chaos of life—the ever-evolving narrative of our lives . . . Without self-created storylines, the trajectory of our lives would feel like a constant scattering of random details . . . An essential question, then, is how our stories are conceived."

That's where I think the secret is. Storytelling. Joan Didion, a master of the craft, puts a finer point on it: "We tell stories in order to live." Stories are as essential as breathing.

So how do we override the neural pathways of a negative storyline and turn it into a positive one? Kessler tells us that we can influence this process by actively changing what occupies our attention. This is where the mind must confront the brain. Attempting to differentiate the two can go some way to helping us understand how slippery it can be.

The distinction between the mind and the brain has yet to come to a firm conclusion. Not that we haven't tried. The subject has been a matter of debate since the dawn of philosophy and science, and one that has become quite heated recently as a result of the groundswell of advances in neuroscience. Now that we have fMRI scans (functional magnetic resonance imaging) that can detect blood flow in the brain to show neuronal activity, we can measure, to some degree, cause and effect. But the neurochemistry of the brain doesn't necessarily predict behavior. "While the scans are dazzling and the technology an unqualified marvel," says Sally Satel, coauthor of *Brainwashed*, "we can always keep our bearings by remembering that the brain and the mind are two different frameworks."

To further complicate the task of separating the mind and the brain, recent studies have proven that our behaviors are driven more by unconscious motives than we previously thought. But we also know that with awareness, we can override those unconscious drives. Our brains may be bossy but they don't necessarily have to be the boss of us. That's where the mind comes in and why the stories we construct have such power.

Keeping the hard science and its limitations as a touchpoint, we can circle back to one of the most important Buddhist concepts. Right Mindfulness is the practice of bringing the mind back to the present. This helps us to not project a future on a given moment, or to dwell on the past, or to measure an experience as pleasant or unpleasant. Instead of looking at something as good, bad, or neutral, the Right Mind acknowledges that it just is. This ties back to the neural pathways the brain creates: the cells don't judge, they just do what they are meant to do. We learn from the Buddha that the seeds of goodness and negativity are in all of us. We have to water the right seeds. If we do that, we can shift our habit energy—that negative loop that contributes to our suffering—into mindfulness. The habit energy when you suck at something tells you to give up, but if you practice Right Mindfulness, you continue without judgment. And that is freedom. Freedom to tell the story you want to tell.

I'm reminded of Lucy Marsden, the oldest living Confederate widow of Allan Gurganus's epic novel, ninety-nine years old and sassy as the day she turned sixteen. About the seductive tale-telling of her husband, Captain Marsden, she famously says, "Know something, Sugar? Stories only happen to the people who can tell them." And what we choose to tell is as important as the stories themselves.

Whether we learn from the made-up character of Lucy Marsden or from the very real Joan Didion, whether of fiction or nonfiction, it's the story that matters. The distinction between fiction and nonfiction is essentially an English language construct anyway, one not so black and white in other languages and cultures. For as far back as eleven thousand years, humans have been telling stories, even if we can't agree what to call them. Ultimately, story is a big part of what makes us human. The kind of humans we want to be depends on the stories we tell and how we tell them.

I have a strong suspicion that this storytelling technique for reversing the effects of negativity is already something almost all of us do intuitively—when we're talking about those parts of our life we assign to leisure, play, and aimlessness. Think about this: what's the story you have that you can pull out and make anyone laugh, at any time? Maybe it's your go-to for a first date, or during a lull in a conversation at lunch. A good icebreaker.

From my experience, there's a very good chance that that story comes from something you love doing—and something you suck at doing. That time you ended up dancing your way from the karaoke stage onto the pool table (and then into the hospital). That time your friend asked you to sing at her wedding. For many of us, our happiest, most joyful stories are from moments when—at the time—we experienced an acute form of failure. Broken bones and embarrassment and chagrin. Then, with time, we turn that putatively negative pathway into a hilarious one. It's just what we do. And it works. I certainly have my own.

PAIN IS INFORMATION

Back on that glorious New Jersey August afternoon in the water, none of these thoughts had worked their way into my brain. All I knew was I wanted a ride and I was going to try like hell to get one.

As the tide filled in, the waves weren't as sketchy as they had been earlier and they were now breaking in deeper water—meaning, there was less chance to connect with the sandy bottom. But, I was getting tired from paddling and missing, paddling and missing. I couldn't get out of the water without a ride, so I decided that I would absolutely go for the next decent wave that came through. I saw my wave building on the horizon, a sizable one for the day. I estimated it would come to me shoulder high, clean. I was well positioned, had priority, and I told myself, this one is mine. When I swung around to paddle for the wave, I knew in my heart that it was going to be hard to make. Hollow waves need late drop-ins, meaning the surfer has to get to her feet just under the lip of the wave and pull in quickly to gain control and lock into the face. This is especially difficult to do on a longboard, which is heavier and slower than a shortboard.

I threw caution to the wind and heeded advice from Erik, whom we met in the last chapter, one of the best surfers I know. He said, "Sometimes it helps to just go for it even when you know you will get thrown over the falls. Once you get worked and survive, you can relax." Of course, this is meant to happen at the beginning of a session, not at the end.

I caught the wave and popped up—joy!—but as soon as I turned down the line, the bottom dropped out beneath me. The lip of the wave swallowed me and my board together, flipping my board around in the process so the deck was down and the fin side was up. A searing pain between my legs told me that the fin had hit me there. The wave had sandwiched the underside of my board to my body and we rolled together toward the shore. After two full turns underwater, I managed to grab the fin with my hand to yank it away from where it was stubbornly lodged against my privates. I remembered this only later, when I noticed the six-inch slice across my right palm. We both (my board and I) got dragged by white water before I came up gasping for air and from the excruciating pain of having been hit by the fin. Oh, and I got clocked in the noggin before surfacing. My board basically fucked me and then hit me on the head. You can't indict a board for aggression, and a wave will always have its way with you, but this was going a step too far.

As I sputtered in the soup—where the waves break and chaotic white water thrashes you about—trying to get my bearings and assess damage, my friend Jimmy was heading back out to the lineup after kicking out gracefully on his 10' log from a sweet little left.

Having witnessed the sorry episode, Jimmy asked, "You okay?"

"I'm not sure yet . . . ," I told him, more gingerly than I meant it to sound. It felt as if my voice was buried where the fin had been only moments before. Then I told him where I got hit.

"Oh, yeah, been there!" he laughed, before turning and paddling back out for the next set. Sympathy is not on a surfer's menu of sentiments, unless it is truly deserved, as in: you are about to die.

Stunned into immobility, I stood for a few moments in the waist-high water, considering whether I should paddle back out. The throbbing pain would subside, I told myself. It was a beautiful day and I wasn't ready to end my session. But the thought of straddling the board gave me a shudder.

The initial blunt trauma was beginning to dull—or my body was in shock—so the next logical question occurred. "Am I bleeding?" I didn't want to bleed in the water when there were so many people out, including my son. Blood in the water with smaller fish just brings in bigger fish. That some sharks can detect prey in one part per ten billion gives pause to whatever twisted logic a surfer's brain conjures to consider surfing with a bleeding wound. Sure, the ocean is big, so the calculus may be meaningless, but our imaginations are bigger. I decided to call it a day.

I looked down to the water swirling around my lower torso. It wasn't pinkish, so I was initially relieved. Once I limped out of the water, I saw the split on my inner thigh. It was bleeding, but not gushing. First assessment: I didn't hit a major vessel, it's only a surface wound. All good. But damn, it was hard to walk.

Having given birth to two children the old-fashioned way, I was not unfamiliar with discomfort from trauma in the area. The throbbing and constant pressure, the terrifying thought of relieving myself when the moment came. You survive and recover, but I knew it was going to be weeks before I got back in the water. Worse, I blamed my sucky self for the wipeout. I uselessly second-guessed my actions, wondering if I'd hesitated before turning down the line and therefore deserved injury.

Hesitation in surfing is a sure mark of a kook. If you go for a wave and hesitate out of fear, you will either miss it completely or wipe out. The nobility of going balls to the wall for a wave, even if it's sketchy, shows the kind of commitment necessary to surf well. Had I been going for it, or kooking out? I replayed the wave over and over again in my mind.

After limping home from the beach, I took a quick shower to prepare for the butterfly bandages my husband was heading out to buy at the local pharmacy. Once I lathered up, the excruciating burning sensation between my legs had me howling in pain. I used a mirror to find out what I didn't want to know: the damage from my fin gave a new meaning to the word gash. I'd torn myself another one, just like that poor surfer I'd heard about, but mine wasn't a rectum. The tissue was raw and bloody like a badly butchered steak and my pussy hurt like a motherfucker.

"Joel," I cried out, "forget the butterfly bandages!"

When I approached the desk in the emergency room to speak with the nurse about my injury, she somehow missed the towel between my legs, held in place by my left hand, but immediately noticed the slice across my right palm.

"Ah, a skeg got you . . . ," she said.

"Oh, yeah," I said.

"My son nearly sliced his ear off with a fin once. Had to have it sewn back on . . ." She was characteristically nonplussed.

"The hand is superficial . . . I'm not here for that." My voice was still buried you-know-where.

The nurse looked at me to question, "Where, then?"

I pointed to the towel between my legs. That got her attention.

She threw her head back with laughter. "Wow-ee!" she hooted. "The docs are going to love this one!" and she guffawed her way to find the attendant in charge of prioritizing. No one was bleeding out or under cardiac arrest, so they pushed me to the top of the list for treatment. I was glad someone was having some fun with this.

An hour and a half later, I shuffled out of the ER with seventeen stitches on my inner thigh and vulva and the chuckling of emergency room attendants in my ear. I mean, it was pretty fucking funny.

I couldn't sit for weeks. I had to stand at my work desk and during meetings. (My colleagues had the same response as the ER staff.) I couldn't put on a pair of pants for a month. When I checked with a mirror to see how the healing was progressing, I saw that my entire genitalia had turned black. I yelled to Joel, "Oh my God, I killed her!"

When I saw Jimmy the day after I got finned and he'd heard the extent of my injury, he admitted, "Yeah, I was wondering what you were doing taking off on that thing. It was steep!" Okay—maybe I did myself proud. Maybe I didn't hesitate. But in my case, the fall goeth before my pride. While I felt momentarily proud that I went for it, and humbled by my failure, Jimmy said something I couldn't shake.

"Hey, man, maybe someone's trying to tell you something. Maybe someone doesn't want you to surf!"

If he weren't a religion teacher and a surfer, I wouldn't have given it another thought. But he may have a direct line to the Man or to the Conductor, as the surfer's myth calls the maestro of the waves. Maybe Jimmy *knew* something.

While it may seem absurd that some higher power gave a damn enough to dictate my right to surf, Jimmy's casual warning stuck to me. Surfing had awoken a latent spirituality in me. I am awed by the ocean's power every time I paddle out. Waiting for a wave is a kind of prayer. And while I wouldn't call it religion, surfing has become a kind of discipline, where every session is a practice for patience, humility, skill. Yet, having been born and raised Catholic, those biblical lessons die hard: maybe someone didn't want me to surf.

That idea stuck in my craw. On further reflection, I realized that that someone was clearly the voice in my own head—where did it come from?—and it hurt much more than the discomfort and pain from the blossom of contusions and swollen tissue.

Pain is useful. It focuses your attention to where it's necessary. It's much worse to not feel pain since if you don't know you are injured, you can't fix what's broken. But the physical, at least in this instance, wasn't nearly as bad as its sister discomfort. Maybe I got hurt, the critic in my head badgered, because I don't deserve to surf at all. So I told myself over the next several days, as I stayed out of the water.

THERE IS A PRICE TO PAY for starting to surf so late in life. I pay part of that price with humiliations. And I accept the fact that I will never surf well. I am getting better at following my own counsel and taking these fuckups as the minor things they are, specks on the passage of time, especially in the context of doing something I love doing. But I struggle too. One source of enduring struggle for me is in feelings of shame, and there's one in particular associated with a sentence from one of the best books on the surfing life, *Barbarian Days* by William Finnegan.

I loved Finnegan's book so much that when I finished it, I went back to the beginning and reread it. I started reading it for the third time but checked myself. I'd become obsessed. The book was both painful and exquisite to me. Painful, because Finnegan lived a surfing life I didn't even know existed until I was too old for it to matter. Exquisite, because it is nearly five hundred pages of brilliant writing, mostly about riding waves. For a writer, publisher, and surfer, this is as close to heaven on the page as it gets. But in the book, Finnegan says something that hurt me as much as the ignominious finning episode.

Finnegan writes of his teenaged girlfriend, "Caryn had no interest in learning to surf, which I thought was sensible. People who tried to start at an advanced age, meaning over fourteen, had, in my experience, almost no chance of becoming proficient and usually suffered pain and sorrow before they quit."

Fourteen. Fourteen! Fourteen? I was forty when I started—which, according to Finnegan, would explain everything. There it was, in black and white, confirmation of my self-delusion and understanding of my pain and sorrow. He even got the name right (though not the spelling). Maybe Finnegan knows something too.

The idea that I had gotten into surfing twenty-six years too late was, at first, darkly funny. But then I realized that the ludicrous number had tapped into something deeper in me. Something deeper than the feeling of catastrophe that attends fuckups. I had learned how to deal with those.

It was this other thing that I was having trouble shaking. Generalized self-doubt. The twenty-six years was obviously an arbitrary thing, a silly number (there are plenty of really good surfers who have started after the age of fourteen), but that wasn't the issue. It resonated with me because it chimed with something I realized was still lurking inside. That I was fooling myself.

Where did this self-doubt come from? I'd always believed I had a core of self-confidence along with a readiness to admit what I didn't know or couldn't do without any attendant bad feelings. I was basically an autodidact, driven by curiosity to follow my interests down rabbit holes of wonder to learn what I hadn't from a more formal education. The four years I spent at college proved somewhat ineffectual as I struggled against the structure of university life. My life as an editor contributed to my lifelong education more than attendance at any institution. But surfing could expose the raw nerves of my insecurities like nothing else. I continually put myself in situations where I am scared shitless. I've been injured to the point where any responsible mother of two ought to question the wisdom of playing in the ocean with what is, essentially, a weapon attached to your body, a surfboard with a leash.

I was completely aware of my skill level and didn't pretend otherwise. But Jimmy's comment tapped into a self-consciousness I didn't think I had and exposed a painful rift in my self-belief.

So much of the problem was that surfing is learned and performed mostly in the public eye, under the scrutiny of other surfers. Even worse, in most cases, they are better surfers than me, and they, understandably, want me out of their way. In trying to understand my mortification due to this injury, I wondered if I'd tapped into an atavistic fear that I had somehow dishonored the tribe I didn't even know I was a part of. Even though we know better, we fear that people are watching and judging when they mostly don't give a shit. They've got more important things to worry about for themselves.

We are all familiar with the impostor syndrome—that innate checkpoint most of us have on our egos that brings with it a fear of being found out, a fear that we won't measure up. This yardstick is a false construct, a blunt instrument where grandiosity butts up against inferiority—where these two things become one and the same. So what if observers care that we suck? We have to learn that our internal problem with that is a story we tell ourselves and it is up to us to deal with it.

"The Sutra of the Arrow is a cool Buddhist riff where we learn that there are two kinds of pain: physical pain, which is real, and psychic pain, which is created," says Jaimal Yogis, slipping comfortably into surfer's jargon to unpack the intricacies of our seeking souls. "You have to recognize the stories you tell yourself and realize that they are created by you," he told me. "And while you might first chastise yourself for having them in the first place, pushing those stories away is where it gets more gnarly." Psychic pain gives us information, too, calling our attention to where it's needed, which is how it *is* like physical pain. The work to be done is to not shut down those stories but to learn how to handle them and to keep them from taking root. We must not water the bad seeds.

Stories—they can be pesky too.

CONFIDENCE TO FAIL

By digging deeper into the science and mystery of self-confidence, I hoped that it might help me to develop the right kinds of stories—the kind that aren't soul-killing, but nurturing instead, the kinds that reset those bad neural pathways.

I was happy to discover that there were other people who had ignored (or were ignorant of) William Finnegan's age-warning. Katty Kay, for instance, took up kitesurfing at the age of forty. And she literally wrote a book on confidence, so I hoped she could shed light from her research on how sucking at something might help us to gain confidence. I also figured she would have some firsthand wisdom to share.

In *The Confidence Code: The Science and Art of Self-Assurance—What Women Should Know*, BBC journalist Katty Kay and ABC news correspondent Claire Shipman look at the links between confidence and what they call "the confidence cousins" of self-esteem, optimism, self-compassion, and self-efficacy. The finning episode had thrown me into a tizzy about exactly all of these attributes. While they all touch on different aspects of how we see ourselves in the world, each quality is tethered to the other. Still, they don't necessarily exhibit together—you can have high self-esteem, for example, but feel a crisis of confidence about performing a certain task. Optimism doesn't guarantee self-efficacy but focuses on the outside world with a belief that everything will ultimately be okay. Confidence points to a belief in oneself to be able to get something done—even if you suck at it. But even though there are nuances of difference between them, confidence, optimism, and self-efficacy are—according to the authors—all "closely tied to a sense of personal power."

As Kay and Shipman learned, personal power gets an assist from a little bit of overconfidence. Since confidence is basically a call to action, having none at all leads to inaction. "Confidence is the stuff that turns thoughts into action," says Richard Petty, Ohio State psychology professor and an expert on the subject. Basically, if we don't do anything or try anything, we don't get anywhere. Overconfidence—which is tied to a kind of optimism—spurs us toward taking action. So, what happens when our overconfidence leads us to try and fail? There is resolution here on the other side of the spectrum. If we accept that we might suck at something, then we don't fear trying or going for it. Sucking at something and overconfidence can balance the seesaw of our egos and give us the temerity to just fucking wing it. "I've got this!" we tell ourselves, and at the same time we say, "And, 'so what' if I don't?"

Kay's understanding of confidence and sucking come from both her extensive research and personal experience. A self-described competitive jock, Kay is a skilled downhill skier and polo player. She admits that she took up the new sport of kitesurfing because "The element of the challenge was appealing. I was defeating my own demons. Not many women were kitesurfing when I started thirteen years ago, and part of the appeal was conquering a sport predominantly done by men."

Kay explained that she became competent in the sport at a specific locale but has never been able to progress to the point of mastery in less familiar spots. She also lamented, "I can't jump. I told myself, I am never going to master this sport and I almost gave up." Jumping is where you are lifted off the water by positioning the kite to catch the wind and then land again, sticking it to continue surfing. Even though Kay can't jump, she's still at it.

"It would be useful," Kay agreed, "to accept that you might always suck at something—or at least in some of what you're trying to accomplish. If you are going to try to be perfect you won't take the risk of doing it at all. If you can go into something and give it a go, then you can try lots of things. If you allow yourself to suck, it can be a pathway to new things." She confirmed that failing at things can lead to confidence, but she emphasized how framing is an important part of the process. "Letting go of the comparison to the skills of others is important," she said. "And in the case of my struggle with kitesurfing, that I could stick to it gave me confidence. I had the fortitude and grit to keep going."

One piece of wisdom I took from my discussion with Kay was that, alas, we may never find a cure for self-doubt. But we might already have the closest thing to a recovery program. What I learned—and what I was able to test on myself—is that self-doubt is always going to be there, but self-compassion can mop it up quickly. Let yourself doubt. Be honest. It's a part of sucking, and we'll never get past it.

But forgive yourself for it.

Don't ignore the "self" in self-compassion. Your tribe won't carry you past your own demons. Your doubt is your own.

Compassion is based in love, and if we love ourselves even in our failing, chances are good we will have the confidence to try again. Here's another way that sucking at something will help us with the things we don't suck at. When we learn to forgive and love ourselves during periods when we fail, we'll know what that feels like when it comes time to forgive ourselves in the other parts of our lives.

Hanh teaches us, "With compassion in our heart, every thought, word, and deed can bring about a miracle."

Self-criticism, on the other hand, is anathema to self-compassion. Once we learn to stop judging ourselves, we can look upon our lesser talents with compassion. This doesn't fly in the face of acknowledging what we suck at—it is saying that we can love and become kinder to ourselves as we try and fail. Criticizing yourself is only ever possible when you have anxious goals in mind. So you start falling behind. You don't measure up. Etc.

Sucking at something is about letting go of those goals and accepting, from the outset, that this is aimless. How can you criticize that?

All of this really counts in situations where the stakes are high. If you can accept yourself as you continue to suck at something that does no harm, you will gain the coping mechanisms necessary to accept and to learn how to productively handle things when the shit hits the fan and it really does matter. Whether it is at work, or as a parent, or as a team member, we are all going to suck sometimes. Make no mistake, I am not saying that it is okay to be cavalier about sucking at things that affect others. I would urge no one to find peace and truth in sucking at, say, being an ER nurse or surgeon or basically anything any of us do as entrusted by others. It's the pointless things, the things that stack ephemera on ephemera, wave on wave, moment on moment—and then wash entirely away—that make great sucking pursuits. But if you practice shifting humiliation into acceptance in the sucking of something, you clear a path that will bring about a better outcome when it becomes crucial.

We tend to focus on our individual experiences and single them out. When we are having a bad day, lose a job, break up with a sweetheart, have to deal with bad health news, our habit is to focus on the singular experience we are having and think, *Why is this happening to me?* But we might ask instead, *Why not me?* An essential part of self-compassion includes an understanding that we are all part of a common humanity—negative experiences happen to everyone.

Jaimal Yogis understands it from his own lifetime of practice: "The story we buy into is that we are these separate individuals who exist apart from other beings—it's always going to suck because the grass is always greener. But enlightenment cannot happen in that constructed ego."

I can attest to this theory of play and resilience because on one trip to Costa Rica, when I'd just returned from an unusually successful session in the water (meaning, I caught and rode a few nice-sized waves) and was feeling pretty chuffed about it, I received an email with the unwelcome news that my business was down. I'd been expecting a pretty brutal postmortem for the year. I knew I had missed my goal, but I hadn't realized that I had missed it by an epic factor. The message threw me off because I usually know where I stand during the year. I look at numbers the same as I do letters: in a cohesive form, they tell a story and I pride myself on knowing my story in numbers. Except I was completely wrong about this year's story. The news made me sick to my stomach and reminded me of a conversation I'd had a few years earlier.

I'd been talking to Alex Dick-Read, the former editor in chief of one of the great, but now defunct, surf magazines, *The Surfer's Path*. We were talking surfing and writing and publishing and I was complaining about not getting enough water time to improve my surfing in any significant way. I often devolve into an internal—and useless—debate: do I leave my professional life in New York City and pare down my life so I can surf every day? Of course, even if I did that, I would still suck at it, so the absurdity of the question would not be lost on anyone. Besides, I couldn't make a living at it, so it's a stupid exercise. Still, I am known to bitch about it to those who I think might be sympathetic. The "grass is always greener" promise is a lying bastard. We all know this. But we tend to go there anyway.

Nevertheless, Alex listened patiently, and then asked, "Well, what would you rather be: a good publisher or a good surfer?"

"A good publisher, of course!" I answered, without even thinking about it.

"Well, then," he said, with a graciousness I didn't deserve, "you are in the right place."

I often think about that conversation when I become petulant about the gross disparity between water time and office time, only to be humbled by recalling my immediate answer to Alex's question. Of course I want to be better at my job than at something I do for fun.

But now, it seemed, I sucked at publishing too. Shit. Like everything else, there's only so much sucking can do for you. I felt like I'd crossed the line.

I spent the better part of the next few days practicing what I do when I am in the water and not catching waves. Sit, breathe, relax. Be. Once I could do that without the noise of fear and anxiety coursing through my brain, I tried to figure out how the hell I could have been so far off base in something I've done every single day for thirty years. I'd spent half of that time in deep training sucking at surfing, which helped me to realize that I could also get through sucking at the thing to which I have devoted my entire professional career.

So, I sat. I breathed, not quite in a meditative way, but in the pushing-aside-the-panic-so-it-didn't-consume-me way. In that space, I found some clarity to the problem. I had some serious work to do, but I was ready to confront it head-on. I had to admit and accept that I had made some less than profitable decisions, and I would have to change my strategy to do better.

A few days later, I received news that the original figures weren't based on updated sales numbers. The newly adjusted ones told the story I expected. I still missed my goal and had work to do, but while I may have sucked at making my numbers, it wasn't by a crazy factor—and I didn't totally suck at knowing what those numbers were and how I missed them. A nuance, perhaps, but one that helped me to focus on the task in front of me. And I was ready to tackle that work, instead of feeling overwhelmed by what I hadn't yet accomplished. I'd just been trying to ride waves for several days, and having a blast doing it. Failure was second nature. Failure wasn't associated with a crawling sense of anxiety. It was associated with warm water, the sun, the surf, and my family.

STORIES BRING GIFTS

Self-doubt plagued my recovery, until a gift of encouragement came from an unexpected place. If there were ever a sign from the universe, this was a direct hit.

I have two boards shaped by the legendary Jim Phillips, who surfed prolifically on the East Coast but who, sensibly, now resides in Southern California. Each board is a single fin 9'3" with one stringer, soft rails, and a scooped-out nose. I love the way the soles of my feet wrap around the slightly raised stringer in the center and top half of the deck like a grip. I have never been happier on a board. I loved the first one I bought from my local surf shop so much—a stunning fuchsia-red with a yellow translucent fin—that I bought its colorless twin, sporting a beautiful blue fin, only a few months later. The fuchsia one lives in Costa Rica for our surf trips south. The demure white beauty stays in New Jersey.

The boards are called Da Copy Cat—a reference to the infamous 1960s Malibu surfer Miki Dora, who walked his longboard as stealthily as a cat. If I thought these things happened, I'd imagine him turning in his grave because I ride a board named after him. Dora scorned anyone who wasn't expert in the surf and was known to glide up to kooks and push them off their boards. This was before the invention of the surf leash, so pushing someone off his board meant the bereaved surfer had to spend time better spent catching waves retrieving his board instead. The insult was an effective deterrent. Dora may have been Da Cat, but he was also an asshole.

Even the vengeful spirit of Miki Dora couldn't prevent the news of my injury from reaching the West Coast. Our New Jersey neighbor has a brother who lives in San Diego. He is an attorney who surfs and he passed along the story of my injury to a fellow attorney, who happened to be a friend of board shaper Jim Phillips. The rather gory details gave this story some legs.

Phillips and I were a connection five times removed, but the reportedly reclusive shaper took the time to write an encouraging email to me as I stood and lay recovering from the wound to my body and my self-confidence. Among his words were these:

". . . I hope your recovery goes quickly, downtime from the waves drags on slowly . . . Be safe, git back on that hoss, don't let it throw you and I can only hope your future surfing days will be more of pleasure, not pain."

As much as his words meant, it was his generosity and consideration to send words of support and to accept me as a fellow surfer that mattered most. I didn't know it, but I was looking for connection.

Although I never set out to become a member of the surfing tribe, by spending so much time in the water, I met other surfers. The sport is democratic enough that while dominated by young(er) men, in most line-ups there are young and old, male and female surfers. Because it took me so long to learn, I initially stayed away from everyone in the water. But, as the years went by, and I became more comfortable, I would see the same faces—and eventually it brought me the joy of new friendships.

The connections ran deep, and yet, I never thought of myself as a surfer until the email from Jim Phillips arrived in my in-box. While I had no intention of quitting, doubt had crept into my mind, which would do me no good on a wave. Lack of commitment is a surfer's curse and I had to will myself back onto a board. Phillips's words of compassion came when I questioned my right to continue surfing at all. In words and deeds, miracles do happen.

Community and connection are where those miracles occur. "The power to will is not enough to sustain change," Dr. Kessler reminds us. "The challenge is to draw strength from something other than mere self-discipline—or condemnation. Lasting change occurs when we let go of such isolating pressures and allow ourselves to feel support and connection instead of preoccupation with the self."

I keep coming back around to the power of story. Whether from the mind of a doctor, a scientist, a seeker, a literary master, or even a fictional character—stories are essential to the way we move through our lives. My first story after getting finned told me that I had no right to be in the water with other, more skilled surfers. I was not worthy. The counter-story, if I swing too far to the other side of my wounded ego, leans on unreliable feelings of pride about getting my ass out there at all (certainly the better of the two). But in the end, both of those trajectories are just distorted mirror images of that ego. In the calmer waters of my soul, the story I tell myself is simply, "I surf."

I couldn't get there on my own, though. I needed an assist from a fellow surfer.

A month later, with Jim Phillips's kind words in my head and his board beneath my body, I paddled out. His message had the healing effect to help me to forgive myself for making a bad wave choice, and to remind me that it isn't skill that keeps me paddling out for another ride. Gingerly straddling my board in the lineup, I waited for a wave to come through. My doctor had cautioned me to wait six weeks before getting back on a board and in the water. But four weeks of ruminating was enough. Pussy be damned. I surf.

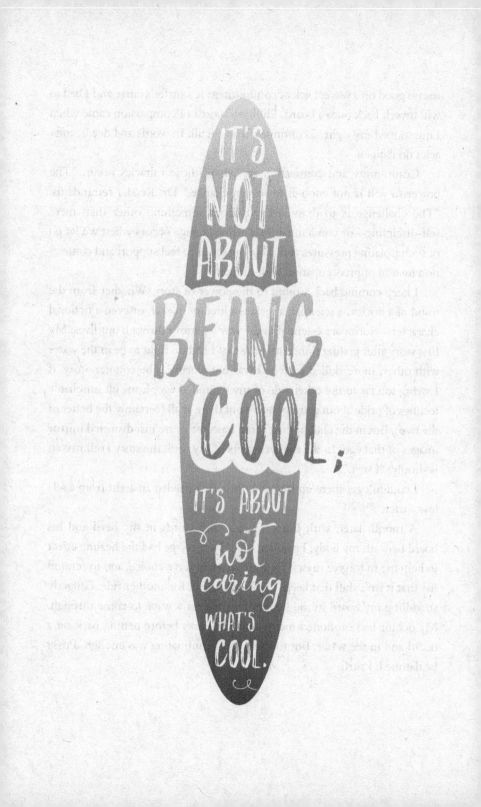

WAVE 4

My Best Wave: Surfing Through Chemo or Whatever Shit May Come Your Way

Rule #4:
You will have to start at the beginning again.

Lesson #4:
Vulnerability makes you stronger.

Benefit #4:
Sucking at something is a reason to live.

My nether parts had healed nicely, and I was back in the water that fall. At least, until the end of October when Superstorm Sandy devastated our Jersey Shore barrier island and we were kept from our home and the ocean for months afterward. The ocean surge swept houses off their foundations, and pushed them around like errant billiard balls, knocking them into *other* houses, and wrecking everything it touched.

Chaos kicked off more chaos: sinkholes opened up in the middle of roads, consuming cars and trucks; flotsam from the destroyed homes—appliances, safes, lumber—got carried by flooding into the bay and the ocean; a post-Sandy fire destroyed a century-old amusement park just a mile from our house. I had grown up going to that park as a child and then as a teenager in the '70s. My father had, too, before me. I took my boys there every summer season. It was a good stretch, but things change.

The night before the storm, we were forced to evacuate our house and the island. We secured what we could and put on a brave face—what else is there to do?—but it was eerie to walk away from a family home with little in tow except the deeds we'd kept there. We didn't bother to take anything with us. I took one last look at the home we loved: a haven for countless family memories—challenges and joys both—and reliable during all, now unceremoniously reduced to its material makeup like everything else in the path of the storm. Just another vulnerable structure, shortly to be battered and possibly broken by wind, and rain, and tide.

"Goodbye, dear house," I spoke to it as though it might respond. "We hope you're still here tomorrow." Then we drove inland.

JOY WHERE YOU LEAST EXPECT IT

The storm wasn't the only force of nature that brought chaos that fall.

In the wake of Sandy and the destruction she brought, I was diagnosed with breast cancer. So if you're keeping track: I gave myself a second vagina in August, Sandy came in October, and I got the diagnosis in December. At the moment when I had regained some self-confidence, my surfing life—and every other aspect of my life—was about to endure a serious wipeout.

Breast cancer hadn't ever been among the bogeymen of my nightmares. There were just too many other things to scare me. Finding myself vulnerable in a way I'd never imagined reminded me that just because we learn to live with the threats we can see, it doesn't mean there aren't others that might manifest—a fin breaks through calm water, a routine checkup gets complicated. Sucking at surfing had primed me to accept that we were never invulnerable, but I was about to learn that our invulnerability contained multitudes. Surfing had been hard on me—but it had always been my choice to paddle into the wave. A challenge and vulnerability that I sought out.

Cancer was another kind of vulnerability.

That wasn't all, though. There was something else that happened after that most vulnerable of winters, when our house and my health were both under siege. It was during this time when I experienced my best ever wave. It was a slow, soft little peeler I shared with Rocco one blessed July morning. It had been five months since I'd been in the water.

JUST BEFORE CHRISTMAS during that season of Sandy, a routine mammogram revealed an aggressive, invasive tumor in my left breast.

Our home had remained mercifully intact as if to prove the (cruel?) randomness of nature. Sandy caused the bay to our west to breach, but her waters stopped three houses away from ours. A swath of houses located in the center of the island were saved from ruin by their fortunate position to receive the least of the wind, ocean swell, and bay tide. While our basement flooded from ground water and we lost what was stored there, the waterline never reached the main part of the house. Many other houses, like my body, would not fare so well.

Multiple surgeries over the course of the next two months resulted in questionable margins. We decided to treat the cancer systemically with chemotherapy before dealing with the localized ductal carcinoma in situ (DCIS) cells stubbornly residing in my breast. Once I was sure that my family would be taken care of in case things went south fast—I was "doing the numbers" again—the question quickly became: *would this be the end of surfing for me?*

In February, before I began my first round of chemo, just four weeks after the last of three surgeries that did not cure me, I surfed Guiones against the recommendation of my physical therapist. Cording had formed in my left arm, a result of the fascia healing too quickly, which created a taut string of tissue between skin and muscle. A visible cord pulled beneath my skin like a guitar string, attaching itself from my wrist along the underside of my forearm and biceps to my armpit. It was hideous and hideously painful, and it prevented my arm from straightening beyond the last thirty degrees. That would make surfing very, very difficult (and I really didn't need any extra difficulty). My doctors were accommodating: they worked

with me to schedule surgeries in anticipation of my travel plans, understanding that getting in the water was paramount for my mental health.
The physical therapist was . . . less so.

When I told her I wanted to surf, she said, "That's ridiculous. You can't
surf with that arm. Besides, you're still recovering from surgery."

"Next option?" I asked her.

"What do you mean?"

"I'm going to surf one way or another, so help me figure out how I
can."

"What's wrong with you people?" she asked. "My boyfriend surfs and
he does stupid things all the time too. Are you all masochists?"

"Not even close."

She instructed me to exercise my arm by making slow crawling mo-
tions with my fingers up a wall while standing sideways against it, up and
down, up and down again. This movement was meant to gently force my
arm to stretch and tear apart the offending tissue. It caused my body to
shudder with pain as the extension of muscle pulled at the taut cord. The
PT told me to perform the exercise before and after every surf session.

That therapy quickly fell by the wayside after the first session in the
Guiones surf. Between paddling and the pull of the breaking waves against
my arm, the stubborn cording was yanked clean. After one particularly
powerful wave, I plunged my face beneath the water to muffle my scream.
By the end of the week, I had my full range of motion back and had regained use of my arm.

My stubborn trip to Guiones with only one functional arm was a critical moment for me coming to grips with my cancer. It's almost embarrassing to admit, but my first thought when I got diagnosed was, "I don't
have time for this." Between work and family life, I couldn't fathom what
would give. Then when it seemed like it might make me stop surfing, I
snapped out of it. I stopped worrying about how I was going to accommo-
date cancer, and I got in the water. It hurt like hell—for a moment. But
there was something about that pain in my arm that made me realize I was

still alive, that I could fight back in local ways, in ways that didn't need a team of doctors and fancy machines and medicines. Getting in the water made my cancer just one more kink in my surfing career, where it joined a crowd. I was used to the kinks.

AN *IT-CHOSE-YOU* ADVENTURE

As soon as you think you've figured cancer out, it reminds you that it's still the big C for a reason.

After the appointment with the radiologist who found and biopsied the tumor, there were visits and consultations with a breast surgeon and a reconstructive surgeon. My breast surgeon recommended an oncologist. A remote pathologist reported on the size, aggressiveness, and type of cells proliferating in my body. There were visits for second opinions, check-ins and checkups with my internist and my ob-gyn. A cardiologist had to make certain my heart was strong enough for treatment. At the treatment clinic, there were nurses and pharmacists who tended to the details of treatments.

No one tells you how to orchestrate which doctor follows which, or what follows what. There was no road map. I was left to follow instincts I didn't have and the advice of others who had been there before me. But of course, no one had been exactly where I was, because my particular set of circumstances resembled no other, as is true for anyone with a diagnosis. Not one of us is an average patient. Although some of us are less average than others. That's the good news and bad news, where hope and despair become close cousins. One of my nurses warned me, as if I had something to do with the matter: "You don't want to be an outlier. Being an outlier in medical treatment isn't a good thing."

I cried only once throughout the entire ordeal, when I became overwhelmed with so many options—even while I understood how very lucky I was to have any options at all. Still, I learned that there was no right way, no wrong way. The decisions were ultimately my own, which baffled me because I had no freaking idea what to do. I felt alone and vulnerable. And

I had an inescapable feeling that I sucked at having cancer. Every once in a while, I wondered if I would die. Almost worse, I wondered if I would have the tenacity to relearn how to surf from scratch. I would have to begin again.

So, I focused on more prosaic concerns. Time became a *bitch*. I kept thinking, "Holy shit! It takes so much *time* being sick!" At first, I couldn't fathom how I would shoehorn the appointments and surgeries and treatments into my work schedule, especially as I wanted to keep the diagnosis private. It was important to me that I maintained my work life unbroken by this new reality. Still, there was no way around it. A diagnosis is a time suck, like an IRS audit or being stuck in traffic. I complained to Joel, "I need an avatar for my cancer."

In lucid moments—and in retrospect—I realized I was thinking myself in circles. My struggle with the new time deficit spoke more to my state of denial. If I could be annoyed by the hours taken away from doing the things I loved or obligations I had, then I wouldn't focus on the terror the diagnosis inspired. What time was I really losing? What about my illness and treatment made it a time suck? What was that time "for" anyway? Had I earmarked it in advance?

I was thinking about it all wrong. I needed a new strategy, so I tried to recast the value judgment on how I was spending my days: Having cancer was like going on an adventure! I tried to look at each hour in this awesomely complex new world as a novel experience. I would learn from it, as we do with any new experience. I would learn to live with this new fear that it brought. What a luxury to become newly acquainted with fear, so as to better understand it. There were dark thoughts, of course, but with acceptance of the adventure came a kind of light. I simply wasn't going to be "good" at having cancer. I could read all the books, learn all the words, ask all the right questions, and I'd still be in the same predicament. With nothing to show for it except a ghoulish new vocabulary.

I also had a surfer's trump card when it came to my psychology. I knew there'd be another wave on the horizon.

VULNERABILITY SUCKS ... OR, MAYBE NOT

For the most part, during the next two months while I continued treatment, I stood, battered, at the water's edge of our battered New Jersey community and mind surfed. I bought a digital SLR camera so I could shoot photos of Rocco while he caught wave after wave. While my body was getting tactically poisoned, his was getting stronger with every session. There were days when just walking through the deep, fine sand to the shoreline of our local break was enough to exhaust me. Rocco's and my weekly hours-long beach walks into the nearby state park became impossible.

Every once in a while, I was strong enough to get out into the water—but almost never strong enough to surf. Getting into the waves was cure enough, a humble blessing, but it also left me feeling more vulnerable than ever before. After the initial burst of fear and anger that came with the diagnosis, and after I embraced the perilous journey aspect of it, I began to feel vulnerable in a way I'd never before. When I found myself sick from the treatments that pushed me to my physical worst, I felt it as a kind of betrayal. My body had turned on itself and now I was sick with the result. This new vulnerability crowded out every other feeling. Rather than try—fruitlessly—to steel myself against the feeling, I decided to accept it. It was close enough to sucking to make me comfortable. I could learn from it—if I could wrap my arms around it.

The word "vulnerable" derives from the Latin *vulnerare*, which means "to wound," so my reflexive response to the physiological insults to my body, both from within and without, followed the origins of the word used to express it. This made sense to me.

And that origin had gotten lost. A wound in our body isn't just a site of destruction. A wound is a site of healing, building, rebounding. At a cellular level, every little laceration or bump on our body is being tended to by bucket brigades of material repairers. The violent action that left the wound is in the past. Every moment that passes is a moment closer to wholeness.

But the only things we call "vulnerable" these days are likely to be fatally compromised or broken. The news cycle consistently proves just how technologically vulnerable we are—hackers accessing private information, enemies threatening to sabotage our utility systems, effective manipulation of social media for gain or influence. Vulnerable things are sites of weakness, paranoia, and fear. Where a system is vulnerable, it is open to what or who may take advantage of it, or at the very least, what might stress it toward breaking, like a badly engineered bridge. And talk about protecting those systems involves identifying those weaknesses in order to safeguard against them.

In this framework, vulnerability in the human emotional experience can be confusing. If we are accustomed to thinking of being vulnerable as the state of being weak, or broken, we miss the value of the feeling and work against it, instead of noticing what it teaches us and the gifts of healing vulnerability brings.

Brené Brown has spent her career unwinding the way in which we pathologize vulnerability. Her TED Talk on the subject is one of the most-watched on the TED website, speaking volumes to how many people not only relate to the issue, but how many clearly struggle with it. It's not a question of whether one feels vulnerable, it's about whether one can accept being vulnerable. Like its broader cultural context, we consider personal vulnerability to be a liability. The synonyms tell the story: "weakness," "defenselessness," "helplessness," "exposure," etc.

Except for one: "openness."

Brown's research has turned those pejoratives into opportunities. Vulnerability, Brown contends, "is the birthplace of love, belonging, joy, courage, empathy and creativity. It is the source of hope, empathy, accountability and authenticity." Those most comfortable with it, according to Brown, are the "open-hearted." These are people who embrace vulnerability rather than run from it. They believe it is what makes them beautiful.

I understood this. I had grasped at it in my amateur way ever since I'd picked up a board. Surfing like a middle-aged kook didn't make me beautiful—but it did open the door to places where I felt vulnerable. Over time, I'd grown accustomed to the fact that I would always be the student, never the master; that I would be among the last in the pecking order and all that signified. Sucking at surfing was a way to practice a (relatively) nonthreatening way of being vulnerable. Somewhat paradoxically, I realized I'd spent so much time being vulnerable that I'd developed a kind of hardiness. It had nothing to do with aptitude. I'd just swallowed my pride and put in the time. I'd permitted myself to live in the open. Even though I would always remain a novice, I would keep trying. I thought I'd been doing the hard work but realized these were but baby steps toward being among the "open-hearted."

I was immediately able to examine some choices I'd made in light of my new, post-diagnosis relationship to vulnerability. For instance: I'd managed to keep my diagnosis to myself and those closest to me for seven long months. By holding the news close, I figured I could push away the feelings of exposure that a cancer diagnosis entailed. I figured I could get to the other side of it and then be able to tell people, "Oh, yeah, I *had* cancer, I *kicked its ass*, and now I'm over it. All good." I wanted badly to talk about it in the past tense: closed, done, finished, never again. But my cancer wasn't past tense yet; it wasn't even nearly past. It was very, very present.

I even chose a chemo protocol that allowed me to keep up the appearance of being healthy. My hair didn't fall out, and with the exception of a few days posttreatment, I could fake it pretty damn well. I looked like hell, but I just told people I was tired.

In retrospect, I realized that I didn't want people to know about my health status because I felt shame. Shame about being weak, defenseless, helpless. Shame about giving my vulnerability a name. In Brown's research into what she calls the "Defense Against the Dark Arts" of shame, she writes, "Shame derives its power from being unspeakable." She advises, "if we speak shame, it begins to wither . . . We can't embrace vulnerability if shame is suffocating our sense of worthiness and connection." Shame makes us feel unlovable and keeps us from accepting our vulnerability— the very thing that opens a path toward love.

We all have a voice in our heads telling us that we aren't good enough, healthy enough, smart enough, strong enough. When something like cancer happens, that voice seems to be . . . correct. It's a terrible feeling, and completely unnecessary. You shouldn't have to live a life totally untouched by misfortune to live openly with yourself. That voice is the wrong one. Shame lives in the center of these perverted measures of self-worth and feeds the monsters of self-doubt and self-criticism. Awareness of this blob of shame is the first step to resisting it. Once we confront those feelings, we can begin to accept our vulnerability and open our hearts to the love we have to give and receive.

JUST WHEN YOU THOUGHT IT WAS SAFE TO GET BACK IN THE WATER . . .

By the time of my final round of chemo, I asked my docs if we could call it quits. Every ounce of my being said, "Enough!" My body was now fully protesting as I approached the clinic on 15th Street in Chelsea with severe bouts of nausea. The nurses began to call me a "tough stick" because my veins would perform a disappearing act, refusing to cooperate, making it extra difficult to tap for the IV push of the chemical cocktail of methotrexate and 5-fluorouracil. I took the "C" part (Cytoxan) of the CMF treatment orally. My body was basically saying, "Fuck this shit!" My mind was saying the same thing.

Instead of having to endure the final treatment, something much worse happened: a second tumor appeared in the same breast. I was reminded of another recurring nightmare about getting into elevators that would take me to unknowable places, moving sideways, or diagonally, or too far up or down. I kept getting on the elevator of vulnerability going down and just when I thought I reached the basement, I found there were subterranean floors to be explored.

Between the double threats of the residual DCIS and the appearance of the new growth, my doctors and I decided that a mastectomy was the best course of action. We will never know if we missed the second tumor in the original diagnosis, or if it broke through the chemo. I prefer to believe the former, because the latter does not bode well for my future.

In either case, the chemo protocol I'd endured was determined to have been ineffectual so I would have to undergo another—basically a do-over—once I recovered from the mastectomy and my immune system rebounded enough to withstand more treatment. Another one of those elevators plunging into darkness.

I was given a welcome two-week respite between the end of the first failed protocol and the mastectomy plus subsequent chemo. Two weeks meant one thing to me: Enough time to get in at least one surf session before being land-bound for another four or five months. In between months of chemically induced rootedness, I got to get into the water and feel my body as it wanted to be. Just for a moment. A moment was enough.

Small, thigh-high waves welcomed me back to our New Jersey break. It was July, eight months since my diagnosis. Rocco and I paddled out through the green Atlantic water together. He stroked easily through gut-less white water and was sitting on his board in the lineup two minutes later. I struggled. Arms powerless, heart pounding, lungs heavy—*holy fuck!* I thought, *this year has kicked my ass.* I couldn't do it.

Choking back a sob, I turned my sleek, white Jim Phillips board around to head back to shore, the same board that had assaulted me a year earlier. When I returned to that beloved board, it felt familiar and stable, like coming home. We'd been through so much together, but now I couldn't honor her with a session because I was wasted from the insults my body sustained over the previous months. An inner voice nagged, *There is no way you can do this.* As I reached shallow water near the shoreline, I suddenly saw myself as my son might have seen me from the lineup: defeated.

Instead of hiking my board out of the water, I swung her back around to face the small crashing waves. I put my head down (which you should never do in the ocean, but even holding my head up took energy I didn't have) and paddled with every bit of juice left in my body. I pushed through past the break.

When Rocco and I first started surfing, we both stayed on the inside, where we would get pushed by the white water to shore. I would position and push him into waves until he was strong enough to propel himself.

When I began to paddle out to catch a few open faces, I would keep watch over him in the white water from beyond the break. When he was very young, he would cry out of fear for my safety if I stayed out too long, or if the current pulled me too far north or south beyond his sightline.

Then, one day when he was thirteen, I was taken completely by surprise to see Rocco in the lineup. We were in Costa Rica where he'd never before been past the break, which is much farther from the shoreline than in New Jersey. It terrified me that he'd paddled out without my oversight. I thought he'd gone safely back to shore.

"How the hell did you get out here?" I asked when he paddled up beside me.

"It took me half an hour, but I made it." He was very proud, as was I. From that day forward, we paddled out together. The tide had turned. I now watch Rocco duck dive and paddle through enormous breaking waves and drop into bombs I do anything to avoid. When the waves get too heavy for me, I surf on the inside while he heads toward the horizon in hope of catching a big one. It still takes every ounce of faith to not panic when he disappears into the swell or with the pull of the drifting current. Surfing with Rocco is as close to heaven as it gets for me, matched by sharing music with Gio (especially our mutual obsession with Bruce Springsteen and Eddie Vedder). But I still struggle with fear for Rocco's safety in the water. I guess you get what you ask for, and heaven and hell are never as far apart as you hope.

On the day that I caught the best wave of my life, Rocco's smile as I approached the lineup gave me the boost I needed to continue. When I glided up to him and straddled my board, he just grinned and said, "You made it," before deftly turning and paddling into a wave.

One wave was all I needed. After bobbing in the surf with my boy for a half hour, a sweet little swell line came my way. I swung my board around to face shore and saw Rocco to my left. He was closer to the peak and had priority. If it had been anyone else, I would have given the surfer the right of way, but I put etiquette aside in favor of sharing a wave with my son, hoping I wouldn't kook out and blow it for him. I paddled harder than seemed necessary to the catch the hip-high bump and caught the energy of the wave, which lifted and pushed me forward as I popped up, turned, and rode along in perfect trim. Now, instead of effort, I let the wave do the work. A board knows what to do on a wave. This one was slow and forgiving, the ocean uncharacteristically merciful. Rocco slid just twenty feet ahead of me. The two of us rode along until the wave unfolded onto the shore. He kicked out the back while I tumbled off the board into the white water.

Breathless from the beauty of that moment, I wept as I headed back out to the lineup. Salty tears mingled with salty ocean water into a brew of emotional release. That I could ride a wave at all seemed a small miracle to me; sharing that wave with Rocco was a kind of grace when I most needed it. I didn't catch another wave during the rest of that session and it would be a long while before I ventured back into the ocean.

In my treatment, the worst was yet to come. While recovering from the mastectomy that would permanently compromise the entire left side of my torso, I endured another two months of a protocol known as "the red devil." But I had experienced being vulnerable. And I knew that beauty and life came with vulnerability, just as surely as risk. When I was too sick to work, or too tired to move, I would close my eyes and ride that one wave with Rocco over and over again.

GRATITUDE: A GATEWAY TO RESILIENCE

The nadir of my physical discomfort from a year that stacked up seven months of chemo and five surgeries came in the final week of that second round of treatment. It was the end of October in a year that rag-dolled me like a bad wipeout. I'd managed to work through the entire ordeal—going to the office kept me distracted and focused on something other than how miserable I felt. I'd shaved my head in anticipation of my hair falling out, still wanting to control what I could (some lessons have to be learned over and over again). Any hope of keeping it private was quashed as soon as I showed up to the office bald. One colleague, upon seeing my shining pate, asked, "Are you okay?"

"No, I'm not," I told her, thinking, *There—I said it!*

Those last few weeks laid me flat out. I could barely walk to the other end of the apartment. In an attempt to comfort me, Rocco would drape his luxurious, to-the-middle-of-his-back hair over my naked head.

I loved it when he did that.

One particularly brutal day, I lay on our living room couch feeling as close to death as I'd ever felt—and I don't say that metaphorically. I literally said to myself as I lay there: "this is what it feels like to die." I tried to conjure the wave with Rocco from three months earlier, but I was so tapped out that I remained on the shore of my imagination. Instead, I found myself counting blessings. At my weakest, I felt my grip loosen on almost everything. There was so little I could *do*. But I could still count.

Gratitude became the only way through. No matter how low I felt, I took comfort that I was still in my home, with my loving family around me. I was relatively safe, except for the cells inhabiting my body that challenged my longevity. I became hyperaware of the infinite circumstances worse than my own and self-pity vanished. In its place came an appreciation for my good fortune to have the care I needed, and the comfort, love, and support from friends and family—no matter the end result. Gratitude became the unexpected benefit of the extreme vulnerability I felt. Once my heart opened up to how vulnerable I was, a path cleared and gratitude was quick to enter. An open heart takes inventory. It's also what you do when you're on an adventure.

One of the most beautiful books written on the subject is neuroscientist Oliver Sacks's final book, a slim but powerful collection of short essays called *Gratitude*, written as he knew he was dying. Upon learning of the metastases that would eventually hasten his end, Dr. Sacks writes, "I cannot pretend I am without fear. But my predominant feeling is one of gratitude." It's especially moving, because he writes as both subject and object, as scientist of his own experiences and experiencer as well.

Dr. Sacks's response to a fatal prognosis may seem extraordinary, but science also tells us that it is not entirely unusual. According to a study of emotions in the wake of 9/11, a group of psychologists found that alongside the fear, anger, and sadness were more positive feelings of gratitude and compassion. The connection between these negative and positive emotion states is explored in University of Michigan psychologist Barbara Fredrickson's "broaden-and-build" theory. Fredrickson espouses how positive emotions "broaden-and-build people's momentary thought-action repertoires and build their enduring personal resources." The more positive resources a person has, the more adaptive they are when shit turns bad. And gratitude is one of the big kahunas of positive thinking.

Gratitude practice leads to more joy, enthusiasm, energy, and feelings of good health. Sometimes it's easy. It's second nature to be thankful for good things. But while thankfulness is a natural response for those experiences that bring us joy, comfort, and security, with practice we can "broaden-and-build" access to those positive feelings in moments of pain, discomfort, and insecurity. Gratitude helps us along the spectrum of experiences to accept what is, rather than spending precious time and resources wishing for what isn't. Years of sucking at surfing readied me for this practice, even though I couldn't have articulated it until I lay dying on the couch.

Until then, I had never grasped the tenets of gratitude practice that involve being thankful for the difficult things in life. Our instinct tells us to push away the nasty stuff. But when we are opened up to our greatest vulnerability, and we make room to feel the positive emotions lurking on the other side of fear or anger or resentment, what comes is an awareness of what we might otherwise take for granted. When we allow deep gratitude into our lives—for both the pain and the solace, in times of great difficulty and those of boundless joy—we help ourselves heal, psychically, and, sometimes, physiologically.

We've all felt how our autonomic nervous system reacts to bad shit with increased cardiovascular activity, jacked heart rate and blood pressure, etc. That's our amygdala at it again, telling us to run or fight. But we can choose to access our more evolved executive function contained in the frontal cortex. That's the newer part of our brain that we can train to override the more primitive in us and to help turn our attention to accentuate the positive. When we are successful, our bodies will respond in kind and physiological stress diminishes. Gratitude helps us to do this.

One of my favorite habits of gratitude came from—who else?—a surfer. Dale Webster holds the title in the *Guinness Book of World Records* of having surfed the most consecutive days. From September 3, 1975, to October 4, 2015—a total of 14,641 days—no matter the weather or swell, in sickness and in health, Webster paddled out and caught at least three waves. Famous for his segment in one of the all-time surf-stoked films even non-surfers enjoy, *Step Into Liquid*, Webster's tenacity isn't what stuck most in my mind. During every session, Webster would honor an ancient Hawaiian tradition by taking a bow to the wave in thanks. No small feat, as he did this by riding backward. Arms spread wide to open his heart to the horizon, he paid his respects to the ocean.

A kidney stone stopped Webster in his forty-first year of surfing every day. I bet he thanked the surf gods anyway. Maybe this time for a break.

WE HAD OPTIMISTICALLY planned a trip to our house in Nosara just four weeks after the final round of that second protocol of chemo. Having canceled the previous two trips that year, I was determined to surf, come hell or high water. I had four weeks to get up enough strength to paddle out.

I started by taking a walk from my apartment to Broadway and back—about twelve blocks round-trip—with Joel by my side. He tried to help keep me upright, but I pushed him away.

"Let me do this on my own . . . ," I told him. ". . . But, catch me if I start to fall."

That walk wore me out. But I made it.

The next day, I went a little farther. My immune system had taken a beating, so I stayed away from the gym and instead focused my efforts on walking longer and farther every day. New York is a great walking city and

I focused on the street theater to keep me alert and entertained as I pushed my body a block or two or ten farther. The thought of getting in the water with my board was enough to keep me going. I knew I was going to have to start from the beginning. New body, new surfer. But I was ready for it. Being a happily bad surfer meant that my pride of accomplishment wasn't hung up on milestones of excellence. Starting over was something I basically did every time I got wet. "Starting over," after two rounds of chemo and five surgeries, sounded really, really great.

If someone had fashioned my circumstances into a "Would You Rather . . . ?" game two years earlier, I am certain I would have chosen keeping my breast over being able to surf. To my great surprise and perverse delight—and maybe this is just survival instinct kicking in, now that my breast was already gone—I felt good riddance to what was giving me grief and threatening all that I hold dear. In the battle of breast vs. surf, I would choose being able to surf as the life-sustaining factor in that equation. Easy.

As the trip approached, I felt myself transitioning mental states once more. I'd been a cancer kook and embraced vulnerability, then I became a battle-tested veteran and relied on gratitude, but now that I was starting to push forward, I was seeking something else. The same thing that I'd cultivated over the years of failures, falls, and washouts on the waves. Nothing more complicated than *resilience*.

When I felt most physically broken, my friend and visionary of body healing, Dr. Eric Goodman, said six magical words to me: "The body *wants* to be healthy." Understanding the body as a resilient system was exactly what I needed. Eric's theory of "complacent adaptation"—basically how we suck at living in our awesome bodies—explains the root cause of our aches and pains. He helps patients heal with the foundational belief in our ability to shift from complacency to resilient adaptation. Our bodies are amazing—but we too often take them for granted. The most fundamental (and the happiest) premise of his work is that we are born with these tools of resilience. Studies have shown that resilience, to echo Dr. Goodman, is innate and not the purview of the exceptional.

So even those of us who suck can reap the rewards of our built-in ability to bounce back.

Because our brains are trainable—we saw this in the discussion of neuroplasticity in the last chapter—we can work to find ways to bolster our ability to deal when things turn bad. Gratitude practice is one of the most effective. This idea brings us back to the Right Mind in Buddhist practice as well. New science and age-old practices dovetail. A little something for everyone.

Someone whose work I came to rely on is Andrew Zolli, whose book, *Resilience*, explored the subject in expansive detail. His background and expertise informed his work, but he also learned best from firsthand experience, like me. After a few years of personal trials that ended with a routine visit to the doctor for the sniffles, Zolli was diagnosed with a nearly always fatal congenital heart condition. He was immediately scheduled for open-heart surgery.

After thirty hours of surgery, Zolli entered what he calls, "My own private island of suckitude as a direct response to that experience." He wondered, "How much disruption will it take until you reach some kind of humility? Eventually you learn your lessons."

Zolli always loved photography, but he had abandoned his own photographic practice for lack of time, talent, and purpose until this health crisis. He told me that his focus on photography, now a big part of his life, was "a direct consequence of his experience of the very edge of existence." Life had given him a deeply personal view of resilience—and a renewed willingness to suck. "I consider this conversation as my afterlife," he told me. "Sucking at something—indeed more than one thing—is part of our continuum of being."

I wondered out loud how sucking could help us to deepen our reserves of resilience. Zolli elaborated, "You're most improvisational when you're first learning something without fear of failure." When disruptions occur—which they inevitably do for everyone, and especially for those struggling to learn something new or improve on something for which they lack talent—"you need to have a reservoir of responses to tap into in order to deal with the situation," he explained. "Being good at improvisation translates into resilience." Zolli calls this *adhocratic* behavior versus *bureaucratic* behavior. This adhocratic response is more like jazz than classical music—less preplanned and more responsive to experiences as they unfold. Resilience works best in an adhocracy.

Zolli's theory translates across all systems and he generously brought it back to my personal working metaphor of surfing. "The lesson of rolling with the waves is true at the level of individuals, groups of people in organizations, and civilizations. It's the ability to release and let go when force is applied. Infrastructure that creates porous concrete, houses that come off their moorings and float . . . the lesson works at every scale." *Don't fight the wave, become it.*

I also knew firsthand that adhocratic systems tend to *thrive* when things go wrong, instead of grinding to a halt. Accessing the potential for resilience in ourselves enables us to lend an assist to others in need and contribute to a ripple effect of the greater good. A resilient community comes together to help those in greatest danger and need. We often see this in the wake of natural disasters where outside agencies are slow to react. I witnessed this in real time when Superstorm Sandy hit our ocean community. Even longtime antagonistic neighbors helped one another and together helped others, creating bonds that lasted beyond the actions necessitated by the state of emergency.

Resilience builds better communities, so those communities can become more resilient in turn. Forward-thinking resilient minds are open to finding ways to create and build resilient systems that benefit all. The improvisational practice of sucking at something, and exercising resilience in the face of it, lends us the opportunity, not only for greater compassion, but also to take action to get beyond what is threatening us as a whole.

COOL AIN'T SHIT

My resilience was about to get tested in the warm Pacific. Just four weeks earlier I'd been immobile from the final round of the second chemo protocol. Rocco wasn't so sure it was a good idea for me to get in the water.

"Mama, maybe you don't want to surf just yet," he cautioned when we were back in Nosara.

"I might not," I told him as we were loading the boards onto the car. (I wasn't strong enough to walk while carrying a board the half mile to the beach.) "But let's bring my board down to the beach just in case."

"I don't think it's a good idea."

"Don't worry, I won't do something stupid," I told him. But Rocco knew better. I did stupid things.

After lugging our boards to the beach, I assured him, "I'm just going to put my board in the water. I won't paddle out, I'll just sit on the inside. I need to be in the water with my board."

"Are you sure?" Rocco was nervous for me. I didn't look so good.

"Yep—don't worry, it'll be fine."

The warm tropical ocean felt like the most comfortable blanket. My body responded instinctively, and I got hit with a rush of dopamine. It felt *good*.

Before Rocco could object, I was lying on my board and windmilling my arms to put some distance between me and the shore. The lineup looked a long way away. A check on my ambition had me notice some smaller waves re-forming on the inside and breaking into less violent white water. With Rocco by my side—he wasn't ready to abandon me even to the inside—I turned my board and let the white water propel me forward. I crawled to my feet and rode my first wave since my best wave, to the shore.

I'd said before that riding white water wasn't surfing, and I stand by that claim. But standing on my board that day in the Guiones surf was a blessed feeling no matter what you call it. I was back to year one in my surfing life. My body had been wounded and put back together—albeit a bit differently from where I started—but I had some muscle memory to lower the learning curve. I was stoked.

By the end of the week, I was making it out to the lineup, but I didn't catch any waves from the outside. My sessions normally lasted from ninety minutes up to three hours; now I was tapped out after half an hour. It didn't help that I had to relearn how to balance prone on my board without putting pressure on the left part of my torso—still tender from the various surgeries and the mastectomy, as well as being nonpliant from the implant. While I would eventually get strong enough again to properly paddle with my back arched and my chest held off the board, I hadn't yet regained the strength in my core to do that. It felt like I was lying on a bruised softball. It sucked.

At the end of our trip, when we were watching clips from Rocco's sessions with the GoPro, I caught a glimpse of a stranger in the background, sitting in the lineup on my beautiful, fuchsia Jim Phillips board.

Hey, who's that on my board? my mind questioned before my more conscious brain registered the answer: *Holy shit!—that's me.*

I looked like Varys, the sly eunuch from *Game of Thrones*: bald, pale, bloated. A shocker to my self-image. There'd been plenty of challenges recently. I was known for my long red hair for the past twenty years and shaving it off was a challenge to my identity as a "redhead." My breasts had given me pleasure in every conceivable way, and now, when I stood naked in front of the mirror, I tried not to flinch as I looked at the Bride of Frankenstein breasts that adorned my body. I was never a beauty in the lineup, but this was a whole new image for me. It brought home, like an anvil of insight, how we hold fast to our personas as a way of clouding what's real. Right now, *real* wasn't pretty. And while it's clear that I have never been cool surfing, I could still pretend at times when I was at least among other surfers, or better yet, when I was alone in the water. I had entered a new low in kookdom. I was the *least* cool person in the lineup.

When I published the suck at something essay in the *New York Times* and posted the video of me surfing, a colleague stopped by my office to gloat.

"So, you really do suck at surfing," she said to me with a modicum of questioning left in her voice, as if I might just be pulling a fast one. No humblebragging from me. I suck, pure and simple.

"You thought I was being modest?"

"Well . . . ," she said, a moment of hesitation in her voice, "I'd thought, *Isn't Karen cool? She surfs, she has a house in Costa Rica*—I mean, I had this image of you . . . ," and she trailed off as if to check that image again in her mind before continuing. ". . . and it wasn't what I saw in that video you posted. You really do suck!" She had convinced herself now.

"And . . . ?" I asked, but I already knew the answer. I just wanted to see if she'd fess up to it.

"It makes me happy to know you suck at it," she said with a wide smile that was not unkind.

I understood. When people hear that I surf, I get a knowing nod of awesomeness from the terra firma–bound. They're picturing me on a thruster, wearing a bikini I don't own, with a body I don't have, carving up and down a wave face until I casually kick out the back with a smile and a hair flip to paddle out to the lineup for another. Instead, picture me in a long-sleeved surf costume on a longboard, my brow furrowed in concentration, paddling like mad and mostly missing waves. When I do finally manage a drop-in, turn, and glide along the face, I end the ride with a clumsy dismount that is the least convincing cool move on earth. The truth is that most surfers don't come close to what we see in highlight videos. But cool's not the point. The point is the patience and perseverance it requires to get back on the board and try again.

"Glad I can be of service," I told my colleague.

Some of the best surfers I know are not cool out of the water. When not getting barreled or carving up and down on a wave, they can be goofy and awkward. The same can be said of many musicians, once the performance is over. Or athletes off the field or court, or any famous people in their quotidian lives to whom we attach fabricated notions of cool. I was mesmerized by a GIF of Elon Musk from a few years ago. While watching the successful launch of one of his rockets from the control center, Musk calmly puts down a bottle of beer on a desk and just walks away. It was the coolest reaction to something extraordinary that I'd ever seen. But there was another video too. In this one, he sprints out of his lab to watch a synchronized landing of a new rocket. If you turn down the resolution, he's indistinguishable from a kid racing out of the house at the jingle of an ice cream truck. That's better than cool.

If I were to catalog the people I know intimately—those whom others might see as cool—they are, to a one, pretty much not cool. Take a moment to do the same—think of all the people you know well to whom others have attached the label "cool" and think about how uncool they are. That's me. That's you. That's them.

So why do we ignore this extremely uncool truth?

Because it helps us to believe that being invulnerable is possible. Watching Elon Musk sip his beer *while his spaceship took off* immediately reignited the old fantasy that I'd tried to leave behind: some people really are totally invulnerable . . . and maybe *I* can be too. "To be cool is to be equipped, and if you are equipped it is more difficult for the next cat who comes along to put you down." That's Norman Mailer in his 1957 essay, *The White Negro*. He was talking about getting laid (of course he was), but the point can be applied to more than Mailer's macho focus.

Being cool—the antithesis of the suck at something ethos—might have a historically very recent, and very specific, origin. There's one fascinating theory that the very basis of cool as a bulwark against vulnerability originated from African American jazz musicians in the '30s and '40s. Joel Dinerstein explains in his book *The Origins of Cool in Postwar America* how "cool" was a survival mechanism against the racism black performers continually confronted. "To play it cool combined performed nonchalance with repressed vulnerability," he wrote.

Dinerstein's brilliant and detailed look at the rich history of cool partly confirms my instincts that coolness is a veil for the ways in which we feel vulnerable, but it does something else too. It confers a profound appreciation for why we love cool and why it has endured for so long. We are drawn to coolness because out of the very vulnerability it seeks to occlude comes creative innovation, not unlike Zolli's improvisation—a key component of jazz. According to Dinerstein, "'playing it cool' was a vernacular phrase picked up from the jazz slang that came to represent a new emotional mode and style: *the aestheticizing of detachment.*" It's the aestheticizing part that makes cool so appealing.

In his TED Talk, Dinerstein tells the story of king of cool saxophonist Lester Young, who protested "Uncle Tomming" by refusing to smile on stage. He hid his eyes—the windows on the soul—by wearing sunglasses onstage and at night. By blocking access to a person's biggest tell, he became unknowable. Sunglasses became a symbol of cool as a protection from giving yourself away.

So, if cool is, in fact, a reaction to that which oppresses us, then we can see how the desire to be cool for cool's sake would keep us from ourselves. Still, we can see why cool is undeniably appealing because from it comes some of our best art. Digging deeper into this unholy matrix of cool and vulnerability might help us to distance ourselves a bit to make room for sucking and the joys it brings.

To help me, I contacted one of the coolest of cool cats, Anthony Bourdain. I knew Bourdain from his early days as a Mr. Fix-it Chef. I published his first book, *Kitchen Confidential* (and the five or so that followed). He was always generous and funny, but also a bit shy and, well, goofy. But in all the good ways, and I wanted to see what he had to say about it all.

I'll put this out there first, since Bourdain was emphatic about one thing above all.

"Simply put?" he said. "I am not cool. I have never been cool."

Admitting to his fair share of recklessness in younger years to overcompensate for awkwardness, fear, and insecurity, Bourdain admitted that doing the most drugs, drinking the most alcohol, and trying to be badder than everybody else as a strategy for social acceptance was never successful. It didn't really make anyone cool. He added, "Any notion or pretense of cool went out the window the second my daughter was born. Thank God."

In trying to dig into cool, Bourdain offered, "I think cool *suggests* the absence of caring," echoing Dinerstein's aestheticizing of detachment theory. But Bourdain saw a more nefarious aspect to it. "It's an almost sociopathic state—the ability to not give a shit about anything . . . In my experience, people are foolishly attracted to people who know what they want. And when all you want is to play blues better than anyone else—or take heroin . . . that, dismayingly, has an appeal to those of us who struggle with our feelings, needs, and desires every day."

But he allowed for there to be something to coolness, something that, to my ears, sounded more like confidence, and a willingness to be confronted (rather than avoidance): "Cool to me is fearlessness, independence, integrity of a sort—the refusal to compromise out of fear or greed or even common sense. David Simon is cool because he makes the television he wants to make and cares little for convention. I congratulated him once on his show *Treme* being renewed by HBO after losing half its viewers. He replied, 'Audiences are for pussies.' *That's* cool." How much daylight exists between that conception of coolness and Brené Brown's vulnerability? Both invite the world in, both exist on the cusp of great creativity.

Bourdain continued, "I finally met and became friendly with my platonic ideal of cool: Iggy Pop. But Iggy needs love. We talk of that a lot. And those of us who *need* love, to be loved, appreciated, can never be really cool." And then Bourdain retreated back to cool's shadow side: "Cool needs nothing. Cool doesn't give a fuck. And *I* give a fuck. I choose to feel, to love, to hurt, to fail. Wouldn't have it any other way."

I asked Bourdain if he thought sucking at something and being cool were mutually exclusive.

"Yes. Cool people appear to be effortlessly great. At everything. If they don't know how to do something, they make sure never to be seen doing it. Because . . . they're too cool for that." I would add to that the reason why so many people won't let themselves suck at something is because, even if they aren't among the "cool people," there's always hope. Hope to be inducted into the hall of coolness—which is sad because it closes the door on so much possibility. In any case, it's a lonely room.

For the self-described man who made "commercially successful pure food porn," excelling is overrated. It shouldn't be surprising, then, that he'd taken up Brazilian jiujitsu. And . . . he regularly got his ass kicked. Bourdain, it turns out, was expert at sucking at something.

"To be at the bottom of an endless learning slope, with no peak. That's deeply satisfying," he explained before turning back to his place of comfort. "It's like being the worst, newest cook in the kitchen again. The satisfactions of learning, in tiny increments, the daily problem solving, the sucking less . . . it's great!"

He paused before continuing, "I'd add something Ferran Adrià said to me: 'I don't want to do things I know how to do. I want to do things I don't know how to do.'"

Maybe it's no coincidence that a lifelong chef developed this positive attitude toward sucking. Nothing will more quickly or more consistently put you face-to-face with your limitations than the kitchen. You'll get scalded and burned, you'll cut your fingers and bleed into the prep, you'll fuck it all up and make shit food even when you get good at it. But—most important—you can't stop trying. We all gotta eat.

And yet, in spite of all that, we sometimes learn in the most painful way how vulnerability and the veneer of cool we project onto others can hide someone's darkest hour. On June 8, 2018, with the news of Tony having taken his own life, I was reminded that the labels we put onto others have no bearing on someone's pain. The best we can do is to expose our own pain to daylight and to pay attention to the twilight messages we might otherwise miss from our loved ones.

Cancer and its ill effects had forced me into dropping even a modicum of cool as had surfing before it. I was somewhat prepared. If I was going to get back out in the lineup looking like a bloated eunuch, there was no way I was going to be able to fake it. I just had to *not care* about being cool. Not in the fake "cool guy" way, but in the way Tony said, by giving a fuck about the important stuff.

If we have to grapple with what cool is and what it isn't, then cool at its best is flexible and resilient, it's improvisational, it's an open response to vulnerability. Cool isn't rigid or unforgiving. It is not the lack of action, but action taken full bore, with no regard for a determined outcome. If it's a mask, it's a transparent one that should facilitate how we see the world rather than manipulate how the world sees us. Tony Bourdain nailed it.

AS OF THIS WRITING, my surfing not only got back to where I was before that crummy year, but it has also improved. I still suck at it, but I suck at it a little bit less. On a recent trip to Costa Rica, I rode three of the biggest waves I've caught so far (four-to-six-foot, *not* Hawaiian!) and rode them with a bit of grace. While improving is not the point of sucking at something, I'll admit it feels good. I am still not cool and I have never been cool, but having to start at the very beginning again is what got me to jump forward. Resilience is its own strength. And the humility to find myself vulnerable and at that very beginning might well be just what I needed to propel me forward.

The same goes for you: as you stumble along, you'll find that you're cool or you don't care if you're cool—because they might be one and the same. It just depends on your starting point.

During the most challenging waves of my life, challenges that exposed almost to the bone just how much of an amateur I was—at surfing, at living, at surviving—I came across these four answers: vulnerability, gratitude, resilience, . . . and being completely uncool. All four have stuck with me (especially the last one). All get me through each day, lift me up, and raise my head above the waterline.

Being resistant to sucking because you want to be cool is not cool:

COOL

is a mask for
VULNERABILITY

without
RESILIENCE
you remain rigid, which is the
opposite of COOL

VULNERABILITY

when hidden, makes it
difficult to feel
GRATITUDE

without
GRATITUDE

—even for the hard
stuff—RESILIENCE
becomes more challenging

Being vulnerable (and sucking at something) is what's cool:

VULNERABILITY

opens you up to feel and practice GRATITUDE

GRATITUDE

creates a path to RESILIENCE

COOL

allows you to be comfortable with VULNERABILITY

RESILIENCE

is what is really COOL

IT'S NOT ABOUT RELIGION; IT'S about BELIEF.

WAVE 5

My God Wave: The Power of Belief

Rule # 5:
Love rules.

Lesson #5:
A witness makes it real.

Benefit #5:
Turn humiliation into humility.

Under the *palapa* at Main Beach, Sunday morning worship had called over fifty people: Ticos and gringos, young and old alike. A preacher wearing board shorts, an unbuttoned Hawaiian shirt, and flip-flops was accompanied by a guitar player. Everyone, both pre- and post-surf stoked alike, sang along in praise to God.

I can think of no better place to give thanks and worship than fifty yards from a great beach break in our small coastal town on the Nicoya Peninsula in Costa Rica, surrounded by families, children, surfers, and frolicking dogs. I'm hardly the first. Thomas Blake, a pioneer surfer from the 1920s, called the ocean "The Blessed Church of the Open Sky." The autodidact Blake, father of the modern surfing lifestyle, had carved *Nature=God* onto a secluded rock face near his hometown. He would have approved of this gathering under a sunny, open sky. Glory, hallelujah!

After my terrible-no-good-very-bad year, I found myself more humbly worshipful when I went down to Costa Rica, or anytime I could get near the water. Gratitude played a part, of course, but I was also starting to touch on something beyond psychology. Something metaphysical.

Maybe it was finally getting myself free from all the scenery of illness, and all the solitude and inwardness of treatment, but I was getting comfortable sharing my recovery with other people, even when those other people were watching me flail and fumble.

My next wave combined two things I'd never thought would flow together: humility and belief. On a warm day, during a miraculous calm moment in the Pacific, I experienced my very own "oceanic moment"— while wonderfully, beautifully, blissfully sucking.

WE WANT PEOPLE TO WATCH

The day offered near-perfect lines of head-high glass. Some outside sets brought overhead waves. Perfect conditions have a downside. A day like this can bring crowds, and for a kook like me, crowds make it very difficult to score a wave. In a crowded lineup, it's much harder to get priority. While some patiently wait for a wave to line up for them, others hunt around restlessly to put themselves in position. Crowds test etiquette. It isn't polite for one surfer to snake another, but there's a bit of survival-of-the-fittest at play in every lineup.

On the occasion of this blessed Sunday session, I did get to drop into a few waves, but hadn't yet enjoyed a decent ride. Then, after about an hour in the water, I got caught inside of a seventeen-wave set (yes, I counted) as the relentless rolling swell dumped waves on my head. I held my breath and ducked under raucous water, pulling the nose of my longboard tightly under my arm to keep it from flying out from my possession and into another surfer. Working hard to push through the heavy white water, I'd come up from under the chaos, jump back onto my board, and paddle hard in an effort to get past the break. Then another wave would break in front of me. Then another, and I'd paddle again. Another. Again. My arms grew weary and I finally decided to give it a rest. *Seventeen*. It was grueling.

The ease or difficulty of access to the lineup depends on a variety of factors. Like any sport or physical endeavor, there are different levels of terrain commensurate with skill level. In surfing, there are pluses and minuses to the different kinds of breaks. Generally speaking there are three setups: beach breaks, reef breaks, and point breaks.

Paddling out at a beach break is particularly challenging. Beach break waves roll in over a shifting sandy floor with no set bottom against which a wave can predictably shoal, making it difficult to predict where a wave will form and how it will break. These are the waves I surf. A competent surfer has the skill to read the ocean to best guess where to paddle out and when. We already know I suck at this.

Despite their added element of randomness, there are definitely upsides of the beach break for perennial beginners. When I inevitably meet the bottom by falling off a wave and I am pushed down by the tons of water on top of me, sand is more forgiving than reef. Also, the very lack of predictability of where a wave will come from and where it will end creates an advantage for the novice by creating more room in the lineup for surfers to spread out. Since beach breaks are so popular, these advantages can be countered by the sheer numbers of surfers in the lineup. I have counted up to a hundred out on a good day.

A reef break's permanent bathymetry (i.e., its unchanging floor composition) makes the takeoff point or points more predictable. There are often access points, sometimes called keyholes, which are cuts in the reef that create a channel through which you can paddle out while avoiding breaking waves. Reefs are scary to me because a meeting with an ocean floor covered with jagged coral heads or rocky spurs after a wipeout can seriously fuck you up.[1]

A point break setup occurs when waves wrap around a headland or outcropping of land and break in semipredictable patterns. Points can be sand or reef bottomed and they, too, are extremely desirable to surfers. Points are competitive, like reef breaks, because the takeoff positions

---

[1] Check out *The Inertia*'s website for their piece on the 5 Goriest Wipeouts to get a visual of superstar surfer Keala Kennelly's face after meeting the reef at Teahupo'o (pronounced CHŌ-poo, "Chopes" for short). Fair warning . . . It's heavy.

are limited. Surfers have to wait their turn to go for one. But everyone is watching and there's serious pressure to make the wave. It's like climbing the tall diving board at the pool when you were a kid—there's no backing down. And everyone else is waiting for their turn. But at least on the high dive, you know where and how far you have to fall. In the ocean, wind, swell direction, and tide make even point break waves changeable, thus increasing the pressure exponentially. Lest we think for one second that the ocean is predictable, it never is.

An important second-order difference among all these breaks (besides the different demands they make on your skill level) is the skill level of everyone else out there. Your witnesses. And, in point break surfing, there's a lot of witnessing. Unless you're lucky or good enough to find and surf reefs and points with no one else out, you're going to be watched. All eyes are on the surfer with priority. This is a world apart from a beach break where a less skilled surfer can somewhat disappear in a spread-out lineup or go for scraps no one else wants away from the prime peaks.

That doesn't mean you don't *want* someone to see you make a wave. But it's a double-edged sword. You might dream of the day when you catch a glorious wave and dozens of other surfers watch you . . . but far more often than not, especially in my case, they're all watching you fail, and fail, and fail (when they're not busy failing themselves). This *seeing* is absolutely a part of surfing. When I finally caught and rode my first real wave, having my son-in-law, Christopher, there to see it solidified the moment in my memory. The desire for having a witness applies to both the least and most important parts of our lives.

"The presence of others who see what we see and hear what we hear assures us of the reality of the world and ourselves," the philosopher Hannah Arendt tells us in her discussion on the private and public realms in her masterwork, *The Human Condition*.

If having a witness solidifies our sense of reality, it becomes a compelling component of our efforts. Witnessing is a big part of surfing and explains a lot about how photography and filmmaking are inextricably tied to the lifestyle. The ephemeral nature of both a wave and the act of riding one contributes to why a surfer wants to be seen in action. *If you catch and ride a wave but no one is there to see it, did you really score?* Having a witness makes it real. Whatever "it" may be: even if it entails failure.

According to Arendt, ". . . the specific meaning of each deed can lie only in the performance itself and neither in its motivation nor its achievement." Admittedly, Arendt's argument is in relation to ancient Greek philosophy and its grappling with greatness. But what if we turn that idea sideways and find application to something other than greatness? She's really talking about the concept of "an end in itself"—a summation of sucking at something (and surfing) if there ever was one.

The surf historian Matt Warshaw said that "Surfing . . . generates laughter at its very suggestion, and this is because it turns not a skill into an art, but an inexplicable and useless urge into a vital way of life." I've come to realize that this laughter is an occasion for celebration, rather than sheepishness. Surfing doesn't suffer because it's pointless; it's the reason why it compels us. I think this uselessness is a key to why it's so excellent to suck at it.

Warshaw's insight can also be said for the call to suck at something, since its promise of vitality is in the act of *doing*, not in the goal of *achievement*. And sucking is certain to generate laughter.

DELICIOUS HUMBLE PIE

In the "performance" Arendt addresses lies the tension between wanting and needing a witness, and our aversion to doing something that might embarrass us. Our resistance to being seen as we fail or struggle has us recoil from public scrutiny for fear of being humiliated. In that space of tension, the potential for joy, or the potential to, say, create art, can be squashed by our self-consciousness. That noisy ego back at it. Think of those people who refuse to dance or sing—I mean who *doesn't* want to dance and sing?—but, instead, hug the sidelines at a party in lonely discomfort. Maybe it's you. It certainly has been me on occasion. But, why?

My friend Aubrey Marcus told me that his professional dancer friends love nothing more than seeing someone letting it all hang out on the dance floor—especially when they lack all semblance of talent. He says it's the surest and clearest expression of pure joy. It's like seeing someone remove their ego, fold it up, and toss it into the corner. At least for a song or two. And that crazy dancer is the perfect model for how we can all turn humiliation into something beautiful. That dancer isn't denying humiliation—he's just zooming right past it. It wouldn't be nearly as joyful to "let it all go" in the privacy of his own room. It's the seeing that makes it special.

Just like "vulnerable" from the last chapter, "humiliation" has come a long way from its proper origin. It's derived from the Latin *humilis* ("lowly, humble"), which in turn comes from *humus*, meaning "ground," "earth," "soil." Though I may prefer the water, I have no problem with the ground. Who would? So why, if we follow the etymology, is being (brought) down to earth considered so terrifying? Don't we admire those we characterize as "down to earth"? When speaking of *others*, we see it as a positive attribute. And yet we see a different facet when we think of ourselves. We fear being "lowly." In our attempt to self-aggrandize out of our insecurities, we want others to see us on an elevated plane or in brighter light—because if others see us as such, then it makes our aggrandizement real. At least that's what our fuzzy logic tells us.

Hannah Arendt pointed out in grander terms the tension between public and private: "Since our feeling for reality depends utterly upon appearance and therefore upon the existence of a public realm into which things can appear out of the darkness of sheltered existence, even the twilight which illuminates our private and intimate lives is ultimately derived from the much harsher light of the public realm. Yet there are a great many things which cannot withstand the implacable, bright light of the constant presence of others on the public scene . . ." She may have rued the effects of the "harsher light" that came from other people, but I have seen how that light can be beautiful, too, even when it illuminates our failures and frailties. Especially when it does so. Sucking in the light of the public realm—washing out in Guiones on a crowded day—feels like throwing open your arms and inviting the world in.

Of course, there are some things that need to happen behind closed doors. I wouldn't have wanted the whole world to watch, for instance, my post-wipeout ER surgery. Not that anyone *would* have.

We are caught, then, between the desire for a public witness to our actions and the privacy we need for our most intimate experiences. We want to be seen but we are also afraid of being seen.

It's the paradox at the heart of the love-hate relationship with social media. That "self," those likes, that empty guarantee of awesomeness (or that horrifying confirmation of anonymity). And yet all of it, we know deep down, is faked. Not just by ourselves, but by complex and clever manipulation by machines and algorithms that are way smarter than we'll ever be. We know better . . . and yet we keep posting, sharing, and liking.

The worst part is, even though we might present our "coolest self" online, this act of persona works just like that mask of cool I wrote about earlier: it *hides* our vulnerability rather than relieving us of our humiliation. It only adds to our fundamental fears that we aren't enough—smart enough, talented enough, pretty enough, strong enough, _____ enough. If we were, we'd feel free to let other people see.

In this framework, sucking at something in public isn't just a panacea; it's also an achievement in itself. If you're able to suck, especially in public, it means that you know you're enough. You don't need the high scores, style, and flash to "make up" for what you don't have. You're enough.

Sucking in public is also a part of what helps us to get over our humiliation. We need to put out there what we really are—fallible beings who are worthy of love.

Every time you see someone fail willingly in public, that person is loudly and clearly and simultaneously telling you something (you may just be missing it): I'm more than enough to account for this failure. And other failures. And anything else. My worth doesn't depend on it.

You can say that, too, anytime you want.

And if we witness others sucking as well, instead of judging them and contributing to an atomic toxicity, we can feel connected to them instead in a joyous unity of mutual sucking. I know I've said it before, but I will keep saying it: Practice. All of this takes practice.

THAT OCEANIC FEELING

Back to that Sunday morning in Guiones—I turned toward shore and took a broken wave in. I needed to catch my breath, drink some water, and look to see if there was an easier spot to paddle out. But I was distracted by something wonderful. I saw the communal gathering of worshippers. Rocco, now eighteen, had come in from the lineup at that same moment. He was going to switch out his shortboard for a hand plane and swim fins so he could bodysurf.

A self-described atheist, Rocco smiled when he saw the group under the palapa.

"Sweet," he said with a nod.

His accepting smile at the gathering on the beach surprised me. Rocco worshipped at the altars of Carl Sagan, Richard Dawkins, and Christopher Hitchens as a teen. He found wonder in the cosmos and had spent time in high school working in the office of Neil deGrasse Tyson at the American Museum of Natural History. Science blew his mind enough to have no need for metaphorical mysticism. With his growing maturity, I'd noticed that he'd softened his previous intolerance of faith. Even my skeptic son could appreciate the beauty of an open-air worship on a sunny Costa Rican Sunday morning.

I was going through my own spiritual maturation. On a trip to Rome just a few months earlier, I'd dragged Rocco to Basilica di Santa Maria, tucked away in the corner of a small piazza in Trastevere. Of the more than nine hundred churches in Rome, this one, built in the fourth century and the first dedicated to the Blessed Mother Mary, was the one I couldn't leave Rome before visiting. I'd been a lapsed Catholic for my adult life and, until recently, wavered between being atheist and agnostic. I'd struggled so much with the politics of the church, and institutionalized religion in general, that I pushed it away. But this ancient church called to me.

In Rome, Rocco had waited in the nave as I entered a small chapel at the back of the unassuming church. Making the sign of the cross (how quickly and instinctively the gesture from my youth returned), I slid into a small pew. It had been decades since I was compelled to seek a moment to kneel in private prayer. I'd attended many weddings, funerals, and bar mitzvahs but in no instance had I heard anything resembling "a call."

So, the feeling I suddenly had in that church caught me by surprise. I felt a *connection* I couldn't quite name.

I'd long relegated my past religious experience—the years I'd spent attending church and catechism, my first Holy Communion, my Confirmation—to an old-world duty my parents felt compelled to honor on my behalf. Once I could make the decision for myself, shortly after my Confirmation, I stopped attending mass regularly. Eventually, I rejected the church wholesale, unable to abide its dogma and patriarchal exclusion of women. Besides, Mary as a virgin seemed ludicrous to me, some feminized ideal no girl or woman could ever live up to. I'd felt it palpably as a youth—that we Catholic girls were bound to fail as women simply because most of us would not (thank heavens) remain virgins. How, my formative mind asked, is it that Mary, as one of the most re-vered females in human history, was worshipped because of her status as a mother *and* a virgin? I've done my research since then—and have plenty to say about it all—but for the purposes of this book, let's just say that my twelve-year-old self figured we Catholic girls were screwed from the get-go. I moved away from the church and found my own spiritual path. Later, the ocean became my cathedral and surfing my way of communing with something bigger than myself.

But things change. Deep inside, settled pieces of our selves shift around, too slowly to notice. Could it have been my recent encounter with cancer? Was it the uncertainty that comes with age? Or, rather, the *certainty* that comes with age that nothing is certain?

It might also just have been Rome. When I stood in front of the *Pietà* in St. Peter's Basilica in the Vatican, Rocco by my side, my breath caught in my throat and tears collected in my eyes. There, among the throngs of people elbowing for a better view, I felt something move at my center. Michelangelo's marble sculpture of Mary holding Jesus, her son's body draped across his mother's lap, *pulled* at me. I wanted to submit to it, and to the immense love I felt for my own sons. That love had always been unambiguous and life-altering, ever since the first moments Rocco and Gio were born, but before this moment in St. Peter's, it didn't feel connected to anything. The many conversations about motherhood with my friends who were also parents, while intimate, didn't alter the solitariness I felt. Not unpleasant or unwelcome, just solitary. I don't think this is unique—I imagine many of us recognize that we love our own children like no one else would or could and therefore feel alone in it. This seems to me the natural order of things.

But standing before the *Pietà*, something lifted. I was imbued with the overwhelming intensity of the mother-child bond. I felt at one with Mary—in her pain and suffering, but also in her love for her son—in a way that all of the liturgical practice and dogma of my youth could never have aroused. I surrendered to it and was overcome by a feeling of serenity and what felt like pure love piercing my heart. I stood, as if pinned in place, tears streaming down my cheeks, until Rocco, aware that I had overstayed the unstated allotted time per visitor to stand front and center at the *Pietà*, pulled at my elbow. "Mama, let's go!"

I collected myself enough to be an orderly tourist. Rocco and I made our way back outside. The feeling stayed with me, though, only gradually trailing away as though evaporating under the Roman sun.

I'd read about "the oceanic feeling" before—I was drawn to the phrase for its reference to the environment that occupied so much of my life. And while I often experience my time in the ocean as a feeling of unity with nature, it had never really touched this. Until my experience witnessing the *Pietà*, I'd never been truly overcome with the oceanic feeling.

The feeling exists—anyone who's had an experience like mine can vouch—but there's never been a consensus on what's actually going on. It's been debated for decades and has drawn in some of the most celebrated public intellectuals of the age. The French novelist Romain Rolland and Sigmund Freud famously debated the concept. The former, who expressed the concept as the source of all religion, explained it as "The simple and direct sensation of the Eternal (which could very well not be eternal, but simply without perceived boundaries and oceanic)." Freud disputed any mystical meaning, defining it as a feeling of "oneness with the universe." He traced this dissolution of self-boundaries back—this will be no surprise—to a regressive narcissistic longing for the primary infant-mother bond. Let me just say to Freud: nope. Whatever I was feeling in Rome wasn't regressive or narcissistic.

The source of the oceanic feeling has been debated endlessly since that original exchange between Rolland and Freud, but from wherever it comes it invites various interpretations making it hard to pinpoint. Author Arthur Koestler illuminates the feeling beautifully: "That higher entity, of which the self feels a part, to which it surrenders its identity, may be nature, God, the anima mundi, the magic of form, or the ocean of sound." From what I can tell, many of our most articulate commentators on the subject have been similarly tamed by its complexity. We're reduced to listing possible explanations rather than forcefully positing just one.

That won't stop me from trying.

For me, there's no doubt that my permeability in the presence of the *Pietà* was a condition I had welcomed into myself through my surfing and sucking. There's a very simple connection. That oceanic feeling, at its most essential, was the presence of something else. Something else that crowded me out for a moment. Something else besides all of my picayune and incidental qualities, my complaints and urges and thoughts. Something that connected me at the root to what really mattered. I don't think we can really call up the oceanic feeling anytime we want. But in order to allow access to it, we need to be receptive to experience something apart from the self, that bossy human peculiarity that's always getting in the way (and getting its way). Even a slight pivot away from our egos can open the door. And sucking at something is exactly that. A brief pivot from our "better-thinking" selves. Our noisy and self-doubting selves.

I might be biased (I am), but there's something in surfing that I think is particularly good at prepping people for this selflessness. There are little mini-oceanic feelings along the way: split-second moments on a wave when gravity and position and wind combine in such a way as to create a momentary suspension of tension and you seem weightless, as if motion slowed to absolute stillness. It's short—gravity and inertia take over quickly—but in that one moment I experience a kind of otherness. It feels like the kind of still point evoked by T. S. Eliot in his poem "Burnt Norton":

> At the still point of the turning world. Neither flesh nor fleshless;
> Neither from nor toward; at the still point, there the dance is,
> But neither arrest nor movement. And do not call it fixity,
> Where past and future are gathered. Neither movement from nor toward,
> Neither ascent nor decline. Except for the point, the still point,
> There would be no dance, and there is only the dance.
> I can only say, there we have been: but I cannot say where
> And I cannot say, how long, for that is to place it in time.

I don't think it's any coincidence that a poem and the *Pietà* are the things that seem to get right to the heart of this concept. Art has the unique power to put us in touch with the ineffable. It is surely not unique that I first encountered it as I gazed upon the *Pietà*. In the witnessing of the sculpture, I participated in an ages-long dialogue—about the story of Jesus and his crucifixion, about a mother's sorrow, about Michelangelo's mastery—and by doing so I experienced a still point of sentience connecting me to thousands of years of human history. It is art's very permanence that creates a connection and stability, as Arendt speculates, "so that a premonition of immortality, not the immortality of the soul or of life but of something immortal achieved by mortal hands, has become tangibly present, to shine and to be seen, to sound and to be heard, to speak and to be read."

But it can't work its magic if we don't put ourselves nearby. Art, like humility, has to be *shared*. And for it to be shared, it needs a witness: someone else to behold the creation by another. Whether it is art as durable material that endures, or art as transitory performance—this "end in itself" is also what makes it matter.

Surfers often talk about surfing as an expressive art. The idiom is "drawing lines" on the face of the wave, referring to the trail momentarily left by a board as the surfer rides along the face of the wave. Every surfer wants to draw a unique line as an expression of individual style. I merely scribble. Still, the same can be said of any creative endeavor. The French artist Jean Cocteau believed that all artwork was the raveling and unraveling of lines to create drawings, poetry, film. Whether that art results in something tangible like a work of poetry, a hand-knit sweater, a piece of pottery, or something intangible like a line drawn in surfing or down a snowy mountain pass—it hardly matters. The pleasure is in making something that wasn't there before. As strong as the act of creation is the desire to share it with others, both to connect us and to make it real. It's elemental, this call to action. When we make something, or when we are humbled before art or performance, we stop asking the question *why are we here?* and feel, even if momentarily, unity with something outside of ourselves. At its deepest connection, we experience that oceanic feeling. But we can't reside there forever.

And that's where sucking at something can have a counterintuitive value in contrast to excellence. Sucking means that as often as you're drawing lines, you're falling. And that falling plants us firmly back on the ground—where we must live—in all of its comfort and discomfort. What if Rocco hadn't tugged at my sleeve in Rome? What if I'd been rooted there in place forever and he left and got on the plane and returned home?

Anthony Storr, author of the modern classic *Solitude*, writes, "If life is to continue, one cannot linger for ever in a state of oceanic tranquillity." People have to adapt to life's exigencies. Without that skill, we wouldn't last long. If we were to remain in an altered mystical state of oneness with the universe, it'd be hard to get up in the morning, get dressed, feed the kids, walk the dog, sit in traffic on our way to work, and all the rest of the daily grind. And while the jury's out for our long-term prospects, in the shortness of a single life span, we adapt or die. It follows that lingering in that oceanic feeling might make us vulnerable in a way that doesn't contribute to our survival. Perhaps it's the fleeting nature of the experience that makes it so transforming. Falling or failing can be as beautiful a line as any. Trying joins us to other people. Maybe Alexander Pope wasn't being pessimistic when he said "To err is human . . ."—maybe it's the best thing about us.

Without humility, we cannot be open to the oceanic feeling, and sucking is nothing if not humbling.

AND THEN GOD ANSWERED

A surf coach, Alex, once told me I had 99 percent of the skill to catch more waves, but he could see me thinking in the lineup, and *that* was what screwed me up every time. He could practically hear from shore the distracting noise in my brain—the one that interfered with my believing that I could surf at all, even though I'd spent thousands of hours in the ocean doing it. Alex helped convince me that I could and I caught a few. Belief was key to scoring.

A few months after my epiphany at the *Pietà*, on that shore break at the edge of the equatorial jungle where the Sunday faithful called to God, I struggled to paddle back out to the lineup. The tide had dropped, making the waves dump with even more ferocity. The relentless swell wore me out, especially as I'd been taking it on the head for an hour before this second paddle out. After getting crushed by ten more waves, I looked beyond the horizon and, inspired by the worshippers now dispersed, I prayed for the first time since my Rome visit.

"Please God," I said aloud, "help me get past the break. I know I am not one of your faithful but show me a sign. Please, help me?"

An oceanographer would be able to explain what happened next in terms of swell period, tide and wave sets, bathymetry, wind speed and direction. But hydrodynamics took a momentary back seat because at the moment I asked God for help . . . The ocean. Stopped. Moving.

Instead of churning white water in front of me and another wave forming behind it and threatening to break on my head, the ocean went totally flat. In place of the chaos that had been kicking my ass, there opened a clear and clean path to the lineup.

Holy shit, I thought, *that worked?*

I zipped past the break. "Thank you!" I yelled heavenward.

Once I was in the lineup, I caught my breath and relaxed. Sitting on my board facing the horizon, I smiled like a lunatic at my success. I knew it wasn't mine alone, which both freaked me out and delighted me at the same time. Tempted to toss the episode into the bin of awesome coincidences, something loosened inside me and I couldn't shake it. What did it *mean* that hours of struggling dissipated the moment I asked God for help?

But there was something more pressing: I still hadn't caught a good wave yet this session and I really, really wanted one.

Was it too greedy to ask for help again? I'd been pushing myself all week, surfing bigger waves than I ever had before, accepting the inevitability of getting worked with each wave I didn't make, or, when I did make the drop and turn, accepting that I didn't always know what to do next. Accustomed to being put in my place by the ocean, I accepted its higher power. Humbled and emboldened, I tried my luck again.

"Just one good ride, God? You got me out here, now can you please help me get *just one*?" I prayed.

You know what happens next.

A peak came my way, head high. It was a bit big for me; I like them waist to chest high, but not wanting to squander this divine gift—if that's what it was—I went for it. I didn't think (thinking hadn't been helping me); but I did believe. With a few strokes, I caught the wave, popped up, and turned left to ride front-side the smooth greenish-blue face of water. I rode as if I believed I could until the wave closed out and I inelegantly, but with a full heart, catapulted over the white water and out the back of the wave. It was another kind of oceanic moment. And I knew I wasn't alone for this one either.

No fucking way! is what I was thinking.

Aloud, I whispered, "thank you," and once safely past the break, I sat on my board in communion with the ocean. For the rest of that session, I was quieted by the realization that in my submission to ask for help, I received it, even if in the form of a deeply felt belief that help was available. I don't know if anyone saw me ride that wave. But in the eyes of God, I felt seen and heard. I had a witness. Maybe that was enough.

I went from not understanding anything about belief, to filling that new opening with an acceptance of its promise. As I sat in the lineup after being humbled by having had answered my rather insignificant request for a wave, I realized that I'd been coming at belief from the wrong side of things my entire life. Belief was its own thing.

I wouldn't go so far as to say that from that moment on I was a Believer, but I began to *believe* in *belief*.

When I recounted this story to Serene Jones, minister, author, and president of Union Theological Seminary, she said she was reminded of the wonderful *New Yorker* piece by Zadie Smith, "Some Notes on Attunement." In the essay, Smith tells the story about finally coming to understand Joni Mitchell's music. Previously, the musician's open tuning and "piping" grated Smith's sensibilities, instead of delighting her. Smith admits she found Joni "incomprehensible." Of the moment it clicked for her, she writes, "As I remember it, sun flooded the area . . . Something had happened to me. In all the mess of memories we make each day and lose, I knew this one would not be lost." This moment for Smith involved "no progressive change, but instead, a leap of faith. A sudden, unexpected attunement."

Serene's insight nailed it. My God wave was "a sudden, unexpected attunement."

Part of what made Smith's piece so relatable to my experience was her previous steadfast inability to hear the beauty of Joni's music. However, the protestations of those before her—*"You don't like Joni?"*—surely primed her to be open to the possibility of attunement. Where progressive change may not be apparent, we are constantly filtering messages and cues from our environment. When an "aha!" moment seems to come out of the blue, it is more likely the culmination of information finally settling into a true understanding.

It seemed clear to me that my struggles with surfing had primed me to be receptive to belief too. Surf coach Alex, in accusing me of thinking on the wave (and getting in my own way), was really telling me that I was trying to control the wave. I was trying to make myself the whole story. If I could just think hard enough, plan enough, predict enough . . . I could surf perfectly. I couldn't. I'm not a one-in-many-millions talent who can do that. Instead, by abandoning that egotism, and submitting to the wave (and to God), I made myself small enough, light enough, to get up and go. Sucking at something makes space for belief.

I KNEW I HAD TO GO to the source of the nature of belief, especially as it intersects with our everyday experiences, and that meant one name: William James.

Way back at the end of the nineteenth century, the philosopher and psychologist put together what remains one of the seminal texts on the subject, *The Will to Believe*. To James, "Faith means belief in something concerning which doubt is still theoretically possible; and as the test of belief is willingness to act, one may say that faith is the readiness to act in a cause the prosperous issue of which is not certified to us in advance."

James trained and taught at Harvard first as a doctor, but found his calling not in the hard sciences, but rather in the new and less grounded science of the human mind. He was one of the most influential Americans studying psychology at a time when the field was relatively unexplored. He is arguing, in *The Will to Believe*, against mathematician William Clifford's own treatise on the subject, called *Ethics of Belief*. Clifford is emphatic that belief isn't a private matter concerning the individual alone and that it is our responsibility to heed the power of belief and its inevitable legacy on future generations. "Into this," he protests, "for good or ill, is woven every belief of every man who has speech of his fellows. An awful privilege, and an awful responsibility, that we should help to create the world in which posterity will live."

Belief is thus acknowledged by both great thinkers as a fundamentally powerful force, but the question is whether we ought to start with it or end with it.

Clifford tries to convince us that "it is wrong always, everywhere, and for anyone, to believe anything upon insufficient evidence." His insistence on certainty is where it all goes wrong for me. This is the kind of framework that shuts down anything new, or incomplete, or unsatisfactory. It's a framework that denies the possibility of growing, or of something becoming true. It's definitely anti-sucking.

The will to believe, on the other hand, helps us to get comfortable with the fact that there can be no guaranteed outcome. James, not in contrast to Clifford, but rather supporting the way of science, writes, "We cannot live or think at all without some degree of faith. Faith is synonymous with working hypothesis. The only difference is that while some hypotheses can be refuted in five minutes, others may defy ages."

What is faith but the willingness to believe? And choosing what to believe can concern something as simple as riding a wave, or something as unfathomable as the Divine. James tells a story about climbing in the Alps that contains something very like the leap of faith necessary in going for a wave. In the story, he questions the value lack of belief would have in a situation where he, hypothetically, finds himself in a precarious situation while climbing "from which the only escape is by a terrible leap." Without having been in the situation before, he can't know with certainty that he can perform the necessary action to save himself. However, if proof of success is necessary before he leaps, he might well doom himself. "But hope and confidence in myself make me sure I shall not miss my aim, and nerve my feet to execute what without those subjective emotions would perhaps have been impossible," he writes. "In this case (and it is one of an immense class) the part of wisdom clearly is to believe what one desires; for the belief is one of the indispensable preliminary conditions of the realization of its object. *There are then cases where faith creates its own verification.* Believe, and you shall be right, for you shall save yourself; doubt, and you shall again be right, for you shall perish. The only difference is that to believe is greatly to your advantage."

His stakes are a little higher than those typical for most of us on any given day, but the spirit is the same. As a proper citizen of the twenty-first century, I didn't just want to stop at philosophy, no matter the class of its vintage. I was also eager to learn what, if anything, science had to offer on the subject, especially neuroscience.

Michael Shermer, publisher and founder of the aptly named *Skeptic* magazine, has written many books trying to unwind why we are susceptible to all kinds of beliefs and how we have the stubborn capacity to reinforce them—even in the absence of proof. In *The Believing Brain*—where the chapter titled "Belief in God" is followed by a chapter titled "Belief in Aliens"—Shermer looks to neuro- and behavioral sciences to track our belief systems across our synapses and the powerful electrical and chemical signals they create. What's interesting in all of the studies around the subject of belief is that brain activity can reveal what areas light up when presented with various stimuli, but the activity is the same for believers and nonbelievers since belief itself is its own stimulus.

Shermer is, no surprise, a skeptic about God. But, even as an expert on the subject, he betrays his concern with the idea of the Divine. Even hard-core atheists can't move away from mystery. Nonbelievers are just passionate believers in nonbelief. Isn't it the same thing?

Shermer even ends part 1 of his book with a kind of prayer:

"Lord, I did the best I could with the tools you granted me . . . Whatever the nature of your immortal and infinite spiritual essence actually is, as a mortal finite corporeal being I cannot possibly fathom it despite my best efforts, and so do with me what you will." This could be read as a kind of joke, but jokes are always at least a little bit true.

Maybe Shermer was inspired by Pascal's Wager, the famous idea that it's better to believe than to not believe. The math is solid (and it's no coincidence that Blaise Pascal worked on probability theory): of all the possible outcomes that combine whether or not you believe, and whether or not God exists, it only puts the odds in your favor to believe. There is an inherent rationality to Pascal's postulate that seems to defy the constructs of faith, but everywhere I turn for elucidation on the subject puts me up against this idea of hope versus rationalism. If hope can be defined as the belief in a positive outcome in the face of all evidence to the contrary, the same logic (or illogic) can be applied to the willingness to continue efforts in the face of sucking at it, since reason has very little to do with it.

There are consequences for our belief choices well before we contemplate the afterlife. We only need to turn to the science of placebos to see how deeply embedded belief is in our neurological function. A placebo effect occurs when a patient is given a nonreactive treatment—a sugar pill, a saline injection, a fake surgery, etc.—but told they are being given a real drug or treatment. Certain placebos are proven to have a profound effect on physiological responses, with patients often reporting a positive outcome: less pain, decreased anxiety, increased performance. By virtue of believing the treatment is going to help, the patient can experience feelings and, in some cases, biological shifts, otherwise created by a real drug or treatment. The opposite is also true, called the nocebo effect, where patients feel adverse effects if they are cautioned about them, even if they are taking an inert substance. The placebo effect is so powerful that randomized double-blind placebo control trials have become the gold standard in many drug studies. The key to these studies is what the patients *believe* they are getting—treatment or no treatment—and points to the power of suggestibility. Or, to put it less scientifically, to belief.

Is it possible to cultivate the kind of mind-set that leaves you open to placebo effects everywhere we might encounter them in the world?

In her book *Cure*, scientist and author Jo Marchant delves into the mystery and science of placebos and nocebos, making a convincing case for the mind-body connection. No longer the purview of suspicious new age enthusiasts, the belief that the mind can influence our physical wellness or contribute to our ill feelings is finally being legitimized by science.

The mind-body connection was made popular by Dr. John Sarno, whose book *Healing Back Pain* sold millions even though it was never embraced—worse, he was often scorned—by the conventional medical community before his death at ninety-three in 2017. He asserted, long before it was popular or acceptable to do so, that much of chronic pain was caused by emotional and psychological stress, which caused the nervous system to create a cascade of responses that contribute to pain. Dr. Sarno treated patients by taking the time to listen to them and by helping them to understand how their emotional state was contributing to their physical discomfort. Having a witness to their pain was the first step to healing his patients. Helping to instill the power of belief that they could heal themselves was the second. Although Sarno didn't run controlled clinical trials or run a research lab, he knew his treatment was effective because his patients got better. Now science has finally caught up with his intuitive and compassionate practice.

In Marchant's book, subtitled *A Journey into the Science of Mind Over Body*, she writes about the importance of caring when it comes to the ministering of people who are suffering. She delves into the power belief has in the mind-body connection, and how it is being studied the world over by neurologists and doctors. Looking at a spectrum of conditions and illness—chronic fatigue, chronic pain, autism, mood disorders, irritable bowel syndrome, and more, Marchant finds that with so many symptoms, it's far more difficult to determine the precise origin than our highly positivist medical profession would have it. There is not always a clear distinction between physical or psychological origins, and manifestations of conditions and the diseases and disorders that we assign to either the body or the mind don't seem to want to be so easily classified.

The connection between healing and believing manifests at the cellular level as well as the spiritual. When Marchant writes about traveling to Lourdes in France, where millions travel to seek its sanctified waters, she asks the question, "Does believing in God make you healthier?" A self-professed atheist, Marchant is moved by what she witnesses in the pilgrimage of believers in an attempt to find some relief in what ails them—even if science can't prove the proclamation of miracles. In the end, she admits, "There are powerful evolutionary forces driving us to believe in God, or in the remedies of sympathetic healers, or to believe that our prospects are more positive than they are. The irony is that although those beliefs might be false, they do sometimes work: they make us better."

The will to believe creates opportunities—for learning, for healing, for openhearted experiences—that the skeptic might not have.

YOU MIGHT WONDER if sucking leads you to belief—or if believing allows you to suck. And what I can say is: I don't know. In my experience with surfing, it's that I've believed, and I've sucked, and believed, and sucked . . . it's been a kind of *ouroboros*. A symbol of unity, renewal, or infinity dating back to ancient Egypt. It most often looks like a snake eating its own tail, and it's taken to be a representation of how one thing feeds another in a never-ending possibility or rebirth. That's what it's felt like over the years.

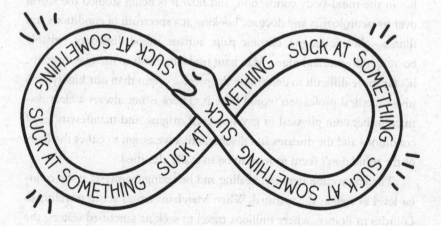

You might have to pretend at the beginning and bet on placebo. As we've already learned, chances are pretty damn good that when you first try something, you'll suck at it. But, if you believe that you'll suck at something and that belief creates resistance to starting, then you're stopped in your tracks before you even start. That kind of belief isn't worth your time. Of course, this entire book is an invitation to push through that barrier in the first place, but our human tendency to resist what we cannot be certain about is difficult to break.

So, instead, relax, and take that little sugar pill of delusion. "Maybe I will be really good at calligraphy!"

That can provide the motivation to get us started. Then, when we inevitably learn—as we did in the first chapter—that it's harder than we thought, our useful belief will transform. Now we might believe that, well, we'll get better. Unless we believe that we might become good at something, we may not be willing to try. It'd be better to start with the assumption that with effort we are likely to improve. And while becoming expert (or being right) is looking too far down the field, advances of any kind would be impossible without this willingness to start something new and to risk being wrong. It may seem like a totally irrational thing, but it can produce wonderfully rational results. This is even true for the very science we often turn to for proof of concept.

The Italian theoretical physicist and luminous writer Carlo Rovelli explains, in a Jamesian type of logic, how this willingness to imagine what *may not be true* can be the very basis of scientific discovery. "The beauty of the scientific enterprise," he explains, "is that we are in touch with the unknown and we try to make steps into it. It works out of beauty, out of intuition, out of imagination, but it has a very solid way, then, of checking. But what it also means is that many beautiful ideas turn out to be wrong." Rovelli doesn't find despair in the wrong turn, but instead celebrates the wonder of it. Being wrong, or sucking, is better than the void of not trying in the first place.

ALL YOU NEED IS LOVE

All of my ruminating on the subject betrays how much my sudden belief in belief confused me. Did it mean that I'd now look to participate in religious practice? I didn't feel the pull toward any particular denomination, even if my dormant Catholic roots began to show signs of new life. But the experience did feel like a kind of awakening. Without the language to articulate what I was feeling, I asked Serene Jones to help me to untangle it all.

"Belief and religion have always been at odds with each other," Serene told me as we sat down to lunch at a café near her office at Union Seminary's campus on the far Upper West Side of Manhattan. "Religion can be an obstruction to belief." Serene was talking about how belief makes us want to share it with others, which leads us to create groups of people who share beliefs. Then those groups create structure and rules around that belief. Ultimately, groups of believers stay close to those who believe in the same thing, which in turn creates walls around believers of that one thing, excluding the beliefs of others. What follow are competition, protectionism, authoritarianism, and the deleterious effects of all those things.

"There are two fundamental qualities of belief," Serene explained. "One is about confronting awe and terror, which leads to humility."

This connection of awe and terror to humility brings me back to our need for a witness and our terror of humiliation. There is awe and terror in the very notion of being alive. Consciousness itself can be terrifying. Maybe this is simply because we all know we will die, or that we are powerless in the face of nature or the universe. I think what Serene was saying is that in the acceptance of awe and terror, we become *less* afraid.

"About the second quality . . . ," Serene continued. "Belief is ultimately about love. Love makes you open to the world. It's about radical openness and wonder. Without belief, there is no love." I didn't start out surfing or writing about it to confront my feelings about belief or love, God or the Divine. I was looking to understand why the hell I kept at it. Maybe to prove I wasn't a fool. I don't know. But everywhere I turned for deeper understanding about what I'd learned from sucking at something led me to mystery, and, occasionally, to divinity.

Surfing has a rich history of these types of glancing encounters with God. Surfing giant Laird Hamilton's Millennium Wave is one of our sport's most iconic moments—one that exemplifies how ultimate success brings humility in its wake. The wave he made was in Tahiti on August 17, 2000. At the time, it was the heaviest wave ever surfed, and it's popularly known as the "Oh-My-God" wave. It changed the sport forever because before that time, no one had ridden anything like it—a backless Teahupo'o monster breaking over a shallow reef. As iconic and delightfully irreverent Greg "Da Bull" Noll—himself a pioneer of big-wave surfing from the '60s—said of Laird's wave: "Man, that shit's impossible. You don't *do* that."

Laird cried after he made that wave. It quieted him. "That was part of it," Hamilton told Surfline on the ten-year anniversary of the ride heard 'round the world. "Riding the unrideable . . . It was also a barrier-breaking moment. It showed both me and others that waves like that *can* be ridden—and they have been by a lot of people since then. You have to believe in the unbelievable . . . That was all about faith. Believing I could."

A big part of what we learn from success can also be thought of as failing or falling short: humility is the common thread. My own little God wave that came to me in prayer helped to turn my humiliation into humility. A transformation I've held on to, and one that I try to spread out across as much of my life as I can.

As Serene and I part from our meeting, I tell her about this pull toward the Divine. Serene smiles and tells me, "You might think of it not as being pulled, but rather, that you are being called."

It would be a sacrilege to say that sucking at something is a calling, but it's no stretch to acknowledge that surfing—in spite of, or maybe even because of, the fact that I suck at it—led to a stirring in my soul.

This is why choosing the thing you are going to suck at (for the long term) should be something you love doing. There may be trial and error before you find that thing, but once you do, it'll be about confronting the awe and terror of your own limits or the limitations of human reason and embracing them with love. I promise it can blow your mind. Or, for the more skeptical among us, it can at least change it.

DURING ONE OF MY favorite sessions with one of my favorite people—the man introduced in chapter 2 as my former contractor and now dear friend, Marion Peri—I was paddling for and missing wave after wave. He finally yelled in frustration for me to go for one that I was hesitating to go for.

"What the hell are you waiting for?" he screamed. "Go! Go! Go! Paddle! Harder! Paddle! Paddle!"

Up to that point, he hadn't ever seen me ride a single wave, so he couldn't know whether I could actually surf or not. But, the sound of someone else's voice louder than the one in my own head was enough to propel me forward.

I learn over and over again, when someone is calling me into waves, how yielding to someone else's belief in me can help me along the way. It's the *yielding* that matters, that surrender to a voice that drowns out self-doubt. A voice that can come from the outside or from within. Self-belief is connected to belief in the larger sense in that they both require a suspension of control toward a specified outcome. Just fucking go for it and see what happens, whether it's a wave, an aspiration, or God.

I made that wave, surfed it well, kicked out, and paddled back out to the lineup where Marion was sitting.

He was laughing.

"What?" I asked him.

"Is that it? You just need someone to yell at you to catch a wave?"

"Sometimes, yeah," I told him and laughed along at how silly that sounded.

Later in that summer of my God wave, Rocco would leave for college, and my privileged eighteen years of raising him were going to metamorphose into another kind of privilege. One of letting him go. That afternoon in the tiny chapel in Trastevere, I had prayed to Mary that I would have the grace to do just that. It wouldn't be easy. I was going to need a lot of help. But at least now I knew how to ask for it. I don't know if I would have been open to the epiphany that help was available if it hadn't been for all of the practice I'd had at failing.

Back in Costa Rica, when I met up with Rocco on terra firma later that morning, I told him about my prayers and how they were answered. I told him that I might start talking to God more often.

He nodded. "Whatever works."

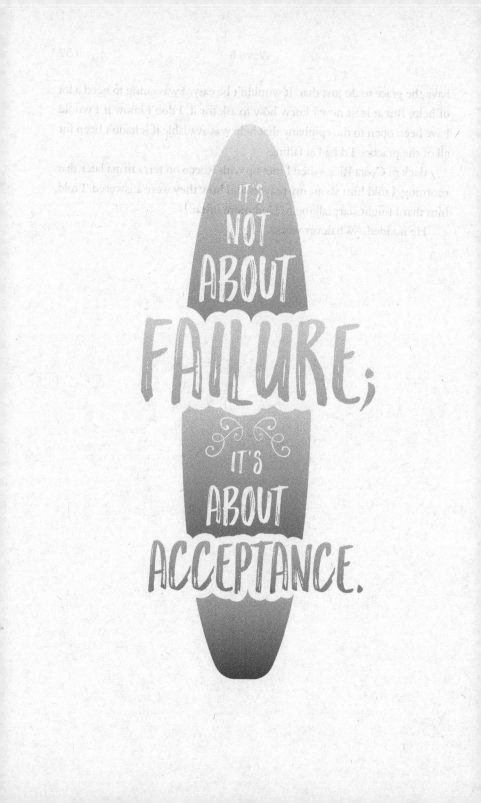

IT'S
NOT
ABOUT
FAILURE;

IT'S
ABOUT
ACCEPTANCE.

WAVE 6
Rocco's Scary Wave: Taking It On the Head

Rule #6:
Do no harm to others in what you suck at.

Lesson #6:
You can't love away someone's pain.

Benefit #6:
You become less of an asshole.

A week after it happened, here's what my friend Paul told me: "If Rocco had been riding your board, he'd be dead."

"That is not helpful," I said. I didn't add that it was almost certainly true, or that I had had that same thought countless times over the past few days.

Sometimes sucking plainly, unquestionably, just sucks. Nevertheless, our affinity for sucking and its gifts can help us remain resilient in those worst of times. I've come to learn that the vulnerability that comes with the spirit of this book isn't something that makes you fragile or brittle—it makes you someone who can live with the realities of failure and move past them. What's the sucking lifestyle except a kind of homeopathic dose of failure? Let its presence make you stronger.

ROCCO AND I WERE SURFING Playa Guiones on a changeable Costa Rican July day. We started out at the southern break called Baker's Beach where the waves tend to be smaller and more manageable than farther up the beach. The first hour was perfect: the wind was down and the waves were clean. But soon a thick river of storm clouds started to flow in from the southeast, creating chop on the surface of the water. We stayed out, hoping the wind might switch again to clean things up. The current pushed us north, so we wound up a kilometer from where we'd started. The waves there were fatter, and the water was more disorganized in general. Conditions became challenging—it was hard to stay lined up and we were bounced around by the choppy, sloshing water—but we weren't interested in giving up on the day just yet.

I went for a wave that closed out and, in the wipeout, the tip of my middle left finger got shaved, probably by the fin. I didn't notice until I was back in the lineup and I saw blood dripping from my finger onto my board. Squeamish about being in the water while bleeding, I told Rocco that I was going to head in. He gave me grief about it. He was already cultivating a toughness that was more or less necessary as he got older and the waves got bigger. It's true that there wasn't enough blood to attract anything with big enough teeth to matter. Still, I told him I would watch from shore.

Back on the beach, I sat on the deck of my board and watched my finger drip pink droplets of salt-watery blood onto the dirty waxed deck of my 8' mysto board. Now that I was out of the water (and my adrenaline was ebbing), the aspirin-sized wound began to sting and burn more than seemed necessary. It was a glorified paper cut. But it hurt.

I peeled my eyes away from the translucent pink splotches on the deck and located Rocco, with difficulty, since he kept drifting even farther north. The water was moving in a lot of different directions and I felt my maternal anxiety starting to mount. I trusted him to navigate heavy water, I just had to remind myself of that. I tried not to project my own fears onto him and tried to fool myself into believing that if I could see him, if I knew where he was in the lineup, nothing bad could really happen. Not quite a superstition, but not quite accurate either.

SHIT GOES WRONG

After a few minutes, I saw Rocco take a sketchy wave. He made the drop but got swallowed by white water as the wave closed out from both sides, pile-driving him beneath the chaotic ocean. I moaned in sympathy as I saw him go down, knowing well the beating he was taking under that turbulence. It took a few moments for him to pop out of the churning foam.

"Okay, there he is, all good," I told myself. But the severity of the fall was made clearer when he didn't turn back around to paddle out for another. That was a signal that something wasn't quite right. Calling the session after a fall was a drastic maneuver. Surfers wait for a last ride to bring them to shore, rather than call it quits after a wipeout and take a belly ride in. I watched as Rocco held the nose of his board, one hand over the other, and rode to shore prone.

Impatient to hear about the wipeout, I got up and walked to meet him up the beach. He was about a hundred yards away, so I didn't see him clearly, but something was wrong. His body was moving oddly. Having been legally blind as a child—and too self-conscious to wear glasses in public when they were prescribed to me at the age of eight—I'd long ago learned to decipher the particular sway of people's movements from afar to be able to distinguish them. My auditory skills compensated as well for my lack of sight. I wear contacts and glasses now, but my early education in body language and mindful listening has stayed with me. It even operates in the water. I can recognize Rocco's specific paddle strokes as he approaches me from behind in the lineup. When I hear the familiar cadence and specific splish-splish-splish of his strokes as he approaches, my body relaxes, and I think, as I did when I saw him surface after this last wipeout, *Ah, there he is. All is fine.* That I can distinguish Rocco's paddle strokes from those of other surfers in the water reminds me of my primal connection to him. When my boys were born, their cries were something I *felt* before I heard.

On this day, I sensed something was wonky before I knew what it might be. When Rocco came into closer view, I noticed that he was holding his body stiffly and strangely straight, like he was balancing something on his head. Stranger still, a group of people had gathered to walk just behind and next to him, an entourage of concerned beachgoers. I thought: *how odd*, and then I blinked hard to focus on his face and torso slick with blood.

I was frozen. He approached me, still walking in a strange, stilted way. His eyes were wide and it seemed like he wasn't blinking at all. Even as the blood streamed into his eyes, he didn't blink. Even stranger yet, I didn't react as much as I made a quick evaluation that is typical of my mothering, and something familiar to the rapid and hyperfocused diagnostic survey made by those who have ever been in any kind of accident: He was out of the water. *Good.* He was walking on his own. *Good.* He seemed to have both of his eyes inside his skull. *Good.* Whatever it is, he is here with me now. *Okay. Okay. Good.*

Then, of all things to do, he smiled a big demented Rocco smile.

He had all his teeth. *Good.*

WHEN ROCCO WAS FOUR MONTHS OLD, I dropped him on his head. It was the most terrifying thing I have ever done. He was in my arms one minute and then falling to the floor with a sickening thud the next. He was fine—if stunned—but I became hysterical, which made him hysterical, which had me convinced I had caused him permanent injury. We literally ran to the hospital. St. Vincent's was still in operation in Greenwich Village and we lived just a few blocks away. After a quick check over Rocco, and assurances that he "would be just fine," the emergency room nurses rolled their eyes and tended to me because while Rocco was fine, clearly his mother was not. I cried for two days after that incident. The docs sent me away with a script for a sedative. As a kind of final joke, I was too anxious to actually fill the script—I was worried it would make me more irresponsible than I already felt.

Some of you already know this, and some of you will eventually learn this—babies are both terrifyingly vulnerable and unexpectedly resilient.

That doesn't mean that it's okay to be careless, but weird shit happens. The most difficult part of parenthood is knowing that you can't protect your child at every moment from every insult to body, heart, and soul. Dropping Rocco manifested my fear in a way that never quite left me. But the broken bones and broken hearts, surgeries, illnesses, and infections that occur in the course of raising children, while not quite *inuring* me to those fears, at least taught me how to put aside my own so as not to exacerbate theirs. When the parent panics, the child panics too. It doesn't accomplish anything.

A friend once told me—before I had children—there were two things about parenthood. Number one: You will drop the baby. Number two: You won't have the luxury of losing your shit when your kid is in trouble.

I accidentally did the first, and never did it again.

It took a while to learn to stop doing the second.

By the time Rocco ambled over to me covered in blood at Playa Guiones, I was getting the hang of it. We'd been through scrapes together. We surfed together. He'd seen me fall, and I'd seen him crash. That familiarity was what allowed him, I think, to still be smiling, even though he'd just taken a scary beating.

TEACH OUR CHILDREN WELL

The proverb "The apple doesn't fall far from the tree" has versions and centuries-old antecedents in languages around the world. It's one of those good ideas that occurred to everyone separately. Otherwise known as common sense.

Our behavior has significant reverb when it comes to our children's well-being. It's one of the places where sucking can have serious detrimental effects. Don't suck at parenting. There's nothing to be gained there. But that doesn't mean it can't teach us and our children something.

The nature/nurture debate seems to have settled firmly in the middle with the latest research showing, not surprisingly, that it's a fifty-fifty proposition. And the apple/tree metaphor is apt as it represents both sides of the debate. While it's hard for parents to not feel a certain inevitability about the personalities of each child, we would all benefit from parental acknowledgment that what our children see us do and hear us say is as important as the tools they are born with. Even with that awareness and understanding—and admittedly the great responsibility that goes along with it—no matter how hard we try, we are still going to fuck up.

Julie Lythcott-Haims, bestselling author of *How to Raise an Adult*, put a fine point on it when I spoke to her about just this subject: "We are their biggest role models—whether we will be the *best* is up to us." So, the questions become: How do we fuck up less? And when we do, how do we handle it?

It has everything to do with being comfortable sucking. Because it's all about how we feel about failure. Inevitable failure. The failure that's built into the way the world works: we get distracted, our hands are sweaty, we suddenly lose our balance—and there goes the baby. What now?

We already know quite a bit about how sucking at something has much to teach *us*. But just as important is what it teaches our children when they witness our struggle. As my prophetic friend made clear to me: We need to be okay with them seeing us as the fallible beings we are. That doesn't mean them seeing us freak out. Because to a kid, that makes it look like we aren't used to messing up. Every time you freak out, you're sending out a signal that *this isn't supposed to happen*. You aren't supposed to face this challenge.

Calmness is the flip side of the sucking mind-set. You know that calmness helps you get out of a sticky situation. But it's especially important when we're modeling behavior for other people, kids particularly (and we are *always* modeling behavior for kids). The same applies for the way we manage at our jobs, and how we behave in friendships and intimate partnerships. We need to be comfortable being less than gods to those over whom we have the most power and with whom our lives are inextricably linked. Because if others see us trying and failing and not losing our shit about it, but rather trying again anyway, they'll learn to do the same.

We need to keep this in mind even when harsh criticism comes our way *from* our children. It's their first lesson by example in resilience. I've had a lot of practice while surfing with Rocco. After one hard-won wave I caught in Nosara, I proudly paddled back into the lineup and asked Rocco if he saw it. I'll admit: my pathetic insecurity was begging affirmation from my son.

"Yeah, I saw it. But you dropped in on that guy," he said, before paddling away from me in disgust.

Dropping in on someone (going for a wave where another surfer has priority) is one of the worst offenses in surfing. It's rude and it's dangerous. Rocco was right—it didn't matter that I made the wave if I made it at the expense of another surfer. There are endless accounts of dropping in throughout surfing's history and one thing is as certain as a crowded lineup on a flawless day: a surfer who drops in habitually and with insouciance quickly becomes a pariah. Even knowing this, I tried to defend my sorry ass anyway by shouting back, "Give your old mother a break, Rocco. I didn't even see him." I probably don't need to tell you that my response did not hit one note of dignity or justification. I was not, at that moment, teaching my child well.

He was teaching me, to be honest.

It wasn't even nearly the first time that happened. I remember once yelling at Gio when he was around eight or nine years old and ending my harangue in a fit of frustration, "You're acting like such a child!"

He shot back, "What are you talking about? I *am* a child."

LYTHCOTT-HAIMS TALKED about this nuance in our lively conversation about sucking and parenting. "We can't expect our kids to make us feel better for our fuckups and we can't burden them with our neediness. So, when we screw up, we need to acknowledge it and then get out of the way. We can get so enmeshed in our own shame that we drag our children into it and we ask them to absolve us."

A good rule of thumb for how we should treat everyone applies ten-fold with regard to our children: we can't make others the stewards for our wounded egos. When we ask our children to fill the black hole of our insecurities, we deny them their own reactions and annihilate their experience. Our failure to fail well doubles down on the wrong message.

What's possibly harder for many parents, however, is not so much having their kids see *them* suck at something, as it is watching *their kids* suck at something. This brings us to the second point—we need to let them struggle and even fail. I always thought of parenting as being like the bumpers of the kids' lane in a bowling alley: Let them roll, throw, or even bounce the ball down the alley however they want to because it doesn't matter whether they succeed in knocking down any pins, we just want to keep their bowling ball (them!) out of the gutter. The key is to stay out of the way, and to avoid making it about you as the parent. Paradoxically, not being afraid of failure, both our own and our children's, helps to inure us and them to fear's useless dominion over our willingness to keep at it in the face of frustrating results.

Helicopter parenting is an all too familiar trend succinctly illustrated in a *New Yorker* cartoon by Bruce Eric Kaplan. Two kids walk in the front door and the father of one is sitting in an armchair. The son says to his friend, referring to his dad: "He's less of a parent and more of a fixer."

This craze of parents getting way up into their children's business was always bound to collapse under the sheer weight of the anxiety it produced. And that was pretty much *all* it produced. Parents trying to game their children's success isn't working, by almost all measurements. Competitive nursery schools, redshirting, overscheduling extracurricular activities, hypervigilance over homework—all of these efforts are meant to give children a competitive advantage. Instead, it's seemed to help form a generation racked by self-doubt and only questionable resilience. Each year, the number of college-aged students seeking help for mental illnesses rises. This is partly the unhappy result of parents who insist on doing and being everything for their kids. Instead of the intended assist, parents wind up sending a message to their children that they are incapable of doing things or succeeding on their own. Clearly this is not the result intended by well-meaning parents who act out of love. But that love can be compromised by ego when we project our own desires and fears onto our progeny. It's a problem with many facets, but at the very least, it should make us all pause and examine how we're raising our children.

Lythcott-Haims spent years as dean of freshmen at Stanford University and what she saw played out over and over again in her work with college students provided plenty of evidence for the kind of projecting parents do onto their children. She explained, "Parents tie their self-worth to the accomplishments of their children, which creates a striving for achievement that is stressing us and our children out."

As a result, kids get a voice in their heads that tells them *someone is always judging me*. It doesn't allow room for experimentation or failure. It doesn't allow for sucking at something. Even when kids do accomplish what they set out to accomplish, they can feel empty. Like they were just performing up to snuff. Like they were performing, period.

I'm not saying the solution is easy. It's definitely a Goldilocks paradox: we need to give them a lot of support, but not *too* much. We need to be honest and transparent, but shouldn't overshare. We want to show them love always, but sometimes a little tough love is called for. Lythcott-Haims told me, "Love is our primary tool, what we want to teach them is love: how to love, to be loving. But there are fine lines, it requires a lot of practice and taking advantage of opportunities to refine the dialogue." That comes from a mixture of love, humility, and, if necessary, an apology. But then we have to move on. We will get it wrong, but we will be familiar with the idea of practice—both our own and our children's—from loving and sucking and being okay with it. This should be familiar to you by this point: the underlying aesthetic of sucking at something is proportion. Things in their place. Attention paid, but not squandered. Let the world come as it is, but do not stop trying to ride its waves.

Lythcott-Haims is familiar with the risks attendant to trial and failure. She confided to me about feeling loved when she is succeeding and unloved when she is failing. This pushed her to spend a lot of time "trying to be great at everything to be worthy of love." Even though she understands that this effort is an old "family imprint" left on her when she was a child, she continues to work to change that automatic response and has some strategies to help her on the way.

A challenging training ground for her turns out to be the *New York Times* crossword puzzle, which she and her husband compete to complete. When they started, she couldn't finish the puzzle at all, but she can now beat him two out of seven times. Still, losing the crossword competition over 70 percent of the time forces her to wrestle with the faulty equation of being worthy of love only by winning. Lythcott-Haims said she's learning. "I do enjoy the win but what I enjoy more is not hating the losses. When I came to the aha realization that winning meant I felt loved, I told my husband. He said, 'Well, if I tell you I love you after I win, will that help?' My answer, which surprised even me, was 'Yes.'"

EIGHTEEN YEARS AFTER I dropped Rocco on his head, on the beach in Nosara, I asked him, "Where did you get hit?" There was so much blood in his eyes and mouth that I couldn't immediately locate the source of trauma.

"Where do you think?" Rocco answered.

"I don't know, Rocco, there is so much blood I can't tell," I told him, trying not to show the panic I felt and to heed the advice of my old friend. He looked at me a bit puzzled. I understood then that he had no idea that he was a mass of gore: he stood there calmly, his surfboard still tucked under his arm as if contemplating another paddle out. Meanwhile, the gathering of strangers was growing, but no one was saying anything, which I thought was weird. *Shouldn't someone be saying something?* I wondered.

"Mama, it's a head wound. That's why there's so much blood," he told me as if explaining why the ocean was blue. Blood bubbled from his mouth as he spoke, which struck me as funny. I actually laughed. That felt weird too.

He put his hand above the wound site and circled it like a halo to indicate where the board hit him and said, "Here . . ."

I parted his hair to reveal a three-inch gaping wound that looked like a bloody mouth. The gash was so deep there was no way to know if it was just a cut or worse. I grabbed his board to put it down and looked for something to press to the wound. I looked to my own body for something I could take off, but the long-sleeved shorty I was wearing was one piece. "Shit," I said, uselessly. Then, "Rocco, take off your rash guard, so we can use it to press against the wound."

"No, that's ridiculous. I'm fine!"

He was shaking now with the rush of adrenaline and the loss of blood, so I yelled at him, "Take off your rash guard *now* and give it to me!"

He had the teenaged temerity to roll his eyes at this burst from his mother, but also the sense to finally listen. I wrung out seawater from the rash guard, and with it the blood that had been absorbed into the fabric. As I saw him acknowledge with surprise how much there was, I pointlessly smirked with a *Yeah, see?* look. I rolled up the rash guard and told him to press it against the wound.

By this time, a Tico surfer, hanging out by the Harmony Hotel palapa where we gathered, came over to help. He told Rocco to go jump in the water to clean off his body from the blood. "The water will wash it away and you'll feel better," he explained. Responding numbly to the directive, Rocco turned to head back to the water. The kid was gushing blood from a hole in his head and we had no idea whether or not his skull had been cracked and this well-intentioned guy told him to go jump in the ocean—which was now at high tide and had a shore break thumping four-foot waves on dry sand.

"Um, I don't think that's a good idea . . . ," I told them, trying to be polite as a cover for how annoyed I was at the suggestion.

Not to be deterred, the Tico grabbed a bottle of water from a gringa and handed it to me. "Okay, then here, take this and wash off some of that blood, it makes it look worse than it is. It is a head wound, it bleeds a lot, but he will be fine."

Rocco gave me a touché look. "See? I told you it's no big deal."

Surfers, like mothers, also do a quick evaluation. If you are not going to lose an eye or a limb, bleed out, or drown, then all is copacetic, and you basi-cally get ignored unless you ask for help. This nonchalance applies to every-one. I've never seen a surfer lose his or her shit when they get hurt. Maybe we figure it's the price to pay for the most wonderful feeling in the world.

"Oh, yeah," the Tico now assured me after he examined the wound, "he's good. He'll need some stitches for sure, but he's fine."

"Does anyone have a phone here? Can someone call Alejandro?" I asked no one in particular, but the locals under the palapa know who I was talking about. There are no lifeguards on duty, no EMS to call for quick response. The community relies on itself to help when people are in trouble; and it works remarkably well considering the nearest hospital is an hour and a half away.

Alejandro is the local doctor who ran a clinic in town. He'd helped us out on numerous other occasions: injuries, earaches, infected bug bites. He is a good doctor, and, almost as important, he is a surfer. He was per-sonally and professionally familiar with plenty of surfing injuries. His practice relied on them.

Now everyone rallied to help. The Tico security guard watching over the palapa called the Harmony Hotel, an eco-friendly, laid-back but cushy hotel just a two-minute walk through a jungle path from the beach. I walked Rocco through the path to the hotel where someone at the front desk had already called the clinic for us. They told me that Alejandro was not available that day, but Leonel would be waiting for our arrival at the clinic. I didn't know Leonel, but he would do.

The kind folks at the Harmony handed Rocco a towel to wipe off some of the blood. I left him there and headed back to the beach. I needed to get my car where we parked it down at the southern beach access and it's faster to retrieve it via the beach than by way of the winding, unpaved muddy roads. Someone offered to take our surfboards for safekeeping at the hotel while I ran the half-mile to pick up my backpack lying under another palapa.

The Baker's Beach entrance is across a small stream that runs out of the forest and onto the sand. We walked through this small copse of jungle to access the beach every day, and while we always watched where we were stepping, we had only seen the purple and orange crabs and lizards that populate the undergrowth there. This time, however, I got a prickly feeling in the back of my neck. I stopped short as I ran up the bank, through the vines and trees. Something told me that it was foolish to run blithely and blindly through this familiar spot. I thought of the caimans that hunt in the river mouths and estuaries in the area and said, *nah, not here. I must be freaked out because of what happened to Rocco.* Still, I zigzagged to my car, remembering advice that this is the way to confuse an alligator or croc if one should be chasing you (yeah, right). I laughed out loud at the ridiculousness of this split-second thought exercise, but I couldn't shake the notion of ambushing crocs. Our paradise felt dangerous right then. I jumped into my car and drove to the hotel so I could pick up my injured son and take him to the clinic in town.

SHIT GOES WRONG THAT HAS NOTHING TO DO WITH YOU

When it comes to facing hard times and challenges, one of the advantages of cultivating something you suck at is that it reminds you how small and ineffective you ultimately are. That might sound like cold comfort, but the opposite is also true: when everything is going wrong, it's much better to remind yourself that you aren't the cause of everything. You have limited powers to set the world right. When it's *not* right, it's not necessarily your fault. Embedded in this idea lives the parallel one that it isn't necessarily anyone else's fault either. You know those people who blame everyone around them for *everything* that goes wrong in their lives? Maybe they would blame others a lot less frequently if they didn't secretly feel that they were the center of the universe. Sucking at something is knowing that we're all just fumbling parts of that gloriously messy universe.

Messiness characterized one particular summer visit to Nosara, a year before Rocco took it on the head.

As I was returning from another funky July session, a surfer ran from the beach through Baker's and passed just behind me, pressing a hand to his eye. Behind him, another surfer followed, asking if he was okay and if he needed a ride somewhere. The first man replied, "No, I'm not okay. Please follow me." I learned later that the man was a local photographer, and he lost an eye that day after the nose of his board gouged him.

That whole trip was an education in the flip side reality behind our beach paradise. Earlier in that week we saw two teenagers get caught in a rip that pulled them a few hundred yards out into an angry ocean. I'd tried paddling out, but something just wasn't right about the way the water was moving so I stayed inside. Rocco himself got sucked past me beyond the break before I could call him back. I got a sickening feeling and asked my friend Nick to go after him to call him back in. Five minutes later, Rocco was beside me in the shore break, breathing hard. "That was the first time I was ever scared," he told me.

Then we couldn't find Nick. A strong swimmer and lifelong surfer, even Nick struggled to get back to shore. When he finally made it, we just stood around watching the water and talking about how funky the current and swell were. That's when we saw the surfboard wash up.

"Uh-oh. That's not good," I said out loud—a mother's worry that all was not copacetic.

A surfboard bobbing around with no owner attached is a sign that something has gone awry. The second clue was the dog pacing nervously along the shoreline. We looked up and down the beach and scanned across the water and out to the horizon, but we couldn't see anyone. Nick climbed a tree for a better look. We thought he was teasing when he yelled down, "I see them, they're way the fuck out there!" When we laughed at what we thought was not a funny joke, he yelled, now noticeably agitated, "No, I'm serious!" Then we saw them, *way the fuck out there*, waving their hands as if in a comedy skit. Tiny, desperate waves to shore: *Somebody save us!*

None of us was expert enough to navigate the tumultuous water and several calls to the police resulted in a no-show. Rocco ran for help from the local surf instructors just off the beach entrance road. Four of them arrived on a quad and with a world-weary manner that betrayed their dedicated focus—this wasn't the first time they'd been called upon to save someone's ass—they paddled out to rescue the kids, who would have surely drowned. Once they all made it safely back to shore, I nearly vomited with relief.

Later that week, we surfed a break, fifteen kilometers north of Guiones—a cleaner but heavier wave than Guiones. Rocco's favorite. It was a perfect, windless day with head-high to a few-feet-overhead waves and all of our friends were catching wave after awesome wave. I could not get past the break. Every time I made some headway, an outside wave would break in front of me and I would get pushed back toward shore. This isn't a new story—but on this day, I was dying to join Rocco and our crew in the lineup we had all to ourselves. Among them was my friend Mike Moore, who had recently been released after nearly three years being held hostage by Somali pirates. He had joined our family on this trip as part of his recovery back to his surfing life.

I finally made it out to the lineup to join everyone after trying for two hours. I was proud of my tenacity and sat (where I thought was) on the outside to catch my breath and regain some energy. I was *so ready* to catch and ride a wave. It turns out I wasn't outside *enough*: an enormous set wave rolled through and I couldn't paddle fast enough to get over the top and out the back. I got caught in exactly the wrong spot, got pulled over the falls and pounded down to the bottom of the ocean, only to resurface to take another two on the head. Trying but failing to keep my head above the thick foam of the broken waves caused me to aspirate some of the aerated water. Exhausted after the effort to get out there and now coughing up saltwater, I couldn't handle the thrashing. Gripping my rails with every last ounce of energy, I let the ocean spit me back to shore. Dizzy and defeated, I sat on the beach feeling despair. Nick and Mike kindly came in to check to see if I was okay. Not wanting to wallow in frustration, I forced a smile to tell them, "Yeah, sure. I'm good." I mean, what's an ocean beating compared to what Mike had endured? Perspective is everything. Still, as happy as I was to share our trip with Nick and Mike, I was reminded that there was no way of being completely safe, anywhere. Not even in paradise.

Later that same day, eight of us piled into our car for the bumpy five-kilometer drive to our favorite restaurant for an end-of-trip celebratory dinner. A few hours later, sated and spent from a day of surfing and a sumptuous meal, we looked forward to getting home and to bed. Instead, we found that two of our car tires had been slashed where the car was parked just outside the restaurant and by the time we got back to our house, someone had broken in, cut the wires of our newly installed security system, smashed into our safe, and stolen all of our stuff—computers, cameras, phones, and more. There were seven of us in the house for that visit, each with our own inventory of technology, so the thieves made a nice score. The security guard we paid to watch over the neighborhood houses saw and heard nothing. The police didn't show up then either; at least not until our friend, who was a local, called them herself.

So, yeah, our paradise was beginning to look a bit hellish. It didn't happen all at once, but after that initial honeymoon period of building a house in a distant place we didn't know the first thing about, where all seemed to go oh-so-smoothly, things started to go wobbly.

Termites built conduits leading inside and back outside of our house and under our roof where they built nest mounds; biomasses of larvae and beehives invaded every orifice and crevice we didn't even know existed—under sinks, behind walls, under the eaves, in window jambs. Scorpions lurked behind every cushion and gigantic flying grasshoppers bombarded us while we cooked. I woke one night to pee and found a tarantula crawling at eye level on our bedroom wall. I said, "Excuse me!" to it on my way to the toilet.

Every space became a nest for some nonhuman creature. While moving the curtain sheers one morning, a gecko fell from the wire and slapped onto my face, before crawling down my neck and arm, eventually leaping to the floor. We awoke one morning to find our white closet, where we kept our clothes, turned completely black with a colony of ants that had taken it over in the course of the night while we slept. A tree frog moved into the toilet and instead of kicking it out of its adopted home, we used the one outside for a few days. Our gardener found a boa sunning itself on the coral stone of our living room. I'm not complaining—I mean, where else would it and all the others go after we cleared the land of their homes to make way for our own?

Mostly, we learned to live with the chaos and tried our best to keep nature from taking over completely while attempting to live in harmony with it. But that's the thing about paradise. The other side of it can be, while not quite hell, something very far from paradisiacal. It's not that we didn't expect the jungle to be a jungle, but you don't get to know its ways until you settle in. A week or two in paradise lulls you into thinking, "If only I could stay *right here*, I would never have another bad day." Like any honeymoon period, you get deliriously convinced that the joy will be forever untouched—even though you know better. That's not to say that after the honeymoon ends, there isn't something wonderful that lingers, like the scent of someone you love on the T-shirt they wore.

During our time spent in Nosara and for every session in the water, I was reminded of the elegance of yin and yang, originally meant to describe opposite faces of a hillside, one in sunlight, the other in shadow. There is no value judgment attached to yin and yang. The hill is still the hill, whether in shadow or light. Instead, it points to the concept of unity as two sides combined to create one whole. And while sometimes we need brightness and other times we need shade, we like to think that it's just a matter of adjustment to volition, as if we can simply change position or location to adjust to our momentary needs. But what *is* is sometimes just that: it just *is*. More often than not, the adjustment is in the form of acceptance, rather than trying to change. Oftentimes, changing a situation is not possible and the only thing we can change is our response to it.

This is especially important for the way we teach our children. If our instinct is to keep them from the harsh realities that will inevitably insinuate themselves along the road of life, how can they come to understand that things going wrong are just as normal as things going our way?

I've hyped up the benefits of sucking at something all throughout this book. Some immediate, some that take a while to show. There's the thrill of trying something new, and the feeling of accomplishment of making incremental progress. Then there are those attitudinal shifts: the embrace of messiness and incompleteness.

There's something else. A long-term effect of sucking at something that I could never have anticipated when I first picked up a surfboard in what seemed by all appearances to be a flight of fancy. It's this, more or less: whether or not we're conscious of it, we all suck at all kinds of things throughout our lives. At least we *ought* to. Getting in touch with that fact isn't doing something radically new; it's learning to turn that truth on its head, like a good thrashing from a wave, and to come up laughing. We beat ourselves up for sucking and then overcompensate in ways that dig ourselves deeper into a hole of inaction, self-castigation, and worse. While we are compelled to suck less, we can't do that if we don't allow and forgive ourselves for sucking in the first place. I mean, it's going to happen so why not live a complete life, full of waves and comedowns both.

If there was something through it all to teach my boys, it's that you take the good with the bad. How clichéd, how trite, how *obvious*. On the other hand, how spectacular that some piece of common sense exists that gets right to that eternal wisdom.

WHEN ROCCO AND I arrived at the clinic, the new doctor—he introduced himself as Leo—was manning the office alone. He invited Rocco to lie down on the patient bed. His upper body slick with congealed blood and his lower body covered in sand, Rocco somehow remained unnervingly cool. I was beginning to worry about the intermixing of sand and blood still pouring from his wound, but Leo's quick assessment was calming. He was a surfer too. "Oh, I have seen much, much worse."

Leo got to work cleaning the wound as a long black and yellow centipede made its way desultorily across the blood-splattered operating room floor. After seven shots of local anesthesia into the wound, Leo ran his surgical glove–covered finger across the hole in Rocco's head to feel his skull.

"Oh, this is good . . . ," he told me, ". . . very good, no fracture. Do you want to see his skull?" Leo asked. I wanted to collapse with relief and my belly fluttered with both relief and anxiety. But I stayed upright.

"Sure!" I said, more game than I actually felt.

And there it was. My son's skull.

I left the room to call Joel and tell him what happened now that all was, in fact, copacetic.

Rocco got nine stitches and was told that he couldn't surf for a week or so. The worst part done with, Leo echoed what we were all thinking: how lucky this happened at the end of our trip. Rocco would just miss the last two days of surfing in Nosara, but he would be back in the water soon after we returned to our fickle and frustratingly non–Costa Rican break in New Jersey.

When we got back to the house, we shared the news and photos with friends and family: Hey, look at the surfing warrior!

BUTTERFLIES AND CHAOS

But here's the thing: I couldn't sleep a wink that night. Instead of being exhausted by the day's events and relieved with the outcome, I stayed agitated and concerned. Everything was going to be fine. The ordeal was over . . . but now the dark thoughts came. My biggest fear, one that I have always had a hard time admitting, is that one day Rocco will paddle out and not come back in. Surfing is dangerous. Living is dangerous. But in surfing, there are just so many things that can go wrong and they do go wrong, for the best surfers and the biggest kooks. Most of the time, everything is, eventually, copacetic. But surfing is a dangerous thing to suck at. Most of surfing literature is about the near miss: the three-wave hold-down, the numbing head-over-heels-over-head wipeout, the brush with an apex predator, a near-fatal fin to the head. They all become the stories we tell. Until we can't.

My own fear of the ocean—which doesn't compel me to stay out of the water, because my love for it is bigger than my fear—puts scary things in my head. I don't fear so much for my safety anymore, but I can't relinquish that fear for my son, in spite of the fact that he is a much better swimmer, a stronger surfer, and a clearer thinker than his kooky, befuddled mother. Mother Ocean and Mother Love, the strongest pulls I know. Each bestow immeasurable joy and immeasurable fear.

I couldn't help but ruminate that night. I knew what I was doing: I was fooling myself into thinking I had more control over the situation than I ever did. The illusion was strong, though. It unlocked countless what-ifs. What if I had stayed out with Rocco in the lineup? Surely he wouldn't have gone for that wave, or maybe I would have been able to call him off it. What if I hadn't wimped out with a small nick to my finger? My boy would have been injury-free. Instead I headed back to shore and left my son to danger. I watched in helpless witness as my own mind looped through this useless and defective logic, aware of the absurdity of believing that we controlled outcomes as random as a fin cut to the head. But the loop is powerful and feels inevitable, like the pull of going over the falls when you don't manage to make it over the top of a cresting wave. A friend, author Karen Karbo, told me, when Rocco was born and I was feeling new terrors that undid me, "Motherhood is a life sentence, with no parole."

I'm not sure she made me feel any better back then, but at least she made me laugh. I have repeated her words too many times as regifted words of wisdom, but mostly in an effort to laugh away the demons of motherhood: words that challenge us to *not* live in a constant state of worry. But we don't want our kids to know we feel this way. It would be too much of a burden for them. They are not here to make us feel better about our vulnerability.

The consolation I seek in those loopy moments is in the idea of *contingency*. A fancy word from the field of history that basically boils down to this: the future does not unfurl in a long, straight, predictable path. It strikes rocks in the way, it curves around obstacles and covers up old paths. It responds, in every instant, to the instant before it, and thus is always in the process of becoming itself. My worries contain all kinds of possible futures—many of them bright and optimistic but others that are catastrophic and grim. And none of them is more or less likely than the infinite other futures that I'm not even capable of imagining. It's contingent. Of all things possible to suck at, all of us suck identically and equally at this: knowing what comes next.

It helps me sometimes to be reminded of my father's favorite thing to say: "It *had* to be." He often invokes this while looking back over some of the hardships of his life of nine decades and, instead of regret, he finds solace. Granted, it's often when we are sitting in our small backyard at the Jersey Shore, a scotch in one hand and a cigar in another and he is counting the blessings of his children and grandchildren. At nearly ninety, he's withstood his share of unpredictability and has come through the other side with the wisdom of a man who has seen much and still knows how to have a good time.

Over two hundred years ago, the philosopher Johann Gottlieb Fichte said much the same thing in his essay on doubt in *The Vocation of Man*: "Had anything at all been even slightly other than it was in the preceding moment, then in the present moment something would also be other than it is. And what caused everything in the preceding moment to be as it was? This: that in the moment which preceded that one everything was as it was then. And that one moment again depended on the one which preceded *it*; and this last one again on *its* predecessor; and so on indefinitely . . . and in the present one, you can think the position of no grain of sand other than it is without having to think the whole, indefinitely long past and the whole indefinitely long future to be different."

As has happened with satisfying regularity in this century, what was once only speculation has now seemed to find its place in scientific fact. What Fichte philosophized in 1800 was echoed in 1960 scientific data by the unexpected results of a meteorological model that proved how tiny changes can trigger enormous outcomes. MIT scientist Edward Lorenz's discovery, now popularly known as "the butterfly effect," helped to reframe the models used to predict outcomes and initially showed how and why long-term weather forecasting was difficult. Lorenz's work went some way to explain how meteorologists get a rap for sucking at accurately predicting the weather. *It's harder than you think.*

Meteorology will always be a surfer's favorite science, but Lorenz's work has become famous in its echoes in other, more flashy fields, like physics and mathematics. As a result, instead of a theoretically predictable scientific model, a new way of looking at things emerged as chaos theory, described by Lorenz as "When the present determines the future, but the approximate present does not approximately determine the future." So, what *is* matters in the sense that it will determine the future but with any incremental change that future changes as well. Common sense, right? But until chaos theory emerged, a linear deterministic model prevailed because linear systems are solvable, and who doesn't like a solvable problem? People don't suck at solving linear problems.

Lorenz turned to fluid dynamics as a way into the complexity of the meteorological conundrum. Fluid dynamics, it's no surprise, are nonlinear and a bitch to solve. It's also an *enduring* bitch. The infamous Navier–Stokes equation, which connects the velocity, pressure, density, and viscosity of fluids, has yet to be proven. But if you have the time (and the brain), it might be worth trying: the elusive solution to the equation, first created early in the nineteenth century, is one of the seven Millennium Prizes, which pays $1 million to the scientist who can prove it. That'd pay for a lot of far-flung surf trips.

"This is the most beautiful problem I have ever worked on," says Stephen Montgomery-Smith, a mathematician at the University of Missouri in Columbia, who has been tackling the equation since 1995. "It has opened my eyes to appreciating aspects of the real world."

Chaos theory and its complexities are beautifully illustrated by how damn hard water is to predict—and so it goes for the rest of the "real world." So much of what we have to deal with in surfing relates to this unpredictability—both with weather and waves. Chaos is a surfer's curse—not the least of which is due to the complexity of fluid dynamics, but unpredictability is also what makes it so rad when the weather, the waves, and the surfer's good fortune arrive at the opportune moment to conspire for a memorable session. Many of the best sessions happen when a surfer least expects them, but we paddle out anyway and sometimes experience the best of what chaos brings to us. Of course, the opposite is true and sometimes we get snaked, or worse. Bad things happen as unpredictably as the good. Chaos, while not quite providing solace, helps, at the very least, with the practice of accepting whatever shit comes our way.

In that way, surfing has been a long education into how the world sucks too. Not in any kind of fatal, nihilistic way, but in a familiar way. It's just as contingent and unpredictable and unreliable as our own selves are. Being out there on the waves and trying becomes exposure therapy to this fact of life: it doesn't work in straight lines. It's fluid, it flows, and the brightest minds at the best schools still have no idea how it works. And—that's okay. It doesn't mean the worst thing will happen. It means *everything can* happen.

The fact that Rocco was resting in his bedroom just thirty feet away from me and not in the ICU in San José Hospital meant that amid the chaos of the day, everything was as good as I could have possibly hoped for. Chaos giveth and chaos taketh away. In this case, it *gave* a fin slice to the head but it *took away* the possibility of severe brain trauma: Framing, as we keep seeing, is everything.

Still, knowing this didn't keep me from lying awake in bed throughout the night, resisting the urge to get up and go to Rocco's room, just to look at him. *He is eighteen years old, for goodness' sake*, I told myself, *not eight, and he is fine.* I couldn't overcome the need to be next to him, to feel his breath, and to watch him sleep through this restless night. But I didn't go to him. I fought every molecule in my body that was homing in on my son and his bruised body. Instead, I stared at the dark outline of trees against the colorless sky of the coming dawn through the glass doors overlooking the jungle.

Rocco told me the next day that he didn't fall asleep until four in the morning. He smiled a smile of understanding when I told him that I lay awake until dawn, arguing with myself about whether I should get up and check on him. There was no roll of his eyes this time, just an appreciative nod of acknowledgment when he said, "You would have found me awake."

Two days after we returned home from that trip, Joel read in a local Nosara report that a few days earlier, a ten-foot crocodile had moved into the entrance of Baker's Beach. Chances are she was there that day I zigzagged to my car.

Another contingency. I was happy to miss that one.

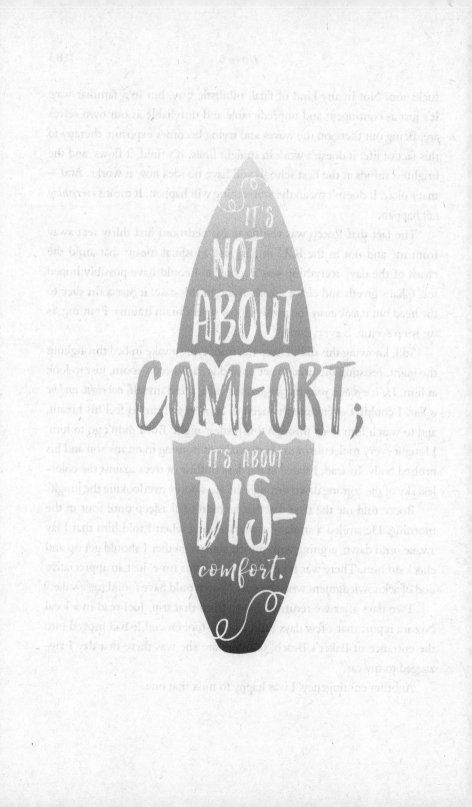

IT'S
NOT
ABOUT
COMFORT;
IT'S ABOUT
DIS-
comfort.

WAVE 7

Mind Surfing: Watching the Waves from Shore

Rule #7:
You will lose something along the way.

Lesson #7:
How something meaningless can be the exact opposite.

Benefit #7:
You'll find beauty where you least expect it.

But there are two kinds of pain in this world, aren't there?

There's the pain of Rocco's scary wave, and the pain of my own surfing wound, but those wounds heal. Our bodies are fragile, but they make up for that with resilience. Bodies bounce back. So, too, our minds when we encounter setbacks. That's what sucking has been about—exercising that part of your person that doesn't *need* consistent success.

But there's that other kind of pain. There's sorrow.

Wisdom from all over the world, from religious tradition and from common sense, pairs sorrow with its opposite. It seems that nearly all our most profound feelings are understood to be Janus-faced: how many times have you heard that there's no joy without sorrow, no pleasure without pain? There's no beauty without evanescence. And what is heaven without a hell to compare it to?

If you're like me, these sayings are more than a little pat. This promised equilibrium between the good and the bad is easy to print in a slogan,

185

and much harder to really *live*. We imagine experiences we haven't had, lives we haven't led, and think we can have a way of only joy, pleasure, and beauty.

Which is why the experiential side of sucking is so important. These hardest, most profound things simply can't be thought through. I'm reminded of the famous statement on the tricky concept of "not-self" by Ajahn Chah, a Buddhist monk and teacher from Thailand: "To understand not-self, you have to meditate. If you only intellectualize, your head will explode."

In that spirit, let's coin our own saying: If there is no sucking, there is no hope.

But now let's go live it. I did.

NO MATTER THE SEASON or weather, Rocco and I would walk barefoot to the ocean to check out the surf. On some days we performed this ritual once in the morning, but on others it could be four or five times over the course of a day depending on the promise of conditions and life's obligations.

In the two-and-a-half-minute walk from our New Jersey home to the ocean's edge, we would listen for the sound of the water before we saw it to guess what it was up to. Silence was definitely not welcome, as it portended no waves at all. An even *shushing* wasn't good either, as it told us that there would be no period swell, just water constantly pushing toward shore. When a crackle, then *boom!* filled the air, followed by a momentary respite, we heard it as a promise of breaking waves. A promise of time in between each wave and set. That meant time to catch and ride a wave. When we heard this particular sound, we looked to each other and raised our eyebrows: *sounds like . . . something!*

In those moments right before the water entered our view, we felt a sweet anticipatory tension. What ocean mood would we find as we crested the dunes? If the conditions were promising—and living at a shore break in New Jersey means that they aren't promising very often—

our conversation would happily switch over to whether we would paddle out right away, or wait for the tide to come in, or go out, and whether the wind would switch direction, or increase or die down. We would immediately get caught up in the little weather obsessions that always come with surfing.

Best of all was when conditions were *just so* and there'd be no need for discussion at all: light off shores, clean sets rolling in and breaking over a sandbar a decent distance from the shoreline. We'd just look to each other and nod, then turn and sprint back to the house to pull on our wet suits (if necessary—which is true for nine months out of the year in New Jersey). We'd grab and wax our boards and head back to the beach for a session.

This routine with Rocco has driven much of my time and energy and joy in the past decade. Catching and riding waves has only been part of this whole crazy journey.

Which is why when he left, I was devastated.

PAIN IS INFORMATION, PART II

The night of our return home after dropping Rocco off for his first year at college, I went to bed with a hole in my heart and a text bidding him goodnight. That mendacious refrain in my mind was insisting: *I am fine, I am fine.* I'd been preparing for this over the past year. *How hard can it be?*

I slept fitfully. I felt a dull ache, like something missing, like a phantom limb, and while I know exactly why that was, I couldn't get comfortable with the feeling. When I woke the next morning, the sight of our wet suits hanging over the shower curtain rod in the bathroom—lifeless and deflated without our bodies to fill them—filled me with sadness. We'd left them there to dry after our last session together the day before our trip north to Massachusetts.

I grabbed a cup of coffee and walked up to the beach alone for a wave check. Hurricane Hermione was working her way up the eastern seaboard and I was excited to see what conditions she'd bring. Surfers wait for hurricane swells and I knew Rocco wouldn't want to miss this one. But now he was landlocked, having forgone a West Coast college experience where he'd be able to surf every day for a small East Coast school a three-hour car ride away. Still, for my sake, I was pleased by his decision to remain close to home.

I'd planned to send him photos of the waves—even knowing full well that he would have already checked the local surf cam online. But having this self-appointed task calmed me. Then I heard the reverb of booming water and said aloud to no one, "There are waves!" I faked a lightheartedness I didn't feel, hoping to convince myself that all was normal. I walked barefoot with a forced steadiness on the splintery boardwalk alongside the protective dunes, but I was anything but stable. The ocean side dunes blocked the view to water, as they had done for the hundreds of times Rocco and I made this walk together. Only when I turned onto the dune path, and I saw the steely green-blue Atlantic and its distant horizon, did his absence hit me like a blow to my solar plexus.

I took a quick inhale to stem a surge of emotion. *You're fine*, I told myself. I stepped off the boarded walkway into deep, white sand and I dug my feet toward the shoreline. The waves were disorganized and crashing loudly, not surfable, but stunning in their stormy churning. A twenty-mile-per-hour wind blew from the north, contributing to the morning's cacophony and pelting sand against my body. This time there was no stopping it: the sight of the ocean swelled my heart and I collapsed to my knees with grief and dissolved into wracking sobs, mercifully drowned out by the waves and the wind.

I missed my boy. I missed him so much that I ceased knowing who I was at that very moment. I was fine, but then I was not. This was sorrow. Not just pain.

The drop-off a day earlier, which promised to be heart-wrenching, was surprisingly calm. No tears were shed. I kept my cool. Rocco, characteristically stoic, betrayed his feelings with a smile of resignation that I shared. Neither of us wanted to make the moment dramatic, so we hugged—with just a moment of lingering—and then we parted awkwardly. My heart tugged as I said goodbye, though my first thought was, *We are so closely connected, physical distance between us will do nothing to alter that.*

Joel, Gio, and I drove back home, chitchatting much of the way. We were all going to miss Rocco deeply as we four became we three—at least in the daily sense. Our nervous conversation and attempts at humor echoed off the well of feelings about leaving our son and brother, a feeble attempt to keep those feelings at bay. We were laughing the demons away.

I was reminded of a wonderful scene in a family favorite film, Hayao Miyazaki's *My Neighbor Totoro.* A father and his two daughters move into a new home to be closer to their mother, who is in a nearby hospital ward recovering from some possibly incurable illness. The house, in its unfamiliarity and previous lack of occupancy, is full of mischievous creatures and possibly haunted. During the family communal bath that evening, the father and his daughters laugh loudly to scare away what may be haunting them. It's a beautiful scene, one that struck several chords in my own life. I know I did plenty of laughing through the fear of having cancer. *Totoro* hit very close to home.

That morning I collapsed on the beach was just hours after we had gotten home from dropping Rocco off. I let myself get folded into the embrace of the deep white sand. I watched the water move in so many directions, agitated and wild, like the beating of my breaking heart. Tears were flowing down my face and I choked on breaths of salty air. Then I laughed. At nothing, really. And this time the laughter didn't push away any of my intense feelings as much as focus them. I felt an old and deep *longing.* Longing—I realized in this very moment—that was only ever conjured in the presence of the ocean. For nearly two decades, this feeling had been all but absent.

I grew up with this ache, when I would spend hours staring at the ocean, and walk along where the waves lost their forward momentum as they reached land. As an adolescent turned teenager, as a young adult, at twenty-something, at thirty-five, whenever I saw the ocean and her horizon, I felt something visceral, a push and a pull inside of me, like the water on the shoreline itself. I never knew the source of this feeling, but I had grown accustomed to it. It became a part of the climate of my life. I'd seek it out whenever possible. I was both happier, and more melancholy, whenever I was by the ocean.

Eventually, these twin feelings coexisted in comfortable dissonance, making me feel alternately that I was either *on the verge of* something, or that I was *missing* something essential in my life. I would theorize. Maybe the expanse of open water helped me to understand both the vastness of possibilities, as well as the tiny station in space and time that we occupy. Perhaps I was tuning in to the opposing nature in everything and the unknowingness or lack of certitude that goes with it.

I got a clue into the nature of these stirrings when they went away. Once I'd had my boys, the longing disappeared. In their place was something else: love, but bigger than love. It was as if an unbalanced weight in the core of my being had steadied, or a vibration quieted, a lifelong hunger quelled. I learned to surf, and to suck, in the shadow of that steadiness. Mother Ocean and Mother Love both found voice inside of me. Until one of them was quieted.

I was going to miss my son in unfathomable ways. But we had shared something together that prepared me for this, just a little bit. Sitting at the stormy water's edge the day after Rocco's start at college, the old longing was back in full force, but now it was tinged with something new at my center. There was a beauty. I understood, in the fury of my tears, this old longing was nothing more than a longing for meaning and purpose I found in my life as a mother. Later, I found it while surfing, or trying to.

Across the span of the past two decades, I'd learned to accept the dangers and fears inherent in both. Still, not having wrestled with this longing for so long had fooled me into thinking that maybe it was gone forever. Its return knocked me off center, a rude awakening that served as a reminder that after all these years my tether to purpose and meaning could be stretched to an uncomfortable limit. I imagined it would return with a new understanding of my roles: as a mother to children on their own, as a surfer in the ocean without her son. Nothing stays the same. Of course it doesn't.

But in this moment of upheaval, I really felt the truth of those old oppositions. Beauty and sadness really did intermingle. Like touching something extremely cold but experiencing it as a burn, in the immediate information your body receives, you can't always make the distinction. Strong emotions are similar—we can't always identify them as one thing or another. Perhaps that's why we sometimes cry when we are happy and laugh when we are scared.

WHAT BEAUTY IS

Irish poet and philosopher John O'Donohue wrote in his book *Beauty: The Invisible Embrace*, "Beauty does not belong exclusively to the region of light and loveliness, cut off from the conflict and conversation of oppositions. The vigour and vitality of beauty derives precisely from the heart of difference."

O'Donohue, a former priest and mystic, whose untimely death in 2008 left us without one of the great minds of our time, said in his last interview as he was talking about the inner landscape of beauty, "[It's] about an emerging fullness, a greater sense of grace and elegance, a deeper sense of depth and also a kind of homecoming for the enriched memory of your unfolding life." Lately, my life had been unfolding like origami in reverse. But it was in that most difficult moment of unfolding, when Rocco left, that I encountered something more than simple sorrow. There was beauty in the waves that day, and I wasn't blind to it. The unfolding had unfolded something I couldn't have predicted, something more complicated than just loss.

I'd seen this idea contemplated before, in a place similarly austere and thoughtful to Donohue's western Ireland.

The Japanese have had a thousand years of refining concepts of beauty that hold heartbreak at its center. *Mono no aware*, which can be translated as "sorrow at evanescence," puts this idea into words. Impermanence is at the heart of so much of Japanese aesthetics since medieval times. Whether the brief flowering of cherry blossoms, the blossom of youth, the maturation of a single wave as it comes to rest on land after traveling great distances across the ocean. That nothing stays the same is seen by the Japanese as a kind of pleasure cherished for this quality of being momentary.

The work *Essays in Idleness*, by medieval Japanese Buddhist monk Yoshida Kenkō, provides an early record of the Japanese aesthetics that gave rise to this culture of reverence for that which can't last, or that which isn't perfect. In his mind, the most profound beauty is not to be found in the perfect or the symmetrical or the permanent, but rather in the anticipation, the imagination, the unexpected, and the impermanent. Kenkō writes, "Should we look at the spring blossoms only in full flower, or the moon only when cloudless and clear? To long for the moon with the rain before you, or to lie curtained in your room while the spring passes unseen, is yet more poignant and deeply moving."

Some of these Japanese concepts have recently traveled into the periphery of popular awareness outside of Japan. *Sabi* represents the imperfect, incomplete, or lonely beauty: a moon unseen may be the most beautiful of all in the desire and wistfulness imagining it may bring. *Wabi* is the beauty that "lurks within" what might otherwise seem impoverished or rough. These terms are often connected, as in *wabi sabi*, and understood as an appreciation for that which is *not* beautiful, or seeing beauty in ugliness. *Kintsugi* is finding beauty in broken pottery, not by repairing it seamlessly to restore it to its original state, but by using gold-dusted lacquer to accentuate the broken bits, creating a new kind of beauty. I'd come to appreciate this way of seeing whenever I looked at my upper body in the mirror after a shower. My once beautiful and functional breasts were now crossed with scars, reconstructed and misshapen, yet I'd learned to see a kind of beauty in them. It's the beauty of endurance in the face of fragility.

I am reminded of these versions of beauty whenever I consider my insistence on doing something that is difficult for me. If we can recognize the beauty of sucking at something, then efforts to improve, while awkward on the surface, embody a kind of beauty of intent. When we struggle at doing something, we ourselves look like a piece of broken pottery. And when we finally achieve a moment of grace, it's as though we are sealing up our broken parts with gold lacquer.

Even for the revered Japanese *shokunin*, the master craftspeople who devote their lives to one pursuit—say, to making a perfect sword blade or sushi rice or piece of pottery—process is everything. It connects past traditions with present action toward a future promise of transcendence.

My friend, photographer Mike Magers, spends a lot of time in Japan and has been working on a photography project about the shokunin for years. When I asked him about how these craftspeople go about spending a lifetime with such unwavering focus, he immediately gets to the heart of why sucking at something is difficult, placing it in terms of its opposite.

"The reason we don't do mastery well in the West is because the distance between success and failure is so defined that people stop even before they start," Mike explains. "Here in the West, we want things to be easy. Innate talent is expected. For the shokunin, it's about refinement, not mastery. It's about making the thing you made yesterday a tiny bit better tomorrow."

A ceramicist Mike was working with told him, "It took ten years to master technique but the rest of my life to connect my soul to my hands." While the shokunin are considered masters by others, from their perspective, they are always learning. If masters of craft can accept their imperfectibility, certainly those of us looking to expand our experiences can learn to accept the process no matter where it leads. If we can find the beauty and meaning in our efforts, then we open our hearts to so much of what life offers. And while hearts will sometimes break, the lacquer that heals them is the joy an open heart summons.

That sense of complementarity is loud and clear in the arts. From the Japanese celebration of imperfection to the Western Renaissance development of chiaroscuro, that pairing of light with dark, it seems the things we create want to contain both experiences. Like the yin and yang we explored earlier—we need both sides to be complete in order to reflect an underlying human condition, or perhaps a condition that extends even beyond us, something in the universe itself.

Nobel Prize–winning physicist Frank Wilczek finds questions of meaning difficult to measure, so he asks instead, "Does the world embody beautiful ideas?" In his search for equations that might help to clarify the universe, he finds beauty in complementarity: the idea that something can embody two very different ideas, not necessarily at the same time, and each one helps to elucidate the other. In particle physics, for example, this applies to qualities of light where at times it behaves like a wave and other times as a particle. Each way of looking at it helps us to have a deeper understanding of light, but you can't apply the different theories at the same time.

Wilczek explains, "Complementarity is both a feature of physical reality and a lesson in wisdom . . . You have to view the world in different ways to do it justice and the different ways can each be very rich, can be internally consistent, can each have its own language and rules, but they may be mutually incompatible, and to do full justice to reality, you have to take both of them into account." Wilczek's framework beautifully applies the rigor of physics to this otherwise mysterious sublimity.

I'm practical about this idea. I don't just want to know that complementarity exists; I want to make use of it. That's what has always drawn me to the famous quote from F. Scott Fitzgerald: "The test of a first-rate intelligence is the ability to hold two opposed ideas in mind at the same time and still retain the ability to function." He might well have been referring to the skills that he—and every novelist—depended on. Without this ability, characters, stories, and their telling would get tedious pretty damn fast. This dissonance isn't easy for most of us. It's instinctual, instead, to seek out simple answers and smooth surfaces. Unity is pleasant, because unity is comfortable. We tend to prefer absurdity to the possibility of having to contain conflicting thoughts in our minds. You'll see it often in the surfing world. It comes in the form of kooks vastly overestimating their skills. Because, after all, if they weren't good at surfing . . . why would they be out there surfing?

Well, I know. And you know. Because sucking is a part of life. And a great part. We can indeed do and fail at the same time.

Sucking at surfing has gone a long way to helping me accept the supposedly opposed ideas of pleasure and discomfort. But when I found myself in emotional turmoil and surfing wasn't an immediate option, I took a more drastic measure to externalize my inner discomfort.

PAIN RELIEVES PAIN

The needle hit the base of my spine. Shock waves shot up the center of my back until they landed and eddied around a single cervical vertebra, right beneath my head. I dared not move a muscle. The trick was to remain still in those moments of acute sensation and pain. My breaths came slowly, deep and steady so as not to raise my rib cage midline, which would make it harder for Angela to get her work done without mistake. My arms wrapped around a pillow placed against a forty-five-degree-angled upright bench, as my face pressed awkwardly into it. Led Zeppelin played through the parlor's speakers and beneath Robert Plant's sexy wail, a soft but persistent buzzing of needles covered the eerie silence. Part of the appeal of getting tattooed is a communal tolerance of pain. Even if you are alone with the artist, you both know it hurts like fuck, especially when the image crosses the base of your spine.

The design started as a small piece adorning the front of my right shoulder, but there was an incompleteness to it, as if the surface pain I'd endured was not enough of a representation of the pain I was feeling inside. I needed to make more of a commitment and it came with getting a full back tattoo. A permanent representation of impermanence is the epitome of ridiculousness, mitigated only by the cold hard truth that the *sakura* blossom tattoo will disappear with the rest of me in due time. While I was still around, I wanted to carry them with me. So much was changing in my life and I was bereft. So, to honor my grieving, and to momentarily distract me from the emotional turmoil I felt, I sought the physical pain and discomfort of being under the tattoo gun.

Gio had been accepted to college through early admission, and while we had another eight months before he left us to an empty nest, the endgame was in view. At least when Rocco left, Gio still graced our daily lives. I wished I could welcome the opportunity of my freedom from their quotidian needs, but I experienced no such feelings.

Compounding that looming loss, we'd sold our beloved home in Nosara. The multiplicity of reasons that led to that decision belongs in another story, but I won't deny that two college tuitions played a significant part. If there ever had been a physical manifestation of the joy that sucking can bring, the home we built from the ground up in Guiones—where I could go and suck to my heart's content—was it. It was simple, humble, and it attracted all manner of creatures from the jungle. It was heaven—even when hellish.

The sakura blossoms being etched into my skin were inspired by our home, which had, in turn, found its inspiration in the seventeenth-century Katsura Villa just outside of Kyoto. A work of extraordinary modernism from over four hundred years ago, I fell in love with the idea of the Villa as the ultimate expression of structural simplicity and felt wonder at its connection to its environment. I'd dreamt about a home that reflected those qualities and took cues from its design for our own.

The Katsura Villa was the home of Prince Toshihito—who spent his life studying *The Tale of Genji*, the Heian period masterpiece by Lady Murasaki Shikibu that epitomizes the concept of *mono no aware*. I didn't make those connections until after I'd built the house. We'd kept the house bare and the walls empty with the exception of an exquisite scroll, or *kakejiku*, we'd found in Kyoto and hung on the wall over a shelf in the living area. Next to it hung a small lopsided vase we'd found in a tiny pottery studio during our visit to Japan.

The design, structure, and process of building that house were connected to my aesthetic education as much as to the resolution of the cosmic dare I put into place when we decided to build it. While I know that attachment to any physical object is lesson numero uno of how not to be enlightened, I had always felt different in that house than I did anywhere else in the world. There is a reason why we often move through houses in our dreams—they symbolize our interior lives, or those we wish we had. The house in Nosara represented the life I longed for—calm, clear, elegant, compact, connected to nature, and close to a great surf break. Casa de las Rosas, inspired by the Katsura Villa, reflected the interior landscape of my soul. Not all joy and sunshine, as you know from the last chapter, but I'd made peace with that part of it. It wasn't a generations-old home that had history held in its walls, but the sheer intensity of our time spent there with family and friends lent potency to each stay. And having raised my boys there over the past years made letting go not so easy.

I choked back sobs during the house closing in the lawyer's office in Guiones when he stood to congratulate us and the new owners on the transaction. A bit like the surge of emotion I felt at the ocean's edge when Rocco left for college, it was a moment that pulled me in many directions. I was sad to see the house go—but it was a moment of intense gratitude too.

Having to part with our home, and all that it symbolized, I found comfort in the Japanese tradition and history from which it sprung. Kenkō writes in his *Essays in Idleness*: "This world is changeable as the deeps and shallows of Asuka River—time passes, what was here is gone, joy and grief visit by turns . . . and even the same house as of old is now home to different people." Amen, brother. Across a vast cultural divide and seven hundred years, Kenkō's words helped me to move on.

THE KINDNESS OF STRANGERS

Impermanence does not apply to the acts of kindness we meet along the way, but beauty most certainly does. Though momentary, kindnesses— both those given and received—can last in our emotional memory and bestow other kindnesses. Community and connection outlive us all.

On one particular July day during our first trip back to Guiones after selling the house, the waves were as perfect as they ever get for me. Shoulder high, gentle, but with enough push and peeling for a good long ride. They rolled in few and far between, so priority got a bit competitive. A nice set wave came my way and a young Tico sitting next to me in the lineup ceded this beauty to me and called me into it.

"This one for you! Go left . . . paddle now, paddle hard, go, go go!"

I paddled and dug as hard as my arms allowed, but he could see that it wasn't going to be enough for me to catch the wave. Without a word, my fellow surfer paddled up behind me and gave a push to my tail (the back rail of the board) to give me the extra momentum I needed to get into the wave. Then he yelled: "Go! Stand now!" There's that voice of belief again, encouraging me to *go*, made sweeter because from a stranger. I felt the plugged-in energy of connecting with the wave, I popped up easily, dropped in, and turned left to ride along its face. I caught a few sections to ride the wave almost to shore, then kicked out the back when the wave finally closed out. That rare feeling of elation came, as it does whenever I make a wave, but this time, it was even better.

I immediately knew why: most times, when people see me in the water and assume, often rightly, that I will likely miss an oncoming wave, they take the good ones for themselves. It's a rite of passage for shitty surfers— make the wave or make way for someone who can. But this local guy, who had absolutely no reason to help a middle-aged gringa kook, not only gave up the wave for me, but put so much effort into helping me make it that his generosity was *just as good* as the ride. Even better.

I'd been thinking a lot about blessings during that first trip back to Nosara since we'd sold our house. Without the sanctuary of our home there, we found ourselves bouncing around to different abodes, trying to find our space. I had to remind myself that I was there for the waves, for the jungle, for the community we'd become part of. Those were the blessings Nosara conferred upon us. It had nothing to do with owning our piece of it. We are all visitors to this world, no matter the circumstances. But this benediction from an unknown Tico in the form of an assist helped me to feel connected to more than the wave.

If I didn't suck at surfing, I wouldn't have enjoyed such kindness because I wouldn't have needed his help. Asking for help doesn't always come easily, but to receive it without asking is one of the most unifying things we can do for each other. (I don't mean we should run around assuming everyone sucks at everything and make a nuisance of ourselves by interfering.) Would communities ever have sprung up in the first place if everyone excelled at everything? Would anyone have *needed* anything from anyone else? Maybe it's time for a brand-new theory of human development. Perhaps it was our deficiencies all along that bound us together as a species, as a civilization, as a family.

I am reminded of the poem by Naomi Shihab Nye called "Kindness":

Before you know kindness as the deepest thing inside,
you must know sorrow as the other deepest thing.
You must wake up with sorrow.
You must speak to it till your voice
catches the thread of all sorrows
and you see the size of the cloth.
Then it is only kindness that makes sense anymore,
only kindness that ties your shoes
and sends you out into the day to mail letters and purchase bread,
only kindness that raises its head
from the crowd of the world to say
It is I you have been looking for,
and then goes with you everywhere
like a shadow or a friend.

I had been feeling a bit lost when we first got to Nosara without our home to ground me, but this gesture of kindness from a person I'd never seen before and will likely not see again changed that in an instant.

By the time I paddled back out to the lineup, my surfing shadow angel was thirty yards south from me. When I saw him across the water he threw a *shaka* and a fist pump my way—the corny kook move that is beautifully universal surf speak for "woo-hoo!" I threw a shaka back to him and shouted, "*¡Muchas gracias, señor!*"

I was reminded that beauty is everywhere if we open our eyes and hearts to receive it. If we do, we'll find that, in our greatest need, we become open to the "kindness that raises its head from the crowd of the world." There are risks, to be sure. As Elizabeth Lesser says, "You can't choose what your heart will feel when you open it."

Lesser, bestselling author of *Broken Open*, has spent her life as a seeker. Her work as cofounder of the Omega Institute in Rhinebeck, New York, has put her in proximity to spiritual and thought leaders from the world over. Her broad and deep perspective comes from insights into the big questions from a multidisciplinary practice. Elizabeth steered me to one of her core teachers, Tibetan Buddhist Chögyam Trungpa, whose words she has lived by and which helped to put my mind around overturning conventional wisdom about fear that keeps us from the beauty of an open heart.

Trungpa Rinpoche wrote, "Conventionally, being fearless means that you are not afraid or that, if someone hits you, you will hit him back. However, we are not talking about that street-fighter level of fearlessness. Real fearlessness is the product of tenderness. It comes from letting the world tickle your heart, your raw and beautiful heart. You are willing to open up, without resistance or shyness, and face the world. You are willing to share your heart with others." If we keep ourselves open to this experience, its energy touches us in both directions and we plug into true beauty.

The practice, then, is to keep an open heart with the understanding that it will feel pain as much as love, sorrow as much as beauty. We might, as a result, feel fear of what an open heart might invite. You can't suck at something without this risk, and yet the beauty we experience in exchange won't come without it. My love for my sons infuses every cell of my being, so my heartbreak at their leaving is a privilege I wouldn't trade for all the world.

Now that Rocco and Gio are launched into adult life, where more of their experiences will be without me—as well they should be—I must recalibrate the cadence and purpose of my days. Of course, they will always be with me, but they will not be with me in the profoundly physical sense as they had been as younger children at home.

The last twenty years of meaning and purpose will shift focus, but I am not yet sure where that focus will land. I have learned to let in the beauty of those moments of sadness, to not fight the discomfort, but to live inside of it. As Lesser asks, "Why do we think closure is a good idea? Why would we close our hearts to feeling?"

AS I WAS WRITING the final chapter of this book, I had the best few days of surfing in seventeen years of trying. A week earlier, that kind Tico pushed my tail into an awesome wave. I'd caught a few over that weekend of smallish swell and was happy for having surfed them, maybe not exactly with style and grace, but with some bit of control and a modicum of hard-won confidence.

The rest of the week was a bust. A large swell brought thumping waves that kicked my ass up and down Guiones. You know this story by now: I'd spent the entire week getting hammered and inevitably wound up in the shore break taking the few re-formed waves that came my way, but I no longer enjoyed the dregs. I'd advanced enough to actually surf, so doing the beginner's thing no longer gave me any pleasure. Instead, I'd sit on the sand and mind surf while Rocco disappeared in the lineup. Even when you improve at the thing you suck at, there's always another level on the horizon. Another level that you will suck at, until you can get past it to the next level. And, as that buddha of surfing Gerry Lopez said, "It never ends."

Here's the thing that maybe I haven't said enough: when you work hard at something you suck at, you *will* get better at it. My skill level at surfing is still rudimentary, but I can and do surf, which just makes me want to surf *better*. I mean, I'm not a masochist. As my now departed friend Tony Bourdain said, "It's about sucking a little bit less." I *want* to suck less. You will want to suck less too. I know I will keep trying, no matter what.

Maybe the universe was trying to tell me something, or maybe it was just fucking with me, but with just a few days before we were set to return to New York and just weeks before I was due to turn in this book to my editor, the swell had dropped and the ocean behaved (unusually) very much to my liking: Waist- to shoulder-high, with some head-high sets. Windless, clean seventeen-second period swell. I could paddle out without getting my hair wet. I caught one wave and rode it well. I paddled out and caught another. Then another, and another. I stacked up *seven* waves—seven waves in one spectacularly beautiful session. (My friend asked me later, "You *counted*?" Fuck yeah, I counted!) Rocco caught twenty-five that day, just to keep perspective, but still, I'd become one with each wave, I rode with style, and with no heart-pounding fear. Instead of fighting the wave, I merged with each one. Although I'd written about this before, this time it happened over and over again—as if I knew what I was doing. Because if you suck at something long enough, you *will* suck a little bit less at it.

Seven waves for seven chapters? I promise you, I tried for more. After my seventh wave, I wanted an eighth. But seven was all I got. So maybe after all of these pages of trying to convince you to suck at something, I finally convinced myself that it was okay being unexceptional at something I loved doing and I relaxed enough to realize that I know what I am doing out there. Making the wave matters, of course it does. But it isn't the most important part.

All along, this sucking business turns out to be about something much bigger than riding a wave. It's about ritual and meaning, beauty and pain, connection and loss and how all of it ties together. Not neatly, into a pretty little bow, but into a Gordian knot no sword can cut through. Life is not for figuring out. It's for *living*. It's for succeeding *and* sucking. And while we are inclined to seek comfort, we are sure to meet with discomfort. Sucking at something embraces that discomfort and turns it into something beautiful.

I am thinking of starting something new to suck at. I've inquired about singing lessons, something I can do with Gio, who is already a better singer than I am. My fantasy of singing in his not yet formed band is probably more suckiness than he can bear, but I'd be game to try. Rocco reminds me that although I surf, I suck at swimming, so why not start a subset of what I already suck at, something that might help me in a meta-way to suck less at surfing? The possibilities are endless. I know now that the journey and those you meet along the way are what counts. Let's start something new and let sucking at something be our path to nowhere at all.

Acknowledgments

Thanks first to John Adams, who said those magic words to Rocco all those years ago while standing outside of PS 41 in Greenwich Village. And to Mike Colombo of Right Coast Surf shop in Seaside Park, New Jersey, whose open heart and mind didn't flinch when I told him I wanted to learn to surf, even though he easily could have told me that it was too late to bother. John and Mike opened the doors to two beginnings without which this book would not have been written.

Thanks to my dear friend and agent, Kim Witherspoon, and her partner at Inkwell, Richard Pine, who listened and read too many iterations before I landed on something that didn't totally suck. Thanks as well and always to Alexis Hurley, and to William Calahan, who lent a discerning and invaluable assist when I was sucking at writing.

Simon Critchley and Peter Catapano generously saw something of value in the notion of sucking at something and shepherded my original essay into The Sporting Section of the *New York Times*. I am grateful to both for another beginning of many.

My editor, Sarah Pelz, has been enthusiastic and the best advocate from our very first meeting. Thanks for the many conversations and attention to detail that saw this book into publication. As an editor who loves being edited, I've had the great fortune to work with one of the best. And even though I do it every day, I'm in awe watching the process from the other side. I am grateful beyond words for the time and the work spent on my book. It's no small thing. I know painfully well the efforts and the sheer number of professionals involved to bring a sin-

gle book out into the world (one day I will count them!). And while I
also know there are those who touched my book I will likely never meet,
I am grateful to every single person involved. Specifically, many thanks
to Sarah's assistant, Melanie Iglesias Perez; associate publisher, Suzanne
Donahue; for marketing and publicity, Ariele Fredman, Bianca Salvant,
Dana Trocker, and to Kristin Fassler for overseeing all of it; and to publisher Libby McGuire and editorial director Lindsay Sagnette. Thanks for
the inspired jacket by Jimmy Iacobelli.

Naomi Shihab Nye generously granted permission to include part of
her luminous poem, "Kindness." I am honored to include her words in
this book.

Thanks to Niege Borges whose delightful illustrations grace these pages.

Thanks to my fellow surfers for the hours of surf talk in and out of the
lineup—much to the annoyance of everyone else around us who doesn't
share our passion—and for the assists, camaraderie, and support in and out
of the water along the way. There are too many to mention everyone but
specifically, to those not thanked elsewhere in these notes, thanks to: Jay
Alders, Erik Antonson, Phil Bacon, Phil Browne, Paul Cassidy, Jimmy and
Chris Courtney, Nick Frankfurt, Eric Goodman, Laird Hamilton, Vanessa
Purpurri, Mark Lukach, Mike Magers, Garrett McNamara, Michael Scott
Moore, Marion Peri, Jim Phillips, Austin Rinaldi, John Sargent, Phil
Shinn, Shelby Stanger, Alex Wilkinson, Thad Ziolkowski (who wrote my
favorite surfing book of all time), and to the generous Tico, whom I will
never meet again, for the tail push into that awesome wave. Most espe-
cially, thanks to my son-in-law, Christopher Meyer, who has tolerated me
alongside him in the lineup on too many occasions to count. Remember,
Chris, "It's only water; it's only cold."

Thanks to all who took the time to speak with me and embrace this
crazy notion of sucking: Tony Bourdain, Susannah Cahalan, Rozanne
Gold, Matt Hussey, Serene Jones, Katty Kay, Elizabeth Lesser, Julie
Lythcott-Haims, Mike Magers, Aubrey Marcus, Andy Martin, Farnoosh
Torabi, Jaimal Yogis, Andrew Zolli, and to countless others. I've had the
privilege of so many conversations with friends, colleagues, fellow writers

(who know innately about sucking), and acquaintances about sucking at something. As a decadelong conversation, to all who have embraced the suck with me, and who helped me make sense of why sucking is so awesome, I am grateful.

Continued thanks as well to Ronnie Peters and Susan Sakin, who have helped me hone my message beyond this book.

Thanks to my friend Chantal Bacon, who welcomed, fed, and sheltered me during the final push to finish the book. Her home and company are an oasis of calm.

Thanks to Micah Starr for help with all the stuff I don't know how to do, even though I should.

Thanks, always, to those whose love and friendship help me to stay centered and relatively sane, reminding me every single day that I am among the sluckiest humans: Colin Dickerman, Joe Dolce, Kassie Evashevski, Rebecca Miller, Chris Padgett, Kristina Rinaldi, and Kim Witherspoon (yes, again!).

Thanks to my squad at Harper Wave, who keep the biggest part of my day going—and all with love, grace, and some really, really good laughs. I'm a lucky sucker for sure.

A special thanks to Tony Bourdain, my friend and author, whose passing while I was writing this book threw me and the entire world into a frenzy of grief. His grasp of sucking was profound and before he died he told me he was working on "sucking less." I hope, wherever you are now, Tony, that your days are filled with the joyful kind of sucking and there is more of the peace and love we all wish for you.

Thanks to my husband, Joel Rose, who has not only tolerated this journey but has been game to go along for the ride—for better and worse, richer and poorer.

My stepdaughters, Celine and Chloé, have graced me with their love and acceptance when there were other options. I am grateful for their tolerance of some things I have sucked at along the way and that they have made room in their lives to include me in spite of it.

Thanks to Kizi and Vince, just because.

Thanks to my parents, Pete and Roseann, who have witnessed plenty of my sucking over the years and love me anyway.

And of course, the deepest gratitude to my sons, Rocco and Gio, who have taught me more than anyone or anything in this life without even trying. I hope that I haven't sucked too badly at parenting them into adulthood. They are the world to me.

Citations and Notes

Introduction

2   *Nobel laureates "were significantly more likely to engage in arts and crafts avocations" than mere members of the National Academy of Sciences:* Root-Bernstein, Robert et al. "Arts Foster Scientific Success: Avocations of Nobel, National Academy, Royal Society, and Sigma Xi Members." *Journal of Psychology of Science and Technology,* vol. 1, no. 2 (January 2008), pp. 51–63, doi:10.1891/1939–7054.1.2.51.

4   *Perhaps that strength is similar to what Josef Pieper, a German philosopher writing shortly after WWII, had in mind when he wrote his classic* Leisure: The Basis of Culture, *in which he said that "The idea of leisure is diametrically opposed to the totalitarian concept of the 'worker,'" and proceeded to celebrate human activity detached from so-called "social usefulness":* Pieper, Josef. *Josef Pieper: An Anthology.* San Francisco: Ignatius Press, 1989, p. 140.

5   *A little while ago the* New York Times *published a piece I wrote called, naturally, "(It's Great to) Suck at Something":* Rinaldi, Karen. "(It's Great to) Suck at Something." *New York Times* (April 28, 2017), www.nytimes.com/2017/04/28/opinion/its-great-to-suck-at-surfing.html.

Wave 1: My First Wave: An Invitation to Suck

15   *Nostalgia was considered a "neurological disease of essentially demonic cause" in the seventeenth century:* Beck, Julie. "When Nostalgia Was a Disease." *The Atlantic* (August 14, 2013), www.theatlantic.com/health/archive/2013/08/when-nostalgia-was-a-disease/278648/.

18 *Hannah Arendt calls action "the one miracle-working faculty of man":* Arendt, Hannah. *The Human Condition*, 2nd ed. Chicago: University of Chicago Press, 1998, p. 246.

20 *In the painfully beautiful novel* The Sense of an Ending, *Julian Barnes writes, "what you end up remembering isn't always the same as what you have witnessed":* Barnes, Julian. *The Sense of an Ending.* New York: Vintage Books, 2012, p. 1.

23 *This curiosity, or drive for novelty, also has a positive effect on longevity in humans; it helps maintain a healthy central nervous system:* Swan, Gary E., and Dorit Carmelli. "Curiosity and Mortality in Aging Adults: A 5-Year Follow-up of the Western Collaborative Group Study." *Psychology and Aging*, vol. 11, no. 3 (September 1996), pp. 449–453. doi:10.1037//0882-7974.11.3.449.

23 *dopamine, the powerful neurotransmitter that makes us swoon as we fall in love, cements over addictions, and, according to behavioral neuroscientist Bethany Brookshire, is what puts the sex, drugs, and rock 'n' roll into sex, drugs, and rock 'n' roll:* Brookshire, Bethany. "Dopamine Is _____ Is it love? Gambling? Reward? Addiction?" *Slate* (July 3, 2013), www.slate.com /articles/health_and_science/science/2013/07/what_is_dopamine _love_lust_sex_addiction_gambling_motivation_reward.html.

28 *Studies show that pro surfers spend only 8 percent of their time in the water actually surfing:* "Surfers Only Spend 8% of the Time Riding Waves." *SurferToday,* www.surfertoday.com/surfing/7653-surfers-only-spend -8-of-the-time-riding-waves. (Access date November 12, 2017.)

33 *He called this striving, "The urge from below to above that never ceases." The driving force behind all human efforts, this striving for perfection, is innate, "something without which life would be unthinkable," Adler writes. Without this striving, humankind would have never survived:* Adler, Alfred et al. *The Individual Psychology of Alfred Adler.* New York: Harper Perennial, 2006, pp. 103–104.

36 *Adler calls it "The un-reluctant search for truth," and ties it back to the idea of perfection: "the ever-unsatisfied seeking for solution of the problems of life belongs to this longing for perfection of some sort":* Ibid.

36   *Adlerian psychologist Sophie Lazarsfeld explains a difference between "sound striving for perfection and the neurotic wanting to be perfect." In psychotherapy, she states, people "learn to face their own imperfection . . . They acquire the courage to be imperfect":* Lazarsfeld, Sophie. "The Courage for Imperfection." *American Journal of Individual Psychology*, vol. 22, no. 2 (1966), pp. 163–165.

37   *Recent studies support the idea that depression and low self-esteem can result from not accepting imperfection:* Shinrigaku Kenkyu. "Relationship Between Two Aspects of Self-Oriented Perfectionism and Self-Evaluative Depression: Using Coping Styles of Uncontrollable Events as Mediators." *Japanese Journal of Psychology*, vol. 75, no. 3 (August 2004), pp. 199–206.

37   *Rudolf Dreikurs, another Austrian-born psychiatrist working in the US, who developed a system for working with troubled children, cautioned in a 1957 address to the University of Oregon that we were becoming:* Dreikurs, Rudolf. *The Courage to Be Imperfect.* Eugene, OR: University of Oregon, 1957.

38   *Dreikurs was not discouraged though, believing that "if we learn to function, to do our best regardless of what it is; out of enjoyment of the functioning, we can grow just as well, even better than if we would drive ourselves to be perfect":* Ibid., p. 289.

40   *Eighth-century Zen master Tennō Dōgo told a novice monk, "If you want to see, see right at once. When you begin to think, you miss the point":* Suzuki, Daisetz T. *Zen and Japanese Culture.* Princeton, NJ: Princeton University Press, 2010, p. 13.

Wave 2: My Pura Vida Wave:
Chasing a Dream and the Demons Away

45   *Buddhist nun and meditation teacher Pema Chödrön teaches in her invaluable book* When Things Fall Apart, *"Reaching our limit is like finding a doorway to sanity and the unconditional goodness of humanity, rather than meeting an obstacle or a punishment":* Chödrön, Pema. *When Things Fall Apart:*

Heart Advice for Difficult Times, 20th anniversary ed. Boulder, CO: Shambhala, 2016, p. 16.

45   *Chödrön explains, "Whether we experience what happens to us as obstacle and enemy or as teacher and friend depends entirely on our perception of reality. It depends on our relationship with ourselves"*: Chödrön, ibid., p. 65.

51   *In the LeRoy Grannis photo, taken in 1968, Farrelly is poised on the nose of his board, feet parallel, knees slightly bent, arms relaxed and held straight in front of him with his hands pressed together and his head bowed, as if in prayer:* Grannis, LeRoy. *Midget Farrelly Surfing Shore Break, Makaha, 1968.*

52   *Inspired by his early conversations with Albert Einstein, Jung became interested in the psychic conditionality of time and space:* Jung, Carl Gustav, and Richard Francis Carrington Hull. *Synchronicity: An Acausal Connecting Principle.* Princeton, NJ: Princeton University Press, 1973, p. xii.

52   *Jung believed that these synchronistic events proved that "the psyche cannot be localized in space, or that space is relative to the psyche":* Jung, ibid., p. 115.

52   *However, Jung believed that these linked occurrences that go beyond mere coincidence or causal circumstances "are so improbable that we must assume them to be based on some kind of principle, or some property of the empirical world":* Ibid., p. 115.

53   *Roth suggests that when we can put aside this need to be in touch with a chain of causality, we become receptive to opportunities that wouldn't otherwise be available to us:* Roth, Remo F. "Introduction to Carl G. Jung's Principle of Synchronicity." Remo F. Roth, PhD, Home Page, 2002, paulijungunusmundus.eu/synw/synchronicity_jung.htm. (Access date December 1, 2017.)

58   *The eighteenth century saw the great Friedrich Schiller, poet and philosopher, warn against being driven purely by work in his* On the Aesthetic Education of Man. *He writes, "Man only plays when he is in the fullest sense of the word a human being, and he is only fully a human being when he plays":* Schiller, Friedrich et al. "Twenty-Third Letter." *On the Aesthetic Education of Man in a Series of Letters.* Oxford: Clarendon Press, 2005, p. 107.

59   *In his* The Play of Man, *Groos lends scientific grounding to Schiller's max-*
      ims. After writing his first study, The Play of Animals, *he concluded "that*
      among higher animals, certain instincts are present which, especially in youth,
      but also in maturity, produces activity that is without serious intent, and so
      give rise to the various phenomena which we include in the word 'play' . . .
      [T]hus, when an act is performed solely because of the pleasure it affords, there
      is play": Groos, Karl. "Introduction." *The Play of Man.* New York:
      D. Appleton & Company, 1901, p. 2.

59   *"Human society reaches its fullness only among well-rounded individualities,*
      since they alone are properly fitted for service to the whole": Groos, ibid.,
      p. 404.

60   *In one of my favorite surfing movies of all time,* Step Into Liquid, *pro-*
      fessional surfer and writer Sam George answers, when asked what purpose
      surfing serves, "If I come out of the water in a much different, better mood than
      when I get into the water, that somehow translates into my life and I end up
      being a happier, nicer person as a result, then I guess you could argue that surf-
      ing is good for society": Step Into Liquid, documentary, directed by Dana
      Brown (Artisan Entertainment, 2003), DVD.

60   *Konrad Lange, another contemporary of Groos, writes, "in the various occu-*
      pations of mankind, as a rule, but a limited number of the mental powers are
      employed, and those not fully so. Innumerable springs of feeling are hidden in
      the human breast untested and untried": Groos, ibid., p. 379.

62   *When I ask him what Sartre would make of sucking at something as a way to*
      combat existential angst, he refers me to Being and Nothingness, *where Sar-*
      tre talks mainly of skiing, then veers off into a consideration of sliding on water.
      "What Sartre is saying is that everyone—when surfing or skiing or whatever—
      is trying to be a Socratic philosopher, which is to say die, transcend and become
      godlike. To overcome our human fallibility. So, when I am skiing, I want to be
      nothing less than the Skier—in some semi-allegorical way. Perfect. Impeccable.
      Sartre's technical way of talking about this is 'the for-itself-in-itself.' Everyone
      wants to be a god. But here we come to the sense of failure built into conscious-
      ness itself. There is an inevitable asymmetry between the dream and the experi-
      ence": Andy Martin, interview by the author (January 15, 2018).

63   *As Sartre says, play is freedom:* Sartre, Jean-Paul. "Freedom: The First
      Condition of Action." *Being and Nothingness: An Essay on Phenomeno-*
      logical Ontology. Translated by Hazel E. Barnes. New York: Washing-
      ton Square Press, 2012, pp. 580–581.

64   *Josef Pieper reminds us that it's bigger than that. He writes, "Leisure, it must*
      be clearly understood, is a mental and spiritual attitude—it is not simply the
      result of external factors, it is not the inevitable result of spare time, a holiday, a
      weekend or a vacation. It is, in the first place, an attitude of mind, a condition
      of the soul . . . .": Pieper, Josef. *Leisure: The Basis of Culture.* San Fran-
      cisco: Ignatius Press, 2009, p. 46.

64   *Influential British economist John Maynard Keynes, in his 1931 essay, "Eco-*
      nomic Possibilities for Our Grandchildren," predicted that by 2028, the global
      economy would be so large and efficient, that the workweek would shrink
      to fifteen hours. The problem, as he saw it, was how people would fill all of
      their leisure time once they had it. "Must we not expect . . . a general nervous
      breakdown?" he asks in his essay. Keynes betrays his lack of confidence in
      the strength of our mental and spiritual attitude that Pieper refers to when he
      writes, "we have been trained too long to strive and to not enjoy": Keynes,
      John Maynard. "Economic Possibilities for Our Grandchildren."
      Revisiting Keynes, edited by Lorenzo Pecchi and Gustavo Piga. Cam-
      bridge, MA: MIT Press, 2008, pp. 22–23.

65   *This effect is encouraged by the tournament style economic system and*
      performance-related compensation systems, which Harvard economist Richard
      B. Freeman explains, "gives the person who puts in an extra hour of work
      a potentially high return": Freeman, Richard B. "Why Do We Work
      More Than Keynes Expected?" Ibid., p. 137.

65   *Freeman writes, "The United States is the most striking counterexample*
      to Keynes's prediction that increased wealth would produce greater leisure."
      He goes on to explain that "Americans are so committed to work that they
      don't take four vacation days from the two weeks that they typically receive,
      whereas Europeans take almost all of their four- to five-week vacations":
      Ibid., p. 136.

66   *In January 2017, France implemented a law stating that employers must give*

the right to employees to stay off work-related emails during nonworking hours:
Close, Kerry. "France Just Gave Workers the 'Right to Disconnect'
from Work Email." *Time* (January 3, 2017), time.com/4620457/france
-workers-disconnect-email/.

66   *There seems to be something so un-American about that French policy, but sta-*
      tistics show that the French work 15 percent less than Americans and are just
      as productive: "Average Annual Hours Actually Worked per Worker."
      OECD.stat, Organisation for Economic Co-Operation and Develop-
      ment, 2018, stats.oecd.org/index.aspx?datasetcode=ANHRS#, https:
      //data.oecd.org/lprdty/gdp-per-hour-worked.htm; https://stats.oecd.org
      /index.aspx?DataSetCode=ANHRS. (Access date November 18, 2018.)

66   *And as for happiness, I guess it depends on where you get your jollies. Ac-*
      cording to Freeman, "Many people go to work for reasons beyond money . . .
      Workplaces are social settings where people meet and interact. On the order of
      40 to 60 percent of American workers have dated someone from their office":
      Freeman, ibid., p. 140.

66   *Another contributor to* Revisiting Keynes, *Columbia University economist*
      Edmund S. Phelps, argues that work positively provides a place for people
      to exercise their minds and develop new talents. In a time of steady technical
      progress, he postulates, "an increasing number of jobs will offer the change and
      challenge that only predominantly capitalist economies, thanks to their dyna-
      mism, can generate": Phelps, Edmund S. "Corporatism and Keynes:
      His Philosophy of Growth." *Revisiting Keynes*, p. 102.

67   *In Gopnik's popular TED Talk,* What Do Babies Think?, *she compares*
      the thinking processes of babies to that of adults: Gopnik, Alison. *What Do*
      Babies Think? TED Global, October 2011, www.ted.com/talks/alison
      _gopnik_what_do_babies_think.

68   *The CDC reports a fivefold increase in psych meds for minors between 1994*
      and 2010: Health, United States, 2013: With Special Feature on Prescrip-
      tion Drugs. Report no. 2014–1232. Hyattsville, MD: National Center
      for Health Statistics, 2014.

73   *Sartre wrote at length about skiing, and he believed that the ideal act of sliding*
      (which happens to be a term regularly used for surfing) "is sliding that does not

leave any trace," i.e., sliding on water: Martin, Andy. "Swimming and Skiing: Two Modes of Existential Consciousness." *Sports, Ethics and Philosophy*, vol. 4, no. 1 (March 11, 2010), doi:10.1080/17511320903264206.

73   *As Martin puts it, "Sartre heaped scorn on all that beachside bewitchment":* Andy Martin, interview by the author, ibid.

73   *Still, Sartre submits that, with regard to water, "sliding appears as identical with a continuous creation." Continuous, that is, until the wipeout. And then we're back to being all-too-human:* Sartre, ibid., p. 746.

Wave 3: My Worst Wave: Tearing Myself Another One

77   *One of the most brutal survival stories is the well-told tale from Susan Casey's book,* The Wave, *of Brett Lickle's near-death experience on a hundred-foot wave when the razor-sharp fin of his tow-in board flayed open the back of his calf:* Casey, Susan. *The Wave: In Pursuit of the Rogues, Freaks and Giants of the Ocean.* New York: Anchor Canada, 2011, p. 282.

80   *Jaimal Yogis, for instance. He's the author and filmmaker of* Saltwater Buddha *and a follow-up book,* All Our Waves Are Water, *two entries in his lifelong quest to tie the two disciplines of spirituality and surfing together to make some sense of the world around him:* Jaimal Yogis, interview with the author (August 15, 2017).

81   *Our original desire, according to Vietnamese Buddhist monk Thich Nhat Hanh, is for our survival once we leave our mother's womb. The Chinese and Vietnamese refer to the womb as the palace of the child:* Hanh, Thich Nhat. *Fear.* New York: HarperOne, 2012, p. 8.

82   *But then, as Thich Nhat Hanh explains, "to say that craving is the cause of all our suffering is too simplistic":* Hanh, Thich Nhat. *The Heart of the Buddha's Teaching: Transforming Suffering into Peace, Joy, and Liberation.* New York: Harmony, 1999, p. 23.

82   *Hanh writes of the Heart Sutra, "If we cannot stop running, we will miss the miracles of life available inside and around us . . . Practicing aimlessness, you don't need to run after anything anymore":* Hanh, Thich Nhat. *The Other*

Shore: A New Translation of the Heart Sutra. Berkeley, CA: Palm Leaves Press, 2017, p. 97.

82   *"When we are in touch with things by means of the mind of love, we do not run away or seek, and that is the basis of freedom. Aimlessness takes the place of grasping"*: Hanh, *Fear*, p. 242.

82   *Letting go of this need for meaning is what can bring freedom and happiness and "freedom is the only condition for happiness"*: Hanh, *Fear*, pp. 78–79.

83   *Neuroplasticity is based on the law that "neurons that fire together, wire together." Donald Hebb, known as the father of neuropsychology, came up with the concept in 1949 to explain how learning happens and habits form*: Cooper, S. J. "Donald O. Hebb's Synapse and Learning Rule: A History and Commentary." *Neuroscience and Biobehavioral Reviews*, vol. 28, no. 8 (January 2005), www.ncbi.nlm.nih.gov/pubmed/15642626.

84   *Kessler asserts that "We can gradually reshape our minds, even transform our way of experiencing the world, though overcoming one form of capture often depends on discovering another"*: Kessler, David A. *Capture: Unraveling the Mystery of Mental Suffering*. New York: Harper Perennial, 2017, p. 267.

84   *Kessler writes, "Over the course of a lifetime, each of us creates a coherent account out of the jumbled, often fragmentary chaos of life—the ever-evolving narrative of our lives . . . Without self-created storylines, the trajectory of our lives would feel like a constant scattering of random details . . . An essential question, then, is how our stories are conceived"*: Kessler, ibid., p. 266.

85   *Storytelling. Joan Didion, a master of the craft, puts a finer point on it: "We tell stories in order to live"*: Didion, Joan. *We Tell Ourselves Stories in Order to Live: Collected Nonfiction*. New York: Everyman's Library, 2006.

85   *"While the scans are dazzling and the technology an unqualified marvel," says Sally Satel, coauthor of* Brainwashed, *"we can always keep our bearings by remembering that the brain and the mind are two different frameworks"*: Satel, Sally. "Distinguishing Brain from Mind." *The Atlantic* (May 30, 2013), www.theatlantic.com/health/archive/2013/05/distinguishing-brain-from-mind/276380/.

86   *I'm reminded of Lucy Marsden, the oldest living Confederate widow of Allan Gurganus's epic novel, ninety-nine years old and sassy as the day she turned sixteen. About the seductive tale-telling of her husband, Captain Marsden, she famously says, "Know something, Sugar? Stories only happen to the people who can tell them":* Gurganus, Allan. *Oldest Living Confederate Widow Tells All: A Novel.* New York: Ivy Books, 1990, p. 211.

92   *Finnegan writes of his teenaged girlfriend, "Caryn had no interest in learning to surf, which I thought was sensible. People who tried to start at an advanced age, meaning over fourteen, had, in my experience, almost no chance of becoming proficient and usually suffered pain and sorrow before they quit":* Finnegan, William. *Barbarian Days: A Surfing Life.* New York: Penguin Books, 2016, p. 123.

93   *"The Sutra of the Arrow is a cool Buddhist riff where we learn that there are two kinds of pain; physical pain, which is real, and psychic pain, which is created," says Jaimal Yogis, slipping comfortably into surfer's jargon to unpack the intricacies of our seeking souls. "You have to recognize the stories you tell yourself and realize that they are created by you," he told me. "And while you might first chastise yourself for having them in the first place, pushing those stories away is where it gets more gnarly":* Jaimal Yogis, ibid.

94   *Katty Kay, for instance, took up kitesurfing at the age of forty. And she literally wrote a book on confidence, so I hoped she could shed light from her research on how sucking at something might help us to gain confidence:* Kay, Katty, and Claire Shipman. *The Confidence Code: The Science and Art of Self-Assurance—What Women Should Know.* New York: HarperBusiness, 2018, p. 40.

94   *But even though there are nuances of difference between them, confidence, optimism, and self-efficacy are—according to the authors—all "closely tied to a sense of personal power":* Kay, ibid., p. 48.

95   *"Confidence is the stuff that turns thoughts into action," says Richard Petty, Ohio State psychology professor and an expert on the subject:* Kay, ibid., 50.

95   *"The element of the challenge was appealing. I was defeating my own demons. Not many women were kitesurfing when I started thirteen years ago, and part*

of the appeal was conquering a sport predominantly done by men": Katty Kay,
interview with the author (August, 24, 2017).

95   *She also lamented, "I can't jump. I told myself, I am never going to master this*
       sport and I almost gave up": Ibid.

96   *Hanh teaches us, "With compassion in our heart, every thought, word, and*
       deed can bring about a miracle": Hanh, *Fear*, p. 173.

97   *Jaimal Yogis understands it from his own lifetime of practice: "The story we*
       buy into is that we are these separate individuals who exist apart from other
       beings—it's always going to suck because the grass is always greener. But en-
       lightenment cannot happen in that constructed ego": Jaimal Yogis, ibid.

101   *"The power to will is not enough to sustain change," Dr. Kessler reminds*
       us. "The challenge is to draw strength from something other than mere self-
       discipline—or condemnation. Lasting change occurs when we let go of such
       isolating pressures and allow ourselves to feel support and connection instead of
       preoccupation with the self": Kessler, p. 267.

Wave 4: My Best Wave:
Surfing Through Chemo or Whatever Shit May Come Your Way

110   *Brené Brown has spent her career unwinding the way in which we pathologize*
       vulnerability: Brown, Brené. *The Power of Vulnerability*. TEDxHous-
       ton, June 2010, www.ted.com/talks/brene_brown_on_vulnerability.

110   *Vulnerability, Brown contends, "is the birthplace of love, belonging, joy, cour-*
       age, empathy and creativity. It is the source of hope, empathy, accountability
       and authenticity": Brown, Brené. *Daring Greatly: How the Courage to Be*
       Vulnerable Transforms the Way We Live, Love, Parent, and Lead, reprint
       ed. New York: Avery, 2015, p. 34.

111   *In Brown's research into what she calls the "Defense Against the Dark Arts"*
       of shame, she writes, "Shame derives its power from being unspeakable." She
       advises, "if we speak shame, it begins to wither . . . We can't embrace vulner-
       ability if shame is suffocating our sense of worthiness and connection": Ibid.,
       p. 67.

116 *One of the most beautiful books written on the subject is neuroscientist Oliver*
     Sacks's final book, a slim but powerful collection of short essays called Grati-
     tude, *written when he knew he was dying. Upon learning of the metastases*
     that would eventually hasten his end, Dr. Sacks writes, "I cannot pretend I am
     without fear. But my predominant feeling is one of gratitude": Sacks, Oliver.
     Gratitude. New York: Knopf, 2015, p. 20.

116 *According to a study of emotions in the wake of 9/11, a group of psychologists*
     found that alongside the fear, anger, and sadness were more positive feelings of
     gratitude and compassion: Fredrickson, Barbara L. et al. "What Good
     Are Positive Emotions in Crises? A Prospective Study of Resilience
     and Emotions Following the Terrorist Attacks on the United States
     on September 11, 2001." *Journal of Personality and Social Psychology*,
     vol. 84, no. 2 (February 2003), www.ncbi.nlm.nih.gov/pmc/articles
     /PMC2755263/.

117 *The connection between these negative and positive emotion states is explored*
     in University of Michigan psychologist Barbara Fredrickson's "broaden-and-
     build" theory. Fredrickson espouses how positive emotions "broaden people's
     momentary thought-action repertoires and build their enduring personal re-
     sources": Fredrickson, Barbara L. "Broaden-And-Build Theory of
     Positive Emotions." *Philosophical Transactions of the Royal Society B*, vol.
     359, no. 1449 (September 2004), p. 1369, doi:10.1098/rstb.2004.1512.

118 *One of my favorite habits of gratitude came from—who else?—a surfer.*
     Dale Webster holds the title in the Guinness Book of World Records *of*
     having surfed the most consecutive days: "Most Consecutive Days Surf-
     ing." *Guinness World Records*, www.guinnessworldrecords.com/world
     -records/most-consecutive-days-surfing (March 4, 2018).

120 *Someone whose work I came to rely on is Andrew Zolli, whose book* Resil-
     ience *explored the subject in expansive detail:* Zolli, Andrew, and Ann
     Marie Healy. *Resilience: Why Things Bounce Back*, reprint ed. New
     York: Simon & Schuster, 2013.

120 *After thirty hours of surgery, Zolli entered what he calls, "My own private is-*
     land of suckitude as a direct response to that experience." He wondered, "How
     much disruption will it take until you reach some kind of humility? Eventu-

ally you learn your lessons": Andrew Zolli, interview with the author (March 8, 2018).

125   *"To be cool is to be equipped, and if you are equipped it is more difficult for the next cat who comes along to put you down." That's Norman Mailer in his 1957 essay,* The White Negro: Mailer, Norman. *The White Negro.* San Francisco: City Lights Books, 1972, lines 221–224.

125   *Joel Dinerstein explains in his book* The Origins of Cool in Postwar America *how "cool" was a survival mechanism against the racism black performers continually confronted. "To play it cool combined performed nonchalance with repressed vulnerability," he wrote:* Dinerstein, Joel. *The Origins of Cool in Postwar America.* Chicago: University of Chicago Press, 2018, p. 24.

126   *In his TED Talk, Dinerstein tells the story of king of cool saxophonist Lester Young, who protested "Uncle Tomming" by refusing to smile onstage:* Dinerstein, Joel. *Why Cool Matters.* TEDxNashville, March 21, 2015.

126   *"Simply put?" he said. "I am not cool. I have never been cool"*: Anthony Bourdain, interview with the author (March 14, 2018).

Wave 5: My God Wave: The Power of Belief

135   *FOOTNOTE: Check out* The Inertia*'s website for their piece on the 5 Goriest Wipeouts to get a visual of superstar surfer Keala Kennelly's face after meeting the reef at Teahupo'o (pronounced CHŌ-poo, "Chopes" for short). Fair warning . . . It's heavy:* Haro, Alexander. "5 of the Goriest Wipeouts in Surfing's History." *The Inertia* (October 31, 2014), www.theinertia.com/surf/5-of-the-goriest-wipeouts-in-surfings-history/.

136   *"The presence of others who see what we see and hear what we hear assures us of the reality of the world and ourselves," the philosopher Hannah Arendt tells us in her discussion on the private and public realms in her masterwork,* The Human Condition: Arendt, ibid., p. 50.

137   *According to Arendt, "the specific meaning of each deed can lie only in the performance itself and neither in its motivation nor its achievement":* Ibid., p. 206.

137   *She's really talking about the concept of "an end in itself"—a summation of sucking at something (and surfing) if there ever was one:* Ibid., 206.

137   *The surf historian Matt Warshaw said that "Surfing . . . generates laughter at its very suggestion, and this is because it turns not a skill into an art, but an inexplicable and useless urge into a vital way of life":* "The Best Surfing Quotes of All Time." *SurferToday,* www.surfertoday.com/surfing/8267-the-best-surfing-quotes-of-all-time (April 8, 2018).

138   *Hannah Arendt pointed out in grander terms the tension between public and private: "Since our feeling for reality depends utterly upon appearance and therefore upon the existence of a public realm into which things can appear out of the darkness of sheltered existence, even the twilight which illuminates our private and intimate lives is ultimately derived from the much harsher light of the public realm. Yet there are a great many things which cannot withstand the implacable, bright light of the constant presence of others on the public scene . . .":* Arendt, ibid., p. 51.

143   *The former, who expressed the concept as the source of all religion, explained it as, "The simple and direct sensation of the Eternal (which could very well not be eternal, but simply without perceived boundaries and oceanic)." Freud disputed any mystical meaning, defining it as a feeling of "oneness with the universe":* Saarinen, Jussi A. "A Conceptual Analysis of the Ocean Feeling." Jyväskylä, Finland: Jyväskylä University Printing House, 2015, p. 10.

143   *Author Arthur Koestler illuminates the feeling beautifully: "That higher entity, of which the self feels a part, to which it surrenders its identity, may be nature, God, the anima mundi, the magic of form, or the ocean of sound":* Koestler, Arthur. "The Three Domains of Creativity." *Philosophy of History and Culture,* edited by Michael Krausz et al., vol. 28 (June 7, 2013), pp. 251–266.

144   *It feels like the kind of still point, evoked by T. S. Eliot in his poem "Burnt Norton": At the still point of the turning world. Neither flesh nor fleshless . . . And I cannot say, how long, for that is to place it in time:* Eliot, T. S. "Burnt Norton." *Four Quartets.* Boston: Mariner Books, 1943.

144   *It is art's very permanence that creates a connection and stability, as Arendt speculates, "so that a premonition of immortality, not the immortality of the soul or of life but of something immortal achieved by mortal hands, has become*

tangibly present, to shine and to be seen, to sound and to be heard, to speak and to be read": Arendt, ibid., p. 168.

145 *The French artist Jean Cocteau believed that all artwork was the raveling and unraveling of lines to create drawings, poetry, film:* Riding, Alan. "Art; Jean Cocteau, Before His Own Fabulousness Consumed Him." *New York Times* (October 5, 2003), www.nytimes.com/2003/10/05/arts/art-jean-cocteau-before-his-own-fabulousness-consumed-him.html.

145 *Anthony Storr, author of the modern classic* Solitude, *writes, "If life is to continue, one cannot linger for ever in a state of oceanic tranquillity":* Storr, Anthony. *Solitude: A Return to the Self.* New York: Free Press, 2005, p. 197.

146 *Maybe Alexander Pope wasn't being pessimistic when he said "To err is human . . ."—maybe it's the best thing about us:* Pope, Alexander. *The Major Works.* Oxford: Oxford University Press, 2006, p. 33, line 525.

148 *When I recounted this story to Serene Jones, minister, author, and president of Union Theological Seminary, she said she was reminded of the wonderful* New Yorker *piece by Zadie Smith, "Some Notes on Attunement":* Smith, Zadie. "Some Notes on Attunement." *New Yorker* (December 17, 2012), www.newyorker.com/magazine/2012/12/17/some-notes-on-attunement.

148 *Serene's insight nailed it. My God wave was "a sudden, unexpected attunement":* Serene Jones, interview with the author (April 26, 2018).

149 *To James, "Faith means belief in something concerning which doubt is still theoretically possible; and as the test of belief is willingness to act, one may say that faith is the readiness to act in a cause the prosperous issue of which is not certified to us in advance":* James, William. *The Will to Believe, Human Immortality, and Other Essays in Popular Philosophy.* Mineola, New York: Dover, 2017, p. 90.

150 *"Into this," he protests, "for good or ill, is woven every belief of every man who has speech of his fellows. An awful privilege, and an awful responsibility, that we should help to create the world in which posterity will live":* Clifford, William K. "The Ethics of Belief." people.brandeis.edu/~teuber/Clifford_ethics.pdf, p. 3.

150 *Clifford tries to convince us that "it is wrong always, everywhere, and for any-one, to believe anything upon insufficient evidence"*: Clifford, ibid., p. 5.

150 *James, not in contrast to Clifford, but rather supporting the way of science, writes, "We cannot live or think at all without some degree of faith. Faith is synonymous with working hypothesis. The only difference is that while some hypotheses can be refuted in five minutes, others may defy ages"*: James, ibid., p. 95.

150 *In the story, he questions the value lack of belief would have in a situation where he, hypothetically, finds himself in a precarious situation while climbing "from which the only escape is by a terrible leap"*: James, ibid., p. 97.

150 *"But hope and confidence in myself make me sure I shall not miss my aim, and nerve my feet to execute what without those subjective emotions would perhaps have been impossible," he writes. "In this case (and it is one of an immense class) the part of wisdom clearly is to believe what one desires; for the belief is one of the indispensable preliminary conditions of the realization of its object. There are then cases where faith creates its own verification. Believe, and you shall be right, for you shall save yourself; doubt, and you shall again be right, for you shall perish. The only difference is that to believe is greatly to your advantage"*: James, ibid., p. 97.

151 *Shermer even ends part 1 of his book with a kind of prayer: "Lord, I did the best I could with the tools you granted me . . . Whatever the nature of your immortal and infinite spiritual essence actually is, as a mortal finite corporeal being I cannot possibly fathom it despite my best efforts, and so do with me what you will"*: Shermer, Michael. "Part I: Journeys of Belief." *The Believing Brain*. New York: St. Martin's Griffin, 2012, p. 55.

153 *The mind-body connection was made popular by Dr. John Sarno, whose book* Healing Back Pain *sold millions even though it was never embraced—worse, he was often scorned—by the conventional medical community before his death at ninety-three in 2017*: Sarno, John E. *Healing Back Pain: The Mind-Body Connection*. New York: Grand Central Life & Style, 1991.

154 *In the end, she admits, "There are powerful evolutionary forces driving us to believe in God, or in the remedies of sympathetic healers, or to believe that our prospects are more positive than they are. The irony is that although those be-liefs might be false, they do sometimes work: they make us better"*: Marchant,

Jo. *Cure: A Journey into the Science of Mind Over Body.* New York: Broadway Books, 2016, p. 256.

155   *The Italian theoretical physicist and luminous writer Carlo Rovelli explains, in a Jamesian-type of logic, how this willingness to imagine what* may not be true *can be the very basis of scientific discovery. "The beauty of the scientific enterprise," he explains, "is that we are in touch with the unknown and we try to make steps into it. It works out of beauty, out of intuition, out of imagination, but it has a very solid way, then, of checking. But what it also means is that many beautiful ideas turn out to be wrong":* Tippett, Krista, and Carlo Rovelli. "On Being with Krista Tippett: Carlo Rovelli—All Reality Is Interaction." *The On Being Project* (May 10, 2017), www.youtube .com/watch?v=jXFbtDR7IF4.

156   *"Belief and religion have always been at odds with each other," Serene told me as we sat down to lunch at a café near her office at Union Seminary's campus on the far Upper West Side of Manhattan. "Religion is an obstruction to belief":* Serene Jones, ibid.

157   *As iconic and delightfully irreverent Greg "Da Bull" Noll—himself a pioneer of big-wave surfing from the '60s—said of Laird's wave: "Man, that shit's impossible. You don't do that":* Haro, Alexander. "Laird Hamilton's Millennium Wave Reshapes How the World Looks at Surfing." *The Inertia,* June 13, 2014, www.theinertia.com/surf/laird-hamiltons -millennium-wave-reshapes-how-the-world-looks-at-surfing/.

157   *Laird cried after he made that wave. It quieted him. "That was part of it," Hamilton told Surfline on the ten-year anniversary of the ride heard 'round the world. "Riding the unrideable . . . It was also a barrier-breaking moment. It showed both me and others that waves like that can be ridden—and they have been by a lot of people since then. You have to believe in the unbelievable . . . That was all about faith. Believing I could":* "This Day In Surfing— August 17th, 2000." *Surfline* (August 17, 2010), www.surfline.com /surf-news/this-day-in-surfing—august-17th-2000—laird-hamiltons -millennium-wave-at-teahupoo_46530/.

Wave 6: Rocco's Scary Wave: Taking It On the Head

166 *Julie Lythcott-Haims, bestselling author of* How to Raise an Adult, *put a fine point on it when I spoke to her about just this subject: "We are the biggest role models—whether we will be the best is up to us":* Julie Lythcott-Haims, interview with the author (June 8, 2018).

168 *Helicopter parenting is an all-too-familiar trend succinctly illustrated in a New Yorker cartoon by Bruce Eric Kaplan. Two kids walk in the front door and the father of one is sitting in an armchair. The son says to his friend, referring to his dad: "He's less of a parent and more of a fixer":* Kaplan, Bruce Eric. *New Yorker* (August 20, 2018).

181 *Over two hundred years ago, the philosopher Johann Gottlieb Fichte said much the same thing in his essay on doubt in* The Vocation of Man: *"Had anything at all been even slightly other than it was in the preceding moment, then in the present moment something would also be other than it is. And what caused everything in the preceding moment to be as it was? This: that in the moment which preceded that one everything was as it was then. And that one moment again depended on the one which preceded it; and this last one again on its predecessor; and so on indefinitely . . . and in the present one you can think the position of no grain of sand other than it is without having to think the whole, indefinitely long past and the whole indefinitely long future to be different":* Fichte, Johann Gottlieb. *The Vocation of Man,* new ed. Translated by Peter Preuss. Indianapolis: Hackett Publishing, 1987, p. 6.

181 *MIT scientist Edward Lorenz's discovery, now popularly known as "the butterfly effect," helped to reframe the models used to predict outcomes and initially showed how and why long-term weather forecasting was difficult:* Gleick, James. "The Butterfly Effect." *Chaos: Making a New Science.* New York: Penguin Books, 2008, pp. 9–32.

181 *As a result, instead of a theoretically predictable scientific model, a new way of looking at things emerged as chaos theory, described by Lorenz as "When the present determines the future, but the approximate present does not approximately determine the future":* Lorenz, Edward N. "Deterministic Nonperiodic Flow," *Journal of Atmospheric Sciences,* vol. 20, no. 2 (January

7, 1963), https://journals.ametsoc.org/doi/pdf/10.1175/1520-0469%2
81963%29020%3C0130%3ADNF%3E2.0.CO%3B2.

182   *The infamous Navier–Stokes equation, which connects the velocity, pressure,
density, and viscosity of fluids, has yet to be proven. But if you have the time
(and the brain), it might be worth trying: the elusive solution to the equation, first
created early in the nineteenth century, is one of the seven Millennium Prizes,
which pays $1 million to the scientist who can prove it:* Moskvitch, Katia.
"Fiendish Million-Dollar Proof Eludes Mathematicians." *Nature: International Weekly Journal of Science* (August 5, 2014), www.nature.com
/news/fiendish-million-dollar-proof-eludes-mathematicians-1.15659.

182   *"This is the most beautiful problem I have ever worked on," says Stephen
Montgomery-Smith, a mathematician at the University of Missouri in Columbia, who has been tackling the equation since 1995. "It has opened my eyes
to appreciating aspects of the real world":* Ibid.

Wave 7: Mind Surfing: Watching the Waves from Shore

186   *I'm reminded of the famous statement on the tricky concept of "not-self" by
Ajahn Chah, a Buddhist monk and teacher from Thailand: "To understand
not-self, you have to meditate. If you only intellectualize, your head will explode":* Achaan Chah et al. *A Still Forest Pool: The Insight Meditation of
Achaan Chah.* Wheaton, IL: Quest Books, 2004, p. 173.

191   *Irish poet and philosopher John O'Donohue wrote in his book* Beauty: The
Invisible Embrace, *"Beauty does not belong exclusively to the region of light
and loveliness, cut off from the conflict and conversation of oppositions. The
vigour and vitality of beauty derives precisely from the heart of difference":*
O'Donohue, John. *Beauty: The Invisible Embrace: Rediscovering the True
Sources of Compassion, Serenity, and Hope.* New York: HarperCollins,
2004, p. 40.

191   *O'Donohue, a former priest and mystic, whose untimely death in 2008 left
us without one of the great minds of our time, said in his last interview as he
was talking about the inner landscape of beauty, "[It's] about an emerging
fullness, a greater sense of grace and elegance, a deeper sense of depth and also a*

kind of homecoming for the enriched memory of your unfolding life": Tippett, Krista, and John O'Donohue. "John O'Donohue—The Inner Landscape of Beauty." *The On Being Project* (August 31, 2017), onbeing .org/programs/john-odonohue-the-inner-landscape-of-beauty/.

192 *Kenkō writes, "Should we look at the spring blossoms only in full flower, or the moon only when cloudless and clear? To long for the moon with the rain before you, or to lie curtained in your room while the spring passes unseen, is yet more poignant and deeply moving":* Kenkō, Yoshida. *Essays in Idleness and Hōjoki.* Translated by Meredith McKinley. London: Penguin Classics, 2014.

193 *"The reason we don't do mastery well in the West is because the distance between success and failure is so defined that people stop even before they start," Mike explains. "Here in the West, we want things to be easy. Innate talent is expected. For the shokunin, it's about refinement, not mastery. It's about making the thing you made yesterday a tiny bit better tomorrow":* Mike Magers, interview with the author (September 6, 2017).

194 *Nobel Prize–winning physicist Frank Wilczek finds questions of meaning difficult to measure, so he asks instead, "Does the world embody beautiful ideas?":* Tippett, Krista, and Frank Wilczek. "Why Is the World So Beautiful?" *The On Being Project* (April 28, 2016), onbeing.org /programs/frank-wilczek-why-is-the-world-so-beautiful/.

197 *Kenkō writes in his* Essays in Idleness: *"This world is changeable as the deeps and shallows of Asuka River—time passes, what was here is gone, joy and grief visit by turns . . . and even the same house as of old is now home to different people":* Kenkō, ibid., p. 33.

199 *I am reminded of the poem by Naomi Shihab Nye called* Kindness: *"Before you know kindness as the deepest thing inside . . . , like a shadow or a friend":* Nye, Naomi Shihab. "Kindness." *Different Ways to Pray.* Portland, OR: Breitenbush Books, 1980.

200 *If we do, we'll find that, in our greatest need, we become open to the "kindness that raises its head from the crowd of the world." There are risks, to be sure. As Elizabeth Lesser says, "You can't choose what your heart will feel when you open it":* Elizabeth Lesser, interview with the author (August 10, 2018).

200   *Trungpa Rinpoche wrote, "Conventionally, being fearless means that you are not afraid or that, if someone hits you, you will hit him back. However, we are not talking about that street-fighter level of fearlessness. Real fearlessness is the product of tenderness. It comes from letting the world tickle your heart, your raw and beautiful heart. You are willing to open up, without resistance or shyness, and face the world. You are willing to share your heart with others":* Trungpa, Chögyam. "The Genuine Heart of Sadness." *The Sun Magazine* (July 2014), www.thesunmagazine.org/issues/463 /the-genuine-heart-of-sadness.

201   *As my now-departed friend Tony Bourdain said, "It's about sucking a little bit less":* Anthony Bourdain, ibid.

Bibliography

Adler, Alfred. *The Individual Psychology of Alfred Adler*. Edited by Ansbacher, Heinz L. and Rowena R. et al. New York: Harper Perennial, 2006, pp. 103–104.

Arendt, Hannah. *The Human Condition*, 2nd ed. Chicago: University of Chicago Press, 1998, p. 246.

Barnes, Julian. *The Sense of an Ending*. New York: Vintage Books, 2012, p. 1.

Beck, Julie. "When Nostalgia Was a Disease." *The Atlantic* (August 14, 2013), www.theatlantic.com/health/archive/2013/08/when-nostalgia-was-a-disease/278648/.

Beckwith, Christopher I. *Greek Buddha*. Princeton, NJ: Princeton University Press, 2017.

Blake, Tom. *Hawaiian Surfriders, 1935*. Redondo Beach, CA: Mountain & Sea Publishing, 1983.

———. *A Surfer's Philosophy*. Walnut, CA: Mount San Antonio College Philosophy Group, 2016.

Bourdain, Anthony. Interview by the author (March 14, 2018).

Brookshire, Bethany. "Dopamine Is _____ Is it love? Gambling? Reward? Addiction?" *Slate Magazine* (July 3, 2013), www.slate.com/articles/health_and_science/science/2013/07/what_is_dopamine_love_lust_sex_addiction_gambling_motivation_reward.html.

Brown, Brené. *Daring Greatly: How the Courage to Be Vulnerable Transforms the Way We Live, Love, Parent, and Lead*. New York: Avery, 2015.

———. *The Power of Vulnerability*. TEDxHouston (June 2010), www.ted.com/talks/brene_brown_on_vulnerability.

Casey, Susan. *The Wave: In Pursuit of the Rogues, Freaks and Giants of the Ocean.* Toronto: Anchor Canada, 2011, p. 229.

Chah, Achaan et al. *A Still Forest Pool: The Insight Meditation of Achaan Chah.* Wheaton, IL: Quest Books, 2004, p. 173.

Chödrön Pema. *When Things Fall Apart: Heart Advice for Difficult Times.* Boulder, CO: Shambhala, 2017.

Clifford, William K. "The Ethics of Belief," people.brandeis.edu/~teuber /Clifford_ethics.pdf. p. 3.

Close, Kerry. "France Just Gave Workers the 'Right to Disconnect' from Work Email." *Time* (January 3, 2017), time.com/4620457/france -workers-disconnect-email/.

Cooper, S. J. "Donald O. Hebb's Synapse and Learning Rule: A History and Commentary." *Neuroscience and Biobehavioral Reviews*, vol. 28, no. 8 (January 2005), www.ncbi.nlm.nih.gov/pubmed/15642626.

Didion, Joan. *We Tell Ourselves Stories in Order to Live: Collected Nonfiction.* New York: Everyman's Library, 2006.

Dinerstein, Joel. *The Origins of Cool in Postwar America.* Chicago: University of Chicago Press, 2018, p. 24.

———. *Why Cool Matters.* TEDxNashville (March 21, 2015).

Dreikurs, Rudolf. "The Courage to Be Imperfect." Eugene: University of Oregon, 1970.

Eich, Eric et al. *Cognition and Emotion.* Oxford: Oxford University Press, 2000.

Eliot, T. S. "Burnt Norton." *Four Quartets.* Boston: Mariner Books, 1943.

Epictetus. *The Handbook (The Encheiridion).* Translated by Nicholas P. White. Indianapolis: Hackett Publishing, 1983.

Fichte, Johann Gottlieb. *The Vocation of Man,* new ed. Translated by Peter Preuss. Indianapolis: Hackett Publishing, 1987, p. 6.

Finnegan, William. *Barbarian Days: A Surfing Life.* New York: Penguin Books, 2016, p. 123.

Frank, Thomas C. *The Conquest of Cool: Business Culture, Counterculture, and the Rise of Hip Consumerism,* paperback ed., Chicago: University of Chicago Press, 1998.

Fredrickson, Barbara L. "Broaden-And-Build Theory of Positive Emotions." *Philosophical Transactions of the Royal Society B*, vol. 359, no. 1449, September 2004, pp. 1367–1378, doi:10.4135/9781412956253.n75.

Fredrickson, Barbara L. et al. "What Good Are Positive Emotions in Crises? A Prospective Study of Resilience and Emotions Following the Terrorist Attacks on the United States on September 11, 2001." *Journal of Personality and Social Psychology*, vol. 84, no. 2 (February 2003), www.ncbi.nlm.nih.gov/pmc/articles/PMC2755263/.

Freeman, Richard B. "Why Do We Work More Than Keynes Expected?" *Revisiting Keynes*, edited by Lorenzo Pecchi and Gustavo Piga. Cambridge, MA: MIT Press, 2008, p. 137.

Gleick, James. "The Butterfly Effect." *Chaos: Making a New Science*. New York: Penguin Books, 2008, pp. 9–32.

Gopnik, Alison. *What Do Babies Think?* TED Global (October 2011), www.ted.com/talks/alison_gopnik_what_do_babies_think.

Gopnik, Alison et al. *The Scientist in the Crib: What Early Learning Tells Us about the Mind*. New York: Harper Perennial, 2001.

Grannis, LeRoy. *Midget Farrelly Surfing Shore Break*. Makaha, 1968.

Groos, Karl. "Introduction." *The Play of Man*. New York: D. Appleton & Company, 1901, p. 2.

Gurganus, Allan. *Oldest Living Confederate Widow Tells All: A Novel*. New York: Ivy Books, 1990, p. 211.

———. *The Heart of the Buddha's Teaching: Transforming Suffering into Peace, Joy, and Liberation*. New York: Harmony, 1999.

Hanh, Thich Nhat. *The Other Shore: A New Translation of the Heart Sutra*. Berkeley, CA: Palm Leaves Press, 2017.

Haro, Alexander. "5 of the Goriest Wipeouts in Surfing's History." *The Inertia* (October 31, 2014), www.theinertia.com/surf/5-of-the-goriest-wipeouts-in-surfings-history/.

———. "Laird Hamilton's Millennium Wave Reshapes How the World Looks at Surfing." *The Inertia* (June 13, 2014), www.theinertia.com/surf/laird-hamiltons-millennium-wave-reshapes-how-the-world-looks-at-surfing/.

Harris, Sam. *Waking Up: A Guide to Spirituality without Religion*. New York: Simon & Schuster, 2014.

Herrigel, Eugen. *Zen in the Art of Archery*. New York: Vintage Books, 1999.

Hume, Nancy G, ed. *Japanese Aesthetics and Culture: A Reader*. Albany, NY: State University of New York Press, 1996.

James, William. *The Will to Believe, Human Immortality, and Other Essays in Popular Philosophy*. Mineola, NY: Dover, 2017, p. 90.

Jones, Serene. *Feminist Theory and Christian Theology: Cartographies of Grace*. Minneapolis: Augsburg Fortress, 2010.

———. Interview by the author (April 26, 2018).

———. *Trauma and Grace: Theology in a Ruptured World*. Louisville, KY: Westminster John Knox, 2009.

Jung, Carl Gustav, and Richard Francis Carrington Hull. *Synchronicity: An Acausal Connecting Principle*. Princeton, NJ: Princeton University Press, 1973, p. 115.

Jung, Carl Gustav, and Anthony Storr. *The Essential Jung*. Princeton, NJ: Princeton University Press, 1983.

Kahneman, Daniel. *Thinking, Fast and Slow*, first ed. New York: Farrar, Straus and Giroux, 2011.

Kay, Katty. Interview by the author (August, 24, 2017).

Kay, Katty, and Claire Shipman. *The Confidence Code: The Science and Art of Self-Assurance—What Women Should Know*. New York: Harper-Business, 2018, p. 40.

Kenkō, Yoshida. *Essays in Idleness and Hōjoki*. Translated by Meredith McKinley. London: Penguin Classics, 2014.

Kessler, David A. *Capture: Unraveling the Mystery of Mental Suffering*. New York: Harper Perennial, 2017, p. 267.

Keynes, John Maynard. "Economic Possibilities for Our Grandchildren." *Revisiting Keynes*, ibid., pp. 22–23.

Koestler, Arthur. "The Three Domains of Creativity." *Philosophy of History and Culture*, edited by Michael Krausz et al., vol. 28 (June 7, 2013), pp. 251–266.

Lazarsfeld, Sophie. "The Courage for Imperfection." *American Journal of Individual Psychology*, vol. 22, no. 2 (1966), pp. 163–165.

Lesser, Elizabeth. Interview by the author (August 10, 2018).

Lynch, Gary et al. *Tom Blake: The Uncommon Journey of a Pioneer Waterman*, edited by William K. Hoopes. Newport Beach, CA: Croul Publications, 2013.

Lythcott-Haims, Julie. *How to Raise an Adult: Break Free of the Overparenting Trap and Prepare Your Kid for Success*. New York: St. Martin's Griffin, 2016.

———. Interview by the author (June 8, 2018).

Magers, Mike. Interview by the author (September 6, 2017).

Mailer, Norman. *The White Negro*. San Francisco: City Lights Books, 1972, lines 221–224.

Marchant, Jo. *Cure: A Journey into the Science of Mind Over Body*. New York: Broadway Books, 2016.

Martin, Andy. Interview by the author (January 15, 2018).

———. "Swimming and Skiing: Two Modes of Existential Consciousness." *Sports, Ethics and Philosophy*, vol. 4, no. 1 (March 11, 2010), doi:10.1080/17511320903264206.

Moskvitch, Katia. "Fiendish Million-Dollar Proof Eludes Mathematicians." *Nature: International Weekly Journal of Science* (August 5, 2014), www.nature.com/news/fiendish-million-dollar-proof-eludes -mathematicians-1.15659.

Neff, Kristin. *Self-Compassion: The Proven Power of Being Kind to Yourself*. New York: William Morrow, 2015.

Nichols, Wallace J., and Celine Cousteau. *Blue Mind: The Surprising Science That Shows How Being Near, In, On, or Under Water Can Make You Happier, Healthier, More Connected, and Better at What You Do*. New York: Little, Brown and Company, 2014.

Nietzsche, Friedrich Wilhelm. *On the Genealogy of Morals and Ecce Homo*. Edited and translated by Walter Kaufmann. New York: Vintage, 1989.

Nye, Naomi Shihab. "Kindness." *Words Under the Words: Selected Poems*. Portland, OR: Eighth Mountain Press, 1995.

O'Donohue, John. *Beauty: The Invisible Embrace: Rediscovering the True Sources of Compassion, Serenity, and Hope.* New York: HarperCollins, 2004, p. 40.

Pauli, Wolfgang, and C. G. Jung. *Atom and Archetype: The Pauli/Jung Letters, 1932–1958.* Edited by C. A. Meier and translated by David Roscoe. Princeton, NJ: Princeton University Press, 2014.

Phelps, Edmund S. "Corporatism and Keynes: His Philosophy of Growth." *Revisiting Keynes,* Ibid., p. 102.

Pieper, Josef. *Leisure: The Basis of Culture.* San Francisco: Ignatius Press, 2009.

Pope, Alexander. "An Essay on Criticism, Part II." 1711.

Riding, Alan. "Art; Jean Cocteau, Before His Own Fabulousness Consumed Him." *New York Times* (October 5, 2003), www.nytimes.com /2003/10/05/arts/art-jean-cocteau-before-his-own-fabulousness -consumed-him.html.

Rinaldi, Karen. "(It's Great to) Suck at Something." *New York Times* (April 28, 2017), www.nytimes.com/2017/04/28/opinion/its-great-to-suck-at -surfing.html.

Root-Bernstein, Robert et al. "Arts Foster Scientific Success: Avocations of Nobel, National Academy, Royal Society, and Sigma Xi Members." *Journal of Psychology of Science and Technology,* vol. 1, no. 2 (January 2008), pp. 51–63, doi:10.1891/1939-7054.1.2.51.

Roth, Remo F. "Introduction to Carl G. Jung's Principle of Synchronicity." Remo F. Roth, PhD, Home Page, 2002, paulijungunusmundus .eu/synw/synchronicity_jung.htm (December 1, 2017).

Saarinen, Jussi A. "A Conceptual Analysis of the Ocean Feeling." Jyväskylä, Finland: Jyväskylä University Printing House, 2015, p. 10.

Sacks, Oliver. *Gratitude.* New York: Knopf, 2015, p. 20.

Sarno, John E. *Healing Back Pain: The Mind-Body Connection.* New York: Grand Central Life & Style, 1991.

Sartre, Jean-Paul. *Being and Nothingness: An Essay on Phenomenological Ontology.* Translated by Hazel E. Barnes. New York: Washington Square Press, 2012.

Satel, Sally. "Distinguishing Brain from Mind." *The Atlantic* (May 30, 2013), www.theatlantic.com/health/archive/2013/05/distinguishing-brain -from-mind/276380/.

Schiller, Friedrich et al. "Twenty-Third Letter." *On the Aesthetic Education of Man: In a Series of Letters.* Oxford: Clarendon Press, 2005, p. 107.

Shermer, Michael. "Part I: Journeys of Belief." *The Believing Brain: From Ghosts and God to Politics and Conspiracies—How We Construct Beliefs and Reinforce Them as Truths.* New York: St. Martin's Griffin, 2012, p. 55.

Shinrigaku Kenkyu. "Relationship Between Two Aspects of Self-Oriented Perfectionism and Self-Evaluative Depression: Using Coping Styles of Uncontrollable Events as Mediators." *Japanese Journal of Psychology,* vol. 75, no. 3 (August 2004), pp. 199–206.

Smith, Zadie. "Some Notes on Attunement." *New Yorker,* December 12, 2017, www.newyorker.com/magazine/2012/12/17/some-notes-on-attunement.

Stearns, Peter N. *American Cool: Constructing a Twentieth-Century Emotional Style.* New York: New York University Press, 1994.

Storr, Anthony. *Solitude: A Return to the Self.* New York: Free Press, 2005, p.197.

Suzuki, Daisetz Teitaro. *Zen and Japanese Culture.* Princeton, NJ: Princeton University Press, 2010.

Swan, Gary E., and Dorit Carmelli. "Curiosity and Mortality in Aging Adults: A 5-Year Follow-up of the Western Collaborative Group Study." *Psychology and Aging,* vol. 11, no. 3 (September 1996), pp. 449–453. doi:10.1037//0882-7974.11.3.449.

Tippett, Krista, and John O'Donohue. "John O'Donohue—The Inner Landscape of Beauty." *The On Being Project* (August 6, 2015), onbeing .org/programs/john-odonohue-the-inner-landscape-of-beauty/.

Tippett, Krista, and Carlo Rovelli. "On Being with Krista Tippett: Carlo Rovelli—All Reality Is Interaction." *The On Being Project* (May 10, 2017), www.youtube.com/watch?v=jXFbtDR7IF4.

Tippett, Krista, and Frank Wilczek. "Why Is the World So Beautiful?" *The On Being Project* (April 28, 2016), onbeing.org/programs/frank-wilczek -why-is-the-world-so-beautiful/.

Tovote, Philip, and Andreas Lüthi. "Curbing Fear by Axonal Oxytocin Release in the Amygdala." *Neuron*, vol. 73, no. 3 (February 9, 2012), pp. 407–410, doi:10.1016/j.neuron.2012.01.016.

Trungpa, Chögyam. "The Genuine Heart of Sadness." *The Sun Magazine* (July 2014), www.thesunmagazine.org/issues/463/the-genuine-heart -of-sadness.

Wilczek, Frank. *A Beautiful Question: Finding Nature's Deep Design*. New York: Penguin Books, 2016.

Yogis, Jaimal. Interview by the author (August 15, 2017).

Zolli, Andrew. Interview by the author (March 8, 2018).

Zolli, Andrew, and Ann Marie Healy. *Resilience: Why Things Bounce Back*. Simon & Schuster, 2013.

About the Author

Photograph © Rocco Rinaldi-Rose

Karen Rinaldi has worked in the publishing industry for more than two decades. In 2012 she founded the imprint Harper Wave at HarperCollins. The feature film *Maggie's Plan* is based on her novel *The End of Men*. Karen has been published in the *New York Times*, Oprah.com, *Time*, Literary Hub, among others. She lives in New York and New Jersey with her family.